MAKING IT

*the text of this book is printed
on 100% recycled paper*

Also by Norman Podhoretz

Doings and Undoings: *The Fifties and After in American Writing*

Breaking Ranks: *A Political Memoir*

The Commentary Reader (EDITOR)

Making It

NORMAN PODHORETZ

HARPER COLOPHON BOOKS
Harper & Row, Publishers
New York, Cambridge, Hagerstown
Philadelphia, San Francisco
London, Mexico City, São Paulo, Sydney

DEDICATION

For Rachel, Naomi, Ruth, and John
To whom this is, in a way, a letter

ACKNOWLEDGMENTS

I am immeasurably grateful to Elizabeth Ames and the Yaddo Corporation for the hospitality they offered me while I was working on this book. I am also grateful for the hospitality offered me at an earlier stage by Paul Horgan and the Fellows of the Center for Advanced Studies at Wesleyan University.

I wish, finally, to acknowledge my immense debt to Lionel Trilling, who has taught me more than he or I ever realized—though not, I fear, precisely what he would have wanted me to learn.

CONTENTS

PREFACE   xi

PART I   A JOURNEY IN BLINDNESS

          1 The Brutal Bargain   3
          2 Culture, Class, and Conversions   28
          3 The Second Lap Across the Sea   62

PART II   MOVING INTO MANHATTAN

          4 The Family Tree   109
          5 Making a Start   137
          6 In and Out of Nihilism (and Uniform)   177

PART III MAKING IT

          7 Working for a Living in New York   197
          8 Writing for a Living in America   236
          9 Becoming a Boss   274
         10 That Last Infirmity   324

INDEX   357

PREFACE

Let me introduce myself. I am a man who at the precocious age of thirty-five experienced an astonishing revelation: it is better to be a success than a failure. Having been penetrated by this great truth concerning the nature of things, my mind was now open for the first time to a series of corollary perceptions, each one as dizzying in its impact as the Original Revelation itself. Money, I now saw (no one, of course, had ever seen it before), was important: it was better to be rich than to be poor. Power, I now saw (moving on to higher subtleties), was desirable: it was better to give orders than to take them. Fame, I now saw (how courageous of me not to flinch), was unqualifiedly delicious: it was better to be recognized than to be anonymous.

This book represents an effort to explain why it should have taken someone like myself so long to arrive at such apparently elementary discoveries. It is not, in other words, a success story, it is the story of an education; and while it is autobiographical in form, it is not an autobiography in the usual sense, being confined very strictly to those details of my life bearing on the question of career.

To be sure, the story I tell here resembles the traditional success story in tracing the progressive rise of a young man up from poverty and obscure origins. In contrast to the traditional success story, however, its purpose is not to celebrate that rise, but rather to describe certain fine-print conditions that are attached to the successful accomplishment of what the sociologists call "upward mobility" in so heterogeneous a society as our own. There are prices to be paid for the rewards of making it in America, some obvious, some not very well advertised. I try in this book to focus attention on a few of the latter, which are grouped together into the metaphor of "conversions."

My second purpose in telling the story of my own career is to provide a concrete setting for a diagnosis of the curiously contradictory feelings our culture instills in us toward the ambition for success, and toward each of its various goals: money, power, fame, and social position. On the one hand, we are commanded to become successful—that is, to acquire more of these worldly goods than we began with, and to do so by our own exertions; on the other hand, it is impressed upon

us by means both direct and devious that if we obey
the commandment, we shall find ourselves falling victim to the radical corruption of spirit which, given the
nature of what is nowadays called the "system," the
pursuit of success requires and which its attainment always bespeaks. On the one hand, "the exclusive worship
of the bitch-goddess SUCCESS," as William James put
it in a famous remark, "is our national disease"; on the
other hand, a contempt for success is the consensus of
the national literature for the past hundred years and
more.* On the one hand, our culture teaches us to shape
our lives in accordance with the hunger for worldly
things; on the other hand, it spitefully contrives to
make us ashamed of the presence of those hungers in
ourselves and to deprive us as far as possible of any
pleasure in their satisfaction.

Nothing, I believe, defines the spiritual character
of American life more saliently than this contradiction,
and I doubt that many Americans, whether they be
successes or failures in their careers, can have escaped
its consequences. I myself have tasted enough success
of one kind or another to know something about success, and more than enough ambition of every kind to
know much of what there is to know about ambition.
But these are not the credentials I offer for presuming to

---

* On this point, see Moses Rischin (ed.), *The American Gospel
of Success;* John G. Cawelti, *Apostles of the Self-Made Man;*
Kenneth S. Lynn, *The Dream of Success;* and, of course, the
American novel *passim.*

write an autobiographical book about the problem of success in America. My claim to expertise in this field is simply that I *am* an American. The fact that I was also born in Brooklyn to East European Jewish parents and that I have made my career in the wilds of literary New York does not, I think, disqualify the story of that career from being considered typical in its underlying contours. On the contrary, my background and my working life have, if anything, conspired to render me unusually susceptible to the suasions of both sides of the contradictory American attitude toward the ambition for and the pursuit of worldly success.

The immigrant Jewish milieu from which I derive is by now fixed for all time in the American imagination as having been driven by an uninhibited hunger for success. This reputation is by no means as justified as we have been led to believe, but certainly on the surface the "gospel of success" did reign supreme in the world of my childhood. Success did not necessarily, or even primarily, mean money; just as often it might mean prestige or popularity. In any case, the concept always referred, as it was originally intended to do, to the possession of goods which had value in the eyes of others. These goods might also have had value in one's own eyes, but that was a secondary consideration, if indeed it was ever considered at all. The main thing was to be *esteemed*, and one would no more have questioned the desirability of so pleasant an estate in life than one would have wondered about the relative merits of ill-ness and good health.

Having grown up with such feelings, I responded with puzzlement to the discovery first forced upon me in college that something which might be called a gos-pel of anti-success, or even a cult of failure, held as powerful a sway over the spoken attitudes, if not always the behavior, of educated Americans as the opposing creed did over the minds of the people I had previously known. Most of the books I read about America assured me—and continue to do so to this day—that success was the supreme, even the only, American value, and yet at Columbia College the word "successful" glided auto-matically into the judgment "corrupt." The books all said that Americans regarded ambition as a major virtue, and yet a system of manners existed at Columbia which prohibited any expression of worldly ambitiousness. To yearn for the applause of posterity may have been legiti-mate, but it was thought contemptible to dream of the rewards contemporary society had to offer, and alto-gether despicable to admit to so low a hunger, except in tones of irony that revealed one's consciousness of how naughty a thing one was doing.

All this made its mark on me and was to be rein-forced by the ethos of New York literary society, where I eventually came both to live and to earn my living as a writer and an editor. Later on, I go into some of the rea-sons for the special prevalence of the gospel of anti-success among literary people and those involved in the arts in general; here I want only to point out that it *has* a special prevalence in such circles. Thus, as someone who was raised in the most notoriously driving of all American subcultures; who then grew to maturity under the influence of ideas which were in the sharpest possible opposition to the values associated with the worship of success; and whose own experience finally pushed him into rebelling against many of the assumptions behind the oppositionist view—I may perhaps lay claim to a particularly good vantage point from which to report on how the two warring American attitudes toward the pursuit of success are likely to reveal themselves concretely in the details of an individual career.

It is a symptom of the predicament I am concerned with describing that only the immensely successful are permitted to talk about their own careers without becoming vulnerable to the charge of tastelessness. "Good" taste in this area prescribes the denigration of one's achievements, and only the immensely successful can afford, or have the right, to be so modest. The rest of us customarily remain silent, for fear of seeming to inflate our own importance or the importance of the work we do. For taking my career as seriously as I do in this book, I will no doubt be accused of self-inflation and therefore of tastelessness. So be it. There was a time when to talk candidly about sex was similarly regarded as tasteless—a betrayal of what D. H. Lawrence once called "the dirty little secret." For many of us, of course, this is no longer the case. But judging by the embarrassment that a frank discussion of one's feelings about one's own success, or the lack of it, invariably causes in polite company today, ambition (itself a species of lustful hunger) seems to be replacing erotic lust as the prime dirty little secret of the well-educated American soul. And since the natural accompaniments of a dirty little secret are superstition, hypocrisy, and cant, it is no cause for wonder that the theme of success rarely appears in our discourse unattended by at least one of these three dismal Furies inherited from Victorian sex.

To the extent that this book is a confessional work, to the extent that it deliberately exposes an order of feeling in myself, and by implication in others, that most of us usually do our best to keep hidden, from ourselves as well as others, it obviously constitutes the betrayal of a dirty little secret and thereby a violation of certain current standards of tastefulness. There are, however, different standards according to which superstition, hypocrisy, and cant are more damaging to the health of the soul than the admittedly painful offenses against "good" taste that are bound to be committed by a confessional writer bent on bringing the secret out into the open and thus helping to weaken its power to shame. It is on such standards that this book relies, and to them that it makes an appeal.

Part I

A JOURNEY
IN BLINDNESS

1 The Brutal Bargain

One of the longest journeys in the world is the journey from Brooklyn to Manhattan—or at least from certain neighborhoods in Brooklyn to certain parts of Manhattan. I have made that journey, but it is not from the experience of having made it that I know how very great the distance is, for I started on the road many years before I realized what I was doing, and by the time I did realize it I was for all practical purposes already there. At so imperceptible a pace did I travel, and with so little awareness, that I never felt footsore or out of breath or weary at the thought of how far I still had to go. Yet whenever anyone who has remained back there where I started—remained not physically but socially and culturally, for the neighborhood is now a

3

Negro ghetto and the Jews who have "remained" in it mostly reside in the less affluent areas of Long Island—whenever anyone like that happens into the world in which I now live with such perfect ease, I can see that in his eyes I have become a fully acculturated citizen of a country as foreign to him as China and infinitely more frightening.

That country is sometimes called the upper middle class; and indeed I am a member of that class, less by virtue of my income than by virtue of the way my speech is accented, the way I dress, the way I furnish my home, the way I entertain and am entertained, the way I educate my children—the way, quite simply, I look and I live. It appalls me to think what an immense transformation I had to work on myself in order to become what I have become: if I had known what I was doing I would surely not have been able to do it, I would surely not have wanted to. No wonder the choice had to be blind; there was a kind of treason in it: treason toward my family, treason toward my friends. In choosing the road I chose, I was pronouncing a judgment upon them, and the fact that they themselves concurred in the judgment makes the whole thing sadder but no less cruel.

When I say that the choice was blind, I mean that I was never aware—obviously not as a small child, certainly not as an adolescent, and not even as a young man already writing for publication and working on the staff

of an important intellectual magazine in New York—
how inextricably my "noblest" ambitions were tied to
the vulgar desire to rise above the class into which I was
born; nor did I understand to what an astonishing extent these ambitions were shaped and defined by the
standards and values and tastes of the class into which
I did not know I wanted to move. It is not that I was or
am a social climber as that term is commonly used. High
society interests me, if at all, only as a curiosity; I do
not wish to be a member of it; and in any case, it is not,
as I have learned from a small experience of contact
with the very rich and fashionable, my "scene." Yet
precisely because social climbing is not one of my vices
(unless what might be called celebrity climbing, which
very definitely *is* one of my vices, can be considered the
contemporary variant of social climbing), I think there
may be more than a merely personal significance in the
fact that class has played so large a part both in my life
and in my career.

But whether or not the significance is there, I feel
certain that my long-time blindness to the part class was
playing in my life was not altogether idiosyncratic.
"Privilege," Robert L. Heilbroner has shrewdly observed in *The Limits of American Capitalism,* "is not an
attribute we are accustomed to stress when we consider
the construction of *our* social order." For a variety of
reasons, says Heilbroner, "privilege under capitalism is

much less 'visible,' especially to the favored groups, than privilege under other systems" like feudalism. This "invisibility" extends in America to class as well.

No one, of course, is so naïve as to believe that America is a classless society or that the force of egalitarianism, powerful as it has been in some respects, has ever been powerful enough to wipe out class distinctions altogether. There was a moment during the 1950's, to be sure, when social thought hovered on the brink of saying that the country had to all intents and purposes become a wholly middle-class society. But the emergence of the civil-rights movement in the 1960's and the concomitant discovery of the poor—to whom, in helping to discover them, Michael Harrington interestingly enough applied, in *The Other America,* the very word ("invisible") that Heilbroner later used with reference to the rich—has put at least a temporary end to that kind of talk. And yet if class has become visible again, it is only in its grossest outlines—mainly, that is, in terms of income levels—and to the degree that manners and style of life are perceived as relevant at all, it is generally in the crudest of terms. There is something in us, it would seem, which resists the idea of class. Even our novelists, working in a genre for which class has traditionally been a supreme reality, are largely indifferent to it—which is to say, blind to its importance as a factor in the life of the individual.

In my own case, the blindness to class always expressed itself in an outright and very often belligerent refusal to believe that it had anything to do with me at all. I no longer remember when or in what form I first discovered that there was such a thing as class, but whenever it was and whatever form the discovery took, it could only have coincided with the recognition that criteria existed by which I and everyone I knew were stamped as inferior: we were in the *lower* class. This was not a proposition I was willing to accept, and my way of not accepting it was to dismiss the whole idea of class as a prissy triviality.

Given the fact that I had literary ambitions even as a small boy, it was inevitable that the issue of class would sooner or later arise for me with a sharpness it would never acquire for most of my friends. But given the fact also that I was on the whole very happy to be growing up where I was, that I was fiercely patriotic about Brownsville (the spawning-ground of so many famous athletes and gangsters), and that I felt genuinely patronizing toward other neighborhoods, especially the "better" ones like Crown Heights and East Flatbush which seemed by comparison colorless and unexciting— given the fact, in other words, that I was not, for all that I wrote poetry and read books, an "alienated" boy dreaming of escape—my confrontation with the issue of class would probably have come later rather than sooner if not for an English teacher in high school who decided that I was a gem in the rough and who took it upon herself to polish me to as high a sheen as she could manage and I would permit.

I resisted—far less effectively, I can see now, than I then thought, though even then I knew that she was wearing me down far more than I would ever give her the satisfaction of admitting. Famous throughout the school for her altogether outspoken snobbery, which stopped short by only a hair, and sometimes did not stop short at all, of an old-fashioned kind of patrician anti-Semitism, Mrs. K. was also famous for being an extremely good teacher; indeed, I am sure that she saw no distinction between the hopeless task of teaching the proper use of English to the young Jewish barbarians whom fate had so unkindly deposited into her charge and the equally hopeless task of teaching them the proper "manners." (There were as many young Negro barbarians in her charge as Jewish ones, but I doubt that she could ever bring herself to pay very much attention to them. As she never hesitated to make clear, it was punishment enough for a woman of her background—her family was old-Brooklyn and, she would have us understand, extremely distinguished—to have fallen among the sons of East European immigrant Jews.)

For three years, from the age of thirteen to the age of sixteen, I was her special pet, though that word is scarcely adequate to suggest the intensity of the relationship which developed between us. It was a relationship right out of *The Corn Is Green,* which may, for all I know, have served as her model; at any rate, her objective was much the same as the Welsh teacher's in that play: she was determined that I should win a scholarship to Harvard. But whereas (an irony much to the point here) the problem the teacher had in *The Corn Is Green* with her coal-miner pupil in the traditional class society of Edwardian England was strictly academic, Mrs. K.'s problem with me in the putatively egalitarian society of New Deal America was strictly social. My grades were very high and would obviously remain so, but what would they avail me if I continued to go about looking and sounding like a "filthy little slum child" (the epithet she would invariably hurl at me whenever we had an argument about "manners")?

Childless herself, she worked on me like a dementedly ambitious mother with a somewhat recalcitrant son; married to a solemn and elderly man (she was then in her early forties or thereabouts), she treated me like a callous, ungrateful adolescent lover on whom she had humiliatingly bestowed her favors. She flirted with me and flattered me, she scolded me and insulted me. Slum child, filthy little slum child, so beautiful a mind and so vulgar a personality, so exquisite in sensibility and so coarse in manner. What would she do with me, what would become of me if I persisted out of stubbornness and perversity in the disgusting ways they had taught me at home and on the streets?

To her the most offensive of these ways was the style in which I dressed: a tee shirt, tightly pegged pants, and a red satin jacket with the legend "Cherokees, S.A.C." (social-athletic club) stitched in large white letters across the back. This was bad enough, but when on certain days I would appear in school wearing, as a particular ceremonial occasion required, a suit and tie, the sight of those immense padded shoulders and my white-on-white shirt would drive her to even greater heights of contempt and even lower depths of loving despair than usual. *Slum child, filthy little slum child.* I was beyond saving; I deserved no better than to wind up with all the other horrible little Jewboys in the gutter (by which she meant Brooklyn College). If only I would listen to her, the whole world could be mine: I could win a scholarship to Harvard, I could get to know the best people, I could grow up into a life of elegance and refinement and taste. Why was I so stupid as not to understand?

In those days it was very unusual, and possibly even against the rules, for teachers in public high schools to associate with their students after hours. Nevertheless, Mrs. K. sometimes invited me to her home, a beautiful old brownstone located in what was perhaps the only section in the whole of Brooklyn fashionable enough to be intimidating. I would read her my poems and she would tell me about her family, about the schools she had gone to, about Vassar, about writers she had met, while her husband, of whom I was frightened to death and who to my utter astonishment turned out to be Jewish (but not, as Mrs. K. quite unnecessarily hastened to inform me, *my* kind of Jewish), sat stiffly and silently in an armchair across the room, squinting at his newspaper through the first *pince-nez* I had ever seen outside the movies. He spoke to me but once, and that was after I had read Mrs. K. my tearful editorial for the school newspaper on the death of Roosevelt—an effusion which provoked him into a full five-minute harangue whose blasphemous contents would certainly have shocked me into insensibility if I had not been even more shocked to discover that he actually had a voice.

But Mrs. K. not only had me to her house; she also —what was even more unusual—took me out a few times, to the Frick Gallery and the Metropolitan Museum, and once to the theater, where we saw a dramatization of *The Late George Apley,* a play I imagine she deliberately chose with the not wholly mistaken idea that it would impress upon me the glories of aristocratic Boston.

One of our excursions into Manhattan I remember with particular vividness because she used it to bring the struggle between us to rather a dramatic head. The familiar argument began this time on the subway. Why, knowing that we would be spending the afternoon together "in public," had I come to school that morning improperly dressed? (I was, as usual, wearing my red satin club jacket over a white tee shirt.) She realized, of course, that I owned only one suit (this said not in compassion but in derision) and that my poor parents had, God only knew where, picked up the idea that it was too precious to be worn except at one of those bar mitzvahs I was always going to. Though why, if my parents were so worried about clothes, they had permitted me to buy a suit which made me look like a young hoodlum she found it very difficult to imagine. Still, much as she would have been embarrassed to be seen in public with a boy whose parents allowed him to wear a zoot suit, she would have been somewhat less embarrassed than she was now by the ridiculous costume I had on. Had I no consideration for her? Had I no consideration for myself? Did I want everyone who laid eyes on me to think that I was nothing but an ill-bred little slum child?

My standard ploy in these arguments was to take the position that such things were of no concern to me: I was a poet and I had more important matters to think about than clothes. Besides, I would feel silly coming to school on an ordinary day dressed in a suit. Did Mrs. K. want me to look like one of those "creeps" from Crown Heights who were all going to become doctors? This was usually an effective counter, since Mrs. K. despised her middle-class Jewish students even more than she did the "slum children," but probably because she was growing desperate at the thought of how I would strike a Harvard interviewer (it was my senior year), she did not respond according to form on that particular occasion. "At least," she snapped, "they reflect well on their parents."

I was accustomed to her bantering gibes at my parents, and sensing, probably, that they arose out of jealousy, I was rarely troubled by them. But this one bothered me; it went beyond banter and I did not know how to deal with it. I remember flushing, but I cannot remember what if anything I said in protest. It was the beginning of a very bad afternoon for both of us.

We had been heading for the Museum of Modern Art, but as we got off the subway, Mrs. K. announced that she had changed her mind about the museum. She was going to show me something else instead, just down the street on Fifth Avenue. This mysterious "something else" to which we proceeded in silence turned out to be the college department of an expensive clothing store, de Pinna. I do not exaggerate when I say that an actual physical dread seized me as I followed her into the store. I had never been inside such a store; it was not a store, it was enemy territory, every inch of it mined with humiliations. "I am," Mrs. K. declared in the coldest human voice I hope I shall ever hear, "going to buy you a suit that you will be able to wear at your Harvard interview." I had guessed, of course, that this was what she had in mind, and even at fifteen I understood what a fantastic act of aggression she was planning to commit against my parents and asking me to participate in. Oh no, I said in a panic (suddenly realizing that I *wanted* her to buy me that suit), I can't, my mother wouldn't like it. "You can tell her it's a birthday present. Or else I will tell her. If I tell her, I'm sure she won't object." The idea of Mrs. K. meeting my mother was more than I could bear: my mother, who spoke with a Yiddish accent and of whom, until that sickening moment, I had never known I was ashamed and so ready to betray.

To my immense relief and my equally immense disappointment, we left the store, finally, without buying a suit, but it was not to be the end of clothing or "manners" for me that day—not yet. There was still the ordeal of a restaurant to go through. Where I came from, people rarely ate in restaurants, not so much because most of them were too poor to afford such a luxury—although most of them certainly were—as because eating in restaurants was not regarded as a luxury at all; it was, rather, a necessity to which bachelors were pitiably condemned. A home-cooked meal was assumed to be better than anything one could possibly get in a restaurant, and considering the class of restaurants in question (they were really diners or luncheonettes), the assumption was probably correct. In the case of my own family, myself included until my late teens, the business of going to restaurants was complicated by the fact that we observed the Jewish dietary laws, and except in certain neighborhoods, few places could be found which served kosher food; in midtown Manhattan in the 1940's, I believe there were only two and both were relatively expensive. All this is by way of explaining why I had had so little experience of restaurants up to the age of fifteen and why I grew apprehensive once more when Mrs. K. decided after we left de Pinna that we should have something to eat.

The restaurant she chose was not at all an elegant one—I have, like a criminal, revisited it since—but it seemed very elegant indeed to me: enemy territory again, and this time a mine exploded in my face the minute I set foot through the door. The hostess was very sorry, but she could not seat the young gentleman without a coat and tie. If the lady wished, however, something could be arranged. The lady (visibly pleased by this unexpected—or was it expected?—object lesson) did wish, and the so recently defiant but by now utterly docile young gentleman was forthwith divested of his so recently beloved but by now thoroughly loathsome red satin jacket and provided with a much oversized white waiter's coat and a tie—which, there being no collar to a tee shirt, had to be worn around his bare neck. Thus attired, and with his face supplying the touch of red which had moments earlier been supplied by his jacket, he was led into the dining room, there to be taught the importance of proper table manners through the same pedagogic instrumentality that had worked so well in impressing him with the importance of proper dress.

Like any other pedagogic technique, however, humiliation has its limits, and Mrs. K. was to make no further progress with it that day. For I had had enough, and I was not about to risk stepping on another mine. Knowing she would subject me to still more ridicule if I made a point of my revulsion at the prospect of eating nonkosher food, I resolved to let her order for me and then to feign lack of appetite or possibly even illness when the meal was served. She did order—duck for both of us, undoubtedly because it would be a hard dish for me to manage without using my fingers.

The two portions came in deep oval-shaped dishes, swimming in a brown sauce and each with a sprig of parsley sitting on top. I had not the faintest idea of what to do—should the food be eaten directly from the oval dish or not?—nor which of the many implements on the table to do it with. But remembering that Mrs. K. herself had once advised me to watch my hostess in such a situation and then to do exactly as she did, I sat perfectly still and waited for her to make the first move. Unfortunately, Mrs. K. also remembered having taught me that trick, and determined as she was that I should be given a lesson that would force me to mend my ways, she waited too. And so we both waited, chatting amiably, pretending not to notice the food while it sat there getting colder and colder by the minute. Thanks partly to the fact that I would probably have gagged on the duck if I had tried to eat it—dietary taboos are very powerful if one has been conditioned to them—I was prepared to wait forever. And in fact it was Mrs. K. who broke first.

"Why aren't you eating?" she suddenly said after something like fifteen minutes had passed. "Aren't you hungry?" Not very, I answered. "Well," she said, "I think we'd better eat. The food is getting cold." Whereupon, as I watched with great fascination, she deftly captured the sprig of parsley between the prongs of her serving fork, set it aside, took up her serving spoon and delicately used those two esoteric implements to transfer a piece of duck from the oval dish to her plate. I imitated the whole operation as best I could, but not well enough to avoid splattering some partly congealed sauce onto my borrowed coat in the process. Still, things could have been worse, and having more or less successfully negotiated my way around that particular mine, I now had to cope with the problem of how to get out of eating the duck. But I need not have worried. Mrs. K. took one bite, pronounced it inedible (it must have been frozen by then), and called in quiet fury for the check.

Several months later, wearing an altered but respectably conservative suit which had been handed down to me in good condition by a bachelor uncle, I presented myself on two different occasions before interviewers from Harvard and from the Pulitzer Scholarship Committee. Some months after that, Mrs. K. had her triumph: I won the Harvard scholarship on which her heart had been so passionately set. It was not, however, large enough to cover all expenses, and since my parents could not afford to make up the difference, I was unable to accept it. My parents felt wretched but not, I think, quite as wretched as Mrs. K. For a while it looked as though I would wind up in the "gutter" of Brooklyn College after all, but then the news arrived that I had also won a Pulitzer Scholarship which paid full tuition if used at Columbia and a small stipend besides. Everyone was consoled, even Mrs. K.: Columbia was at least in the Ivy League.

The last time I saw her was shortly before my graduation from Columbia and just after a story had appeared in the *Times* announcing that I had been awarded a fellowship which was to send me to Cambridge University. Mrs. K. had passionately wanted to see me in Cambridge, Massachusetts, but Cambridge, England was even better. We met somewhere near Columbia for a drink, and her happiness over my fellowship, it seemed to me, was if anything exceeded by her delight at discovering that I now knew enough to know that the right thing to order in a cocktail lounge was a very dry martini with lemon peel, please.

II Looking back now at the story of my relationship with Mrs. K. strictly in the context of the issue of class, what strikes me most sharply is the astonishing rudeness of this woman to whom "manners" were of such overriding concern. (This, as I have since had some occasion to notice, is a fairly common characteristic among members of the class to which she belonged.) Though she would not have admitted it, good manners to Mrs. K. meant only one thing: conformity to a highly stylized set of surface habits and fashions which she took, quite as a matter of course, to be superior to all other styles of social behavior. But in what did their superiority consist? Were her "good" manners derived from or conducive to a greater moral sensitivity than the "bad" manners I had learned at home and on the streets of Brownsville? I rather doubt it. The "crude" behavior of my own parents, for example, was then and is still marked by a tactfulness and a delicacy that Mrs. K. simply could not have approached. It is not that she was incapable of tact and delicacy; in certain moods she was; and manners apart, she was an extraordinarily loving and generous woman. But such qualities were neither built into nor expressed by the system of manners under which she lived. She was fond of quoting Cardinal Newman's definition of a gentleman as a person who could be at ease in any company, yet if anything was clear about the man-

ners she was trying to teach me, it was that they operated
—not inadvertently but by deliberate design—to set one
at ease *only* with others similarly trained and to cut one
off altogether from those who were not.

While I would have been unable to formulate it in
those terms at the time, I think I must have understood
perfectly well what Mrs. K. was attempting to communicate with all her talk about manners; if I had not understood it so well, I would not have resisted so fiercely. She
was saying that because I was a talented boy, a better
class of people stood ready to admit me into their ranks.
But only on one condition: I had to signify by my general deportment that I acknowledged them as *superior* to
the class of people among whom I happened to have been
born. That was the bargain—take it or leave it. In resisting Mrs. K. where "manners" were concerned, just as I
was later to resist many others, I was expressing my refusal to have any part of so brutal a bargain. But the
joke was on me, for what I did not understand, not in
the least then and not for a long time afterward, was
that in matters having to do with "art" and "culture"
(the "life of the mind," as I learned to call it at Columbia), I was being offered the very same brutal bargain
and accepting it with the wildest enthusiasm.

I have said that I did not, for all my bookishness,
feel alienated as a boy, and this is certainly true. Far
from dreaming of escape from Brownsville, I dreaded
the thought of living anywhere else, and whenever my

older sister, who hated the neighborhood, began begging my parents to move, it was invariably my howls of protest that kept them from giving in. For by the age of thirteen I had made it into the neighborhood big time, otherwise known as the Cherokees, S.A.C. It had by no means been easy for me, as a mediocre athlete and a notoriously good student, to win acceptance from a gang which prided itself mainly on its masculinity and its contempt for authority, but once this had been accomplished, down the drain went any reason I might earlier have had for thinking that life could be better in any other place. Not for nothing, then, did I wear that red satin jacket to school every day. It was my proudest possession, a badge of manly status, proving that I was not to be classified with the Crown Heights "creeps," even though my grades, like theirs, were high.

And yet, despite the Cherokees, it cannot be that I felt quite so securely at home in Brownsville as I remember thinking. The reason is that something extremely significant in this connection had happened to me by the time I first met Mrs. K.: without any conscious effort on my part, my speech had largely lost the characteristic neighborhood accent and was well on its way to becoming as neutrally American as I gather it now is.

Now whatever else may be involved in a nondeliberate change of accent, one thing is clear: it bespeaks a very high degree of detachment from the ethos of one's immediate surroundings. It is not a good ear alone, and perhaps not even a good ear at all, which enables a child to hear the difference between the way he and everyone else around him sound when they talk, and the way teachers and radio announcers—as it must have been in my case—sound. Most people, and especially most children, are entirely insensitive to such differences, which is why anyone who pays attention to these matters can, on the basis of a man's accent alone, often draw a reasonably accurate picture of his regional, social, and ethnic background. People who feel that they belong in their familiar surroundings—whether it be a place, a class, or a group—will invariably speak in the accent of those surroundings; in all likelihood, indeed, they will never have imagined any other possibility for themselves. Conversely, it is safe to assume that a person whose accent has undergone a radical change from childhood is a person who once had fantasies of escaping to some other world, whether or not they were ever realized.

But accent in America has more than a psychological or spiritual significance. "Her kerbstone English," said Henry Higgins of Eliza Doolittle, "will keep her in the gutter to the end of her days." Most Americans probably respond with a sense of amused democratic superiority to the idea of a society in which so trivial a thing as accent can keep a man down, and it is a good measure of our blindness to the pervasive operations of class that there has been so little consciousness of the fact that America itself is such a society.* While the broadly regional accents—New England, Midwestern, Southern—enjoy more or less equal status and will not affect the economic or social chances of those who speak in them, the opposite is still surely true of any accent identifiably influenced by Yiddish, Italian, Polish, Spanish—that is, the languages of the major post-Civil War immigrant groups, among which may be included American-Irish. A man with such an accent will no longer be confined, as once he would almost automatically have been, to the working class, but unless his life, both occupational and social, is lived strictly within the milieu in whose tone of voice he speaks, his accent will at the least operate as an obstacle to be overcome (if, for example, he is a schoolteacher aspiring to be a principal), and at the most as an effective barrier to advancement (if, say, he is an engineer),

* On the other hand, the New York *Times* reported on May 8, 1966, that "A real-life Professor Higgins" had "descended upon Harlem in search of Eliza Doolittles." The *Times* went on: "Every Saturday afternoon the portly 45-year-old professor of comparative education at Teachers College of Columbia University, Dr. George Z. F. Bereday, directs 10 Negro girl seniors from Benjamin Franklin High School on the upper East Side in a series of classes in grooming, dress, make-up, speech, poise, rhythmics, and general deportment and culture." Explained Dr. Bereday: "The theory is that there are factors other than skin color in racial discrimination. These factors are class differences and they are more immediately manageable. They oil their hair and chew gum. Maybe a girl can get a good job as a secretary, but if her hair smells like coconut oil. . . ." (Dr. Bereday himself speaks with a thick Polish accent, which makes him acceptably foreign rather than unacceptably lower class.)

let alone to entry into the governing elite of the country. For better or worse, incidentally, these accents are not a temporary phenomenon destined to disappear with the passage of the generations, no more than ethnic consciousness itself is. I have heard third-generation American Jews of East European immigrant stock speaking with thicker ethnic coloring even than their parents.

Clearly, then, while fancying myself altogether at home in the world into which I was born, I was not only more detached from it than I realized; I was also taking action, and of a very fundamental kind, which would eventually make it possible for me to move into some other world. Yet I still did not recognize what I was doing—not in any such terms. My ambition was to be a great and famous poet, not to live in a different community, a different class, a different "world." If I had a concrete image of what greatness would mean socially, it was probably based on the famous professional boxer from our block who had moved to a more prosperous neighborhood but still spent his leisure time hanging around the corner candy store and the local pool room with his old friends (among whom he could, of course, experience his fame far more sharply than he could have done among his newly acquired peers).

But to each career its own sociology. Boxers, unlike poets, do not undergo a cultural change in the process of becoming boxers, and if I was not brave enough or clever enough as a boy to see the distinction, others who knew me then were. "Ten years from now, you won't even want to talk to me, you won't even recognize me if you pass me on the street," was the kind of comment I frequently heard in my teens from women in the neighborhood, friends of my mother who were fond of me and nearly as proud as she was of the high grades I was getting in school and the prizes I was always winning. "That's crazy, you must be kidding," I would answer. They were not crazy and they were not kidding. They were simply better sociologists than I.

As, indeed, my mother herself was, for often in later years—after I had become a writer and an editor and was living only a subway ride away but in a style that was foreign to her and among people by whom she was intimidated—she would gaze wistfully at this strange creature, her son, and murmur, "I should have made him for a dentist," registering thereby her perception that whereas Jewish sons who grow up to be successes in certain occupations usually remain fixed in an accessible cultural ethos, sons who grow up into literary success are transformed almost beyond recognition and distanced almost beyond a mother's reach. My mother wanted nothing so much as for me to be a success, to be respected and admired. But she did not imagine, I think, that she would only purchase the realization of her ambition at the price of my progressive estrangement from her and her ways. Perhaps it was my guilt at the first glimmerings of this knowledge which accounted for my repression of it and for the obstinacy of the struggle I waged over "manners" with Mrs. K.

For what seemed most of all to puzzle Mrs. K., who saw no distinction between taste in poetry and taste in clothes, was that I could see no connection between the two. Mrs. K. knew that a boy from Brownsville with a taste for Keats was not long for Brownsville, and moreover would in all probability end up in the social class to which she herself belonged. How could I have explained to her that I would only be able to leave Brownsville if I could maintain the illusion that my destination was a place in some mystical country of the spirit and not a place in the upper reaches of the American class structure?

Saint Paul, who was a Jew, conceived of salvation as a world in which there would be neither Jew nor Greek, and though he may well have been the first, he was very far from the last Jew to dream such a dream of transcendence—transcendence of the actual alternative categories with which reality so stingily presents us. Not to be Jewish, but not to be Christian either; not to be a worker, but not to be a boss either; not—if I may be forgiven for injecting this banality out of my own soul into so formidable a series of fantasies—to be a slum child but not to be a snob either. How could I have explained to Mrs. K. that wearing a suit from de Pinna would for me have been something like the social equivalent of a conversion to Christianity? And how could she have explained to me that there was no socially neutral ground to be found in the United States of America, and that a distaste for the surroundings in which I was bred, and ultimately (God forgive me) even for many of the people I loved, and so a new taste for other kinds of people—how could she have explained that all this was inexorably entailed in the logic of a taste for the poetry of Keats and the painting of Cézanne and the music of Mozart?

2 Culture, Class, and Conversions

It did not, of course, happen all at once, and the process by which it did happen was masked and complicated—more, perhaps, than it would have been if I had been living in a campus dormitory during my four undergraduate years, and certainly more than it would have been if I had not also been attending a college of Jewish studies at the same time. I lived at home because my parents couldn't afford anything else, my father being employed in those days as a milkman for about sixty dollars a week; and I went to the Seminary College (which might be described as the undergraduate liberal-arts division of the Jewish Theological Seminary) because . . . well, to this day I am still uncertain of the reason. Unlike most of my classmates, I was neither especially religious nor much of a Zionist; nor did I have any intention, as the great majority of them did, of entering the rabbinate or becoming a Hebrew-school teacher. Yet there I was, every Tuesday night and every Thursday night and every Sunday afternoon, attending classes conducted in Hebrew (a language I never really succeeded in mastering), preparing assignments and taking exams —all at a time when I was having the greatest difficulty in keeping up with my work at Columbia.

I used to tell myself that I was doing it to please my father, and at least to some extent that was true. My father, like many young immigrants from Eastern Europe of his generation who had been raised in fanatically Orthodox homes, had arrived after a time in America at a curious point in his relation to Jewish religious observance. Not especially observant himself—except for the dietary laws and certain of the major holidays—he respected observance in others and encouraged it in me, less, I think, out of any religious conviction than out of a commitment to Jewish survival that was more instinctual than reasoned and consequently all the greater in its force.

A skeptical, reticent, highly private man, he never got caught up, as so many of his contemporaries did on their journey from East European orthodoxy to Western-style modernity, either in socialism or in any one of the organized varieties of ideological Jewish nationalism. He was sympathetic to socialism but not a socialist; he was a

Zionist, but not a passionate one; Yiddish remained his first language, but he was not a Yiddishist. He was, in short, a Jewish survivalist, unclassifiable and eclectic, tolerant of any modality of Jewish existence so long as it remained identifiably and self-consciously Jewish, and outraged by any species of Jewish assimilationism, whether overt or concealed.

The point was to be a Jew, and the way to be a Jew was to get a Jewish education; never mind about definitions, ideologies, justifications. There were, to be sure, limits; he would not, for example, yield to his father-in-law's demand that I be sent to a *yeshiva:* had he cut off his own earlocks in order that his American son should grow a pair? And his son, make no mistake about it, was and would be an American. On the other hand, he was determined not to settle for the usual course of instruction leading to and ending with the bar mitzvah ceremony at the age of thirteen. It was with such a course that he started me off as a boy of eight in the local synagogue, but by the time I was twelve, he had contrived—I no longer remember by what means of persuasion—to enroll me in a Hebrew high school which had a branch a few miles away.

I didn't mind going at first, but after a while I began to resent what more and more seemed a purposeless infringement on my freedom. Everyone else could fool around in the streets after school and on Sunday; why did I alone have to miss out on all the fun? Not that compensations were entirely lacking. It was pleasant being the adored darling of yet another group of teachers; and while my Jewish education only progressed at a sluggish rate at best, my sexual education moved forward in Hebrew high school with giant strides, thanks to the daughter of a rabbi, the first in a series of quietly smoldering rabbis' daughters I was to come upon in institutions of higher Jewish learning who (blessings upon them all) made my adolescent sex life far more abundant than the fiercely pragmatic chastity of the girls in my own neighborhood would otherwise have permitted. If not for this, I doubt that even paternal pressure could have kept me in Hebrew high school to the end. As it was I stayed, graduating at fifteen as valedictorian—an honor which only signified that my classmates had miraculously managed to learn even less Hebrew, less Bible, less Talmud, and less Jewish history than I.

But honors or no honors, rabbis' daughters or no rabbis' daughters, I had had enough. The summer following my graduation, my father, to the degree that his reticence would allow, argued, pleaded, cajoled, but all to no avail: I would not go on to the Seminary. Then early one morning in September, just as the new academic year was starting, he had a heart attack while delivering the milk on his route; a few days later, as he lay in an oxygen tent, as close to death as a man can get whose time has not yet come, I told him that I had decided to go to the Seminary after all. It is not impossible that I took his eventual recovery as a sign that his very life depended on my obedience to his wishes in the matter of being a Jew. But be that as it may, I was to remain at the Seminary for five years, the last four coinciding with my undergraduate term at Columbia; and all the while I lived at home, spending more than two hours a day in transit between Brownsville and Morningside Heights, where both Columbia and the Seminary are located.

In some respects, life at the Seminary was perfectly continuous with the life I had always known. Most of the students came from families much like mine, and the faculty was mostly composed of East European Jews who differed from the ones among whom I had been raised only in being far better educated. The curriculum too was familiar, being made up largely of texts to which I had already been exposed—though the emphasis now fell rather more on meaning and ideas than on the tedious fundamentals of the Hebrew language. The Seminary was not without its intellectual excitements, but they were undercut and diluted by this element of continuity. Columbia, on the other hand, represented an almost total break with the familiar, not only in the kind of people who studied and taught there, but also in the curriculum and the way in which it was treated.

Oddly enough for a boy of literary bent, I had read almost nothing before Columbia but popular novels and a few of the standard poets. I had never heard of most of the books we were given to read in Humanities and Contemporary Civilization—the two great freshman courses for which the college is deservedly famous—let alone of the modern authors whose names were being dropped so casually all around me. Though I had been writing poems and stories ever since I could remember, I did not know what men were doing when they committed words to paper. I did not know that there was more to a poem than verbal prettiness and passion, or that there was more to a novel than a story. I did not know what an idea was or how the mind could play with it. I did not know what history was, thinking of it as a series of isolated past events which had been arbitrarily selected for inclusion in the dreary canon of required knowledge. I did not know that I was the product of a tradition, that past ages had been inhabited by men like myself, and that the things they had done bore a direct relation to me and to the world in which I lived. All this began opening up for me at Columbia and it set my brain on fire.

Columbia College, unlike the university of which it forms the undergraduate liberal-arts division (for men), is a small school. Total enrollment in my day was about two thousand and classes were rarely larger than twenty —which, of course, permitted them to be run as seminars rather than lecture courses. The other unusual characteristic of the college which is relevant here is that many of the university's most distinguished faculty members taught these small classes. This meant that most of us, even as freshmen, came into intimate contact with such

important senior professors as Moses Hadas, Irwin
Edman, and Mark Van Doren.

I yearned with all my soul to be equal to them and
what they stood for, and I feared with all my soul that I
wasn't. Accustomed to effortless preeminence in school, I
suddenly found myself as a Columbia freshman staggering under an incredibly heavy load of assignments and
surrounded by classmates who knew more about everything than I did or clearly ever would. I was sure I would
fail. They would take my scholarship away. I would be
disgraced. Amazingly, it did not work out that way.
After a shaky start and many night-long porings over
strange and difficult books, I gradually learned to pace
myself; and after a few initially timid ventures in classroom discussion had elicited a certain familiar glow in
the eyes of several professors, I began jumping in with
both feet whenever I could get the chance. This did not
endear me to my classmates, but that was a small price to
pay for catching the attention of my teachers, which I
certainly succeeded in doing.

Utterly open, limitlessly impressionable, possessed
of something like total recall and a great gift for intellectual mimicry, I also succeeded, and without conscious intent, in writing papers for each of my professors in a different style—one which invariably resembled his own.
And finally, it turned out that I had a remarkable talent
for examinations of the essay type. Where others were
semiparalyzed by the impossibility of showing how good

they were in a mere three hours, I was never so fluent, never so coherent, never so completely in command of my powers of imitation as when I opened a blue book and started racing the clock. Given all this, and given also the intensity with which I worked, it is no wonder—though it was a great and glorious wonder to me then—that A + 's (an unusual grade at Columbia outside courses in the sciences) should have begun appearing on my record almost as regularly as A's.

Nor, given all this, is it any wonder that I aroused so much hostility among certain Columbia types: the prep-school boys, those B students who rarely said anything in class but who underwent such evident agonies over the unseemly displays of pushiness they had to endure from the likes of me; the homosexuals with their supercilious disdain of my lower-class style of dress and my brash and impudent manner; and the prissily bred middle-class Jews who thought me insufferably crude. All of them were lumped indiscriminately together in my mind as "snobs," and though their hostility got to me often enough to cause me considerable pain, I had friends of my own to lean on who, while they too regarded me as something of a barbarian and perhaps also something of an opportunist, at least regarded me as a likeable one: a Julien Sorel or a Rastignac, let us say (Columbia literati having been very fond of such analogies), rather than a Sammy Glick or a Flem Snopes.

I can see now, of course, that I must have caused the

"snobs" as much pain as they caused me. If I envied them their social composure and their apparent self-assurance, they must have envied me my freedom from the scruples which governed them and the consequent torrent of unhindered energy on which I was able to call. These scruples had nothing to do with morality; they had to do only with the code of manners governing ambitiousness which seemed to bind everyone at Columbia but me. It was a code which forbade one to work too hard or to make any effort to impress a professor or to display the slightest concern over grades. Since most of the "snobs" in question were serious students, however, the code hemmed them in, and since most of them were also ridden with ambition—quite as much, I think, as I—it forced them into secret transgressions, made them feel guilty, hypocritical, and ashamed. Yet I, a flagrantly open violator, instead of being punished, was being rewarded; I would probably even wind up, a "snob" once bitterly remarked to one of my friends, with Columbia's choicest prize, a Kellett Fellowship: "Can you imagine *him* at Oxford or Cambridge? Sammy Glick in the *Agora!*" (Columbia literati were not only fond of analogies, they also tended to a romantic Anglophilia, entertaining, as I was later to discover, an altogether exaggerated idea of the polish of English society.)

There was, to be sure, nothing unusual in the prevailing attitude toward ambitiousness at Columbia: it was a fair reflection of a widespread American sentiment.

And yet it does seem odd that in America, where the word ambition has traditionally been used as an honorific, ambitiousness itself should be so generally considered an unattractive quality and the signs of it looked upon as a personal deformation. According to William H. Whyte in *The Organization Man,* overt ambitiousness has even come to be frowned upon among businessmen, the very class of people who have been held responsible for exalting it to the status of a major virtue. Whyte, of course, ascribes this change to the growth of organization; in a large corporation, he says, the young executives compete with one another in being cooperative. But it is entirely possible that the new attitude toward ambition represents not a revolutionary development at all, but rather a return to normal after an aberrant historical episode brought about by the rapid and uncontrolled industrialization of the country following the Civil War. There is enough reason, God knows, for thinking that it is in the nature of man to be ambitious, but this quality has, after all, more generally been associated with the darker than with the lovelier side of human nature. Thus it is altogether typical that in the contest for popular support between Brutus and Mark Antony after the assassination of Julius Caesar, Antony (at least in Shakespeare's version) should have been able to win by refuting Brutus' charge, advanced in justification of the murder, that Caesar had been an ambitious man.

So far as the characteristic upper-class disdain for

ambitiousness is concerned—the species of disdain I encountered in youthfully exaggerated form at Columbia—
no doubt it was originally adopted as a weapon to be used
by those whose wealth was inherited or whose position
was secure against those who were occupied with accu-
mulating the one or acquiring the other. To become
aware of the origins of this disdain is to be let in on the
comedy of certain situations whose humor might otherwise not be apparent: for example, the frequently voiced
complaint of old-stock Massachusetts Yankees, privileged descendants of some of the most rapacious mer-
chants history has ever known, over the terrible "ruthlessness" of the Kennedy family.

This same "ruthlessness" also bothered many liberals whose discomfort over it probably derived from more
strictly ideological considerations. But whatever the
source of their discomfort, they dealt with it while John
F. Kennedy was still alive by persuading themselves that
the President was exempt from the family stigma, the
whole of that unworthy legacy having been inherited by
his brother Robert. This, in spite of the fact that John
F. Kennedy, like any man who goes far, and especially in
the vocation of politics, must not only have been ambitious but also not inconveniently troubled by delicate
scruples in the pursuit of his ambition. Once in the White
House, of course, Kennedy did carry himself like a *gentleman* (the kind of person, as Yeats once said, who is
thought not to be too much occupied with getting on),

and taking him for such (his famous "style"), most liberals finally came to adore him. Ambition, ruthlessness, unscrupulousness—all these unpatricianlike qualities were simply projected onto Bobby, who, we can be sure, is richly endowed with them, but, as we can be equally sure, no more than his brother was and possibly even less. If Bobby had not existed, the liberals would either have had to invent him or forgo the luxury of worshiping Jack.

Such attitudes toward ambition were not, when I was an undergraduate, without their effect on me; nor was I anywhere near as free of the Columbia code as the "snobs" believed me to be. But my hunger for success as a student, which was great enough in itself but might yet have yielded to discipline, became absolutely uncontrollable when I began to realize that I would never make the grade as a poet. I had a small talent for verse, yet try as I did for more than two years, there was finally no concealing the fact from myself that as compared with Allen Ginsberg, John Hollander, and a dozen other Columbia poets of the time, I rated at the most generous estimate a grudging honorable mention. (Even Mark Van Doren, who admired *everyone's* poetry, clearly thought little of mine: the only B I ever got in English at Columbia was in a creative writing course I took with him.) This was not an easy discovery to take for a boy who since the onset of puberty had been in the habit of telling girls that he would kill himself at twenty-five—Keats again—if he had decided for certain by then that he was not a great poet. Yet there was a truth concealed in those adolescent histrionics: the truth was that I could not bear the idea of not being great. Poetry had once seemed the only way to greatness, but now Columbia taught me that it was neither the only nor the right way for me.

Then what do you want to be now when you grow up, little boy? *A literary critic.* An unlikely answer today, perhaps, for anyone so ambitious as I was at nineteen, but in the late 1940's, the opening years of what Randall Jarrell was later to call "The Age of Criticism," nothing could have been more natural for an undergraduate who was doing well in English than to look forward to a career as a critic, while supporting himself, of course, by teaching. The physical sciences apart, literary criticism in those days was probably the most vital intellectual activity in America, and the most vital branch of literature itself; or if it was not in actual fact more significantly alive than philosophy or theology or history or the social sciences or poetry or fiction or the theater, it was certainly felt to be so by a great many young men of the time who aspired to the academic life. In my circle at Columbia, for example, we awaited the arrival of the quarterlies in which criticism flourished— magazines like *Partisan Review* and *Kenyon Review*— with the avidity of addicts, and we read the essays of such "New Critics" as Cleanth Brooks, R. P. Blackmur, and Allen Tate with an excitement that equaled, if indeed it did not surpass, the passion we brought to the poems and novels they were writing about. If we could all quote at length from the poetry of T. S. Eliot, we could also quote at length—and with, in truth, a greater feeling of assurance—from his critical essays.

And so with the critics on the Columbia faculty itself —the late Andrew Chiappe, the late Richard Chase, F. W. Dupee, and especially Lionel Trilling—who became our mentors, our models, our gods. In the classroom as on paper, the critics were not only our guides to the secret riches of literature, they were our guides to philosophy, theology, and politics as well. As explicators of difficult texts, they taught us a method of reading and gave us a veritably gnostic sense of power; as theoreticians of literature, they introduced us to the thrilling metaphysical categories which, banished from the philosophy department by the triumph of logical positivism, found a new home in criticism. As implicit polemicists for a neo-conservative (the New Critics) or neo-Marxist (the *Partisan Review* critics) point of view, they extended the boundaries of literature in general and their own work in particular to take in this world, as it were, along with the next.

In such an atmosphere, the vocation of critic-teacher seemed a genuine alternative to the vocation of poet, and with the record I already had behind me in English as I entered my senior year, there was every reason to believe that it was the right career for me. But it was only the ultimate certification I received that year from Trilling and Dupee that settled the matter for good. Trilling in particular was known as a tough grader and he was said to be automatically suspicious of students who came to his classes with great reputations behind them. The A+ he gave me in his course on the English Romantics, coupled with another A+ from Dupee in a course on contemporary literature, removed any lingering doubt as to what my future would be. All that remained for the moment was to decide where I would go to graduate school, and that question was settled—the "snobs" had been right—by a Kellett Fellowship and then a Fulbright Scholarship to boot.

The first lap of that journey I was making from Brooklyn to Manhattan had most definitely been completed; the second lap would be a generously financed three-year stay at the ancient university of Cambridge.

II   In his book about Columbia, *The Reforming of General Education,* Daniel Bell speaks of the "conversion experience" which the college seems to induce in many of its students. They are shocked, he says, into "a new appreciation of the dimensions of thought and feeling," and they are thereby converted, "so to speak, to culture." Certainly something of this kind happened to me at Columbia; I discovered, and really for the first time, that there were more things in heaven and earth than were dreamt of in the philosophy of Brownsville, that the world offered a greater range of possibilities than I or the people among whom I had been raised had ever imagined it to contain. And in time I came to see that some of these were possibilities for *me*.

Bell is also right in saying that the conversion was to "culture"—the more so in that he attaches no qualifying adjectives to the term. To be sure, Columbia itself did attach a qualifying adjective, no bones ever having been made there about the fact that it was the heritage of *Western* Civilization to which we were being introduced. And yet the idea of Western Civilization seemed so broad and generous, so all-embracing of whatever might be important or good or great or noble in the world, that most of us thought of the adjective as merely a polite tautology, a kind of elegantly liberal nod at the poor old Orient. To our minds, this culture we were studying at Columbia was not the creation or the possession of a particular group of people; it was a repository of the universal, existing not in space or time but rather in some transcendental realm of the spirit—that very realm I had dreamed of in the days of Mrs. K.

But if for me Columbia represented universality, the Seminary stood just as sharply for parochialism—and not only because of its continuity with the life I had always known. Unlike the Rabbinical School and the Teachers Institute, its sister divisions within the Jewish Theological Seminary, the Seminary College was theoret-

43

ically committed to what Jewish tradition calls *Torah lishma,* learning for its own sake, but in actual fact its purposes were very far from being disinterestedly academic. The literal meaning of *Torah lishma* may be "learning for its own sake," but the true, the theological, meaning of the idea is "studying the revealed word of God for the sake of heaven." The Seminary College did not, I think, consider that it was teaching the revealed word of God for the sake of heaven; it did, however, consider that it was teaching the heritage of the Jewish people as a way of ensuring the survival of that people (my father knew what he was doing when he sent me there). This is not to imply that there was anything covert or devious going on; on the contrary, most professors at the Seminary simply and frankly took it for granted that their business was to deepen the Jewish commitment of their students by making them more fully aware of the glories of the Jewish heritage. They were not training minds or sensibilities; they were training Jews.

To my adolescent eyes, guided by several extraordinary teachers at Columbia (the greatest of whom, the late Moses Hadas, was a lapsed rabbi: the ironies here are manifold), Western Culture made what the Seminary had to offer look narrow, constricted, provincial, and finally less relevant to me personally than the heritage of what was, after all, a Christian civilization, and one which had up until—how long? a minute before?—been at literally murderous odds with the heritage, not to mention the bodies, of my own people. And in this sense, too, I suppose one might speak of a conversion in describing what happened to me at Columbia.

But whether or not the word is appropriate (and probably it is several shades too harsh), it was not long before I grew restless and resentful at having to attend the Seminary. I was determined, because of my father, to stay on to the end, but it all seemed utterly pointless. A few of the courses were easily equal to any at Columbia —Bible with H. L. Ginsberg, Jewish history with Abraham S. Halkin—and could even be thought of as fitting in with my beloved Western Civilization (which—further proof of its universality—took even the best of the Jewish tradition into its generous and transcendent embrace). But the strident note of apologetics and defensiveness which entered into the least detail of almost every other aspect of the Seminary curriculum, the endless pep talks disguised as scholarship, the endless harping on the sufferings of the Jews: all this made my Columbia-trained sensibilities raw. And the students: the bright ones who were going cynically into the rabbinate because it offered an easy, protected way of life; the dull ones who were going solemnly into the rabbinate because they were afraid to dare the outside world; the fanatical Hebraists who would admonish one to "Speak Hebrew!" as they marched by in the halls (one of these, it was rumored, would announce to his wife, *"Hineh zeh bah"*—"Behold, it cometh"—as he reached a climax in the act of love)—what had I to do with such people or they with me?

And there is yet a third sense, deeper in the long run than the other two, in which the word conversion might be applied in describing what happened to me in the course of those four years at Columbia. But here I must tread warily. I have already said that the Seminary was frank in its parochialism, that it made no pretense either to itself or to its students as to the purposes it was pursuing. I knew perfectly well that the Seminary was in the business of making Jews, and I understood perfectly well what that meant. But the suggestion that Columbia, High Temple of Culture and Civilization, might be pursuing certain restricted social purposes of its own would have struck me as an absurdity, a contradiction in terms. And yet it was. "One of the commonest references that one hears with regard to Columbia," wrote the Dean of the College, Frederick P. Keppel, in 1914,

> is that its position at the gateway of European immigration makes it socially uninviting to students who come from homes of refinement. The form which the inquiry takes in these days of slowly dying race prejudice is, "Isn't Columbia overrun with European Jews who are most unpleasant persons socially?" . . . [But] what most people regard as a racial problem is really a social problem. The Jews who have had the advantages of decent social surroundings for a generation or two are entirely satisfactory companions. . . . There are, in-

deed, Jewish students of another type who have not had the social advantages of their more fortunate fellows. Often they come from an environment which in any stock less fired with ambition would have put the idea of higher education entirely out of the question. Some of these are not particularly pleasant companions, but the total number is not large, and every reputable institution aspiring to public service must stand ready to give to those of probity and good moral character the benefits which they are making great sacrifices to obtain.*

Of course, Keppel was writing at a time when Columbia was the college of Old New York society—a kind of finishing school for young gentlemen who would soon enter the governing elite of the nation. By the end of the Second World War, when I arrived, the composition of its student body had become more diverse, both geographically and ethnically, and the G.I. Bill had brought in many veterans who would otherwise have been unable to afford the tuition. To be sure, the number of Jews admitted to the college was still limited by an unacknowledged quota (about 17 percent), but the only anti-Semitism I personally ever encountered there was among some of the Jewish students themselves.

If, however, anti-Semitism as such was dead at Columbia, at least one of the major assumptions contained in Keppel's remarks of 1914 was still very much alive in

* Frederick P. Keppel, *Columbia,* New York, Oxford University Press, 1914.

1946, and this was that the adoption of a liberalized admissions policy by Columbia, as a "reputable institution aspiring to public service," carried with it the responsibility to make "satisfactory companions" out of such of their students who had not "come from homes of refinement" and had not enjoyed "the social advantages of their more fortunate fellows." It was, then, the business of Columbia College to make a gentleman out of any young man of "foreign stock" on whom it chose to confer the benefits of a higher education. In other words, me.

Maurice Samuel once wrote a whole book, *The Gentleman and the Jew*, to show that the idea of the gentleman, however variously it might have been defined at different times and in different places, was always consistent in one detail: that it stood in opposition to the idea of the Jew. Keppel's remarks are a good example of how this opposition worked, but in subsequent Columbia usage of the term, the element of class disappears and the gentleman Columbia now wishes to produce is described as "the honorable and responsible citizen of enlightened and gracious mind." * These are fine and resounding abstractions, but if one wishes to determine

---

* This is Lionel Trilling's paraphrase of Columbia thinking on the matter. It is perhaps worth noting that Trilling was the first Jew ever to be given a permanent appointment in the Columbia English department, which was among the last holdouts against Jews of all the departments in the university. As late as 1937, it was thought that a Jew could teach philosophy or even Greek, but that no one with such shallow roots in Anglo-Saxon culture could be entrusted with the job of introducing the young to its literary heritage.

whether they are quite so free of any class bias as they appear to be, one has only to ask what the type they envisage would in all probability look like. He would not, I imagine, be a person who ate with his fingers, or whose accent bore the traces of an immigrant slum, or whose manners clashed significantly with the oppressively genteel atmosphere of the Columbia Faculty Club. He might once have been such a person, and as such a person he would once have been barred altogether from the possibility of ever being considered a "gentleman." Now, however, in a more liberal and tolerant age, his origins would no longer be held against him—so long, that is, as he could learn to comport himself like a reasonable facsimile of an upper-class WASP.

When I was in college, the term WASP had not yet come into currency—which is to say that the realization had not yet become widespread that white Americans of Anglo-Saxon Protestant background are an ethnic group like any other, that their characteristic qualities are by no means self-evidently superior to those of the other groups, and that neither their earlier arrival nor their majority status entitles them to exclusive possession of the national identity. In the absence of this realization, Columbia had no need to be as fully conscious of the social implications of the purposes it was pursuing as, on its side, the Seminary necessarily was. The demand being made on me as a student of Jewish culture was concrete, explicit, and unambiguous: "Become a good Jew!" The demand being made on me as a student of Western Culture, by contrast, was seductively abstract and idealized: "Become a gentleman, a man of enlightened and gracious mind!" It is not that Columbia was being dishonest in failing to mention that this also meant "Become a facsimile WASP!" In taking that corollary for granted, the college was simply being true to its own ethnic and class origins; and in nothing did this fidelity show itself more clearly than in the bland unconsciousness that accompanied it.

As for me, I was even less conscious of the social meaning of Columbia's intentions toward me than Columbia itself was—which, of course, only made those intentions easier to realize. My personal deportment did not change. Far from coming to look or act like a facsimile WASP, I continued to dress in the Brownsville manner, resisting my Columbia friends now, as I had resisted Mrs. K. before, when they tried to prod me into adopting the "proper" style. Similarly with the dietary laws, which I insisted on observing in spite of much ridicule and long after I had ceased to believe in them. So too with the obscenities I constantly used, after the Brownsville fashion, in casual conversation. And so especially with my ambitiousness, which only grew more ostentatious with every kindly counsel that I try to conceal it. Back home, on weekend nights and any others I could spare, I continued to bum around with the gang—most of them now working at menial jobs and some of them attending night-school classes in accountancy or engineering at one of the City Colleges—living the old life of street corners, pool rooms, crap games, poker games, sports talk, sex talk. I was, to all appearances, the same kid I had been before entering Columbia, only a little older, a little more sure of myself, a little less anxious over my status as one of "the boys." With my parents, also, relations were as good on the surface as ever. We still talked a great deal, I still went on dutiful visits to relatives with them, and I still did not complain about having to live at home without a room of my own to work in.

And yet and yet: we all knew that things were not the same. They knew—it was in their eyes—that I was already halfway out of their world and that it was only a matter of time before I would be out of it altogether. And I? What did I know? I knew that the neighborhood voices were beginning to sound coarse and raucous; I knew that our apartment was beginning to look tasteless and tawdry; I knew that the girls in quest of whom my friends and I hornily roamed the streets were beginning to strike me as too elaborately made up, too shrill in their laughter, too crude in their dress.

Notice: it was my *sensibilities* which were being offended, and by things which had been familiar to me my whole life long; it was the lower-classness of Brownsville to which I was responding with irritation. To wean me away from Brownsville, all Columbia had had to do was give me the superior liberal education it did: in giving me such an education it was working a radical change in my tastes, and in changing my tastes it was ensuring that I would no longer be comfortable in the world from which I had come. For taste is an overwhelmingly important sociological force, capable by itself of turning strangers into brothers and brothers into strangers. What did it matter that I genuinely loved my family and my friends, when not even love had the power to protect them from the ruthless judgments of my newly delicate, oh-so-delicate, sensibilities? What did it matter that I was still naïve enough and cowardly enough and even decent enough to pretend that my conversion to "culture" had nothing to do with class when I had already traveled so far along the road Mrs. K. had predicted I would—when I had to all intents and purposes already become a snob?

And finally there was a fourth conversion—this one to the Columbia code. Though largely social in its origins, the Columbia code was much reinforced among the literati in the college by the contemptuous attitude toward success which inevitably seems to develop out of the study of literature. There are several reasons for this, but the widely entertained idea that the Western literary heritage itself inculcates such an attitude is most assuredly not one of them. For the truth is that if Western literature teaches any consistent lesson on this score— which of course it does not—it would be that wealth, power, and especially fame are immensely desirable things to have. Certainly the Greeks thought so; certainly the Elizabethans thought so; and certainly the great nineteenth-century novelists thought so too. Contemporary literature is admittedly another matter, but even there the case is rather more ambiguous than many people appear to think.

What then are the reasons for the connection between the study of literature and the contempt for success? The noblest of them is undoubtedly that the study of literature encourages a great respect for activity which is its own reward (whereas the ethos of success encourages activity for the sake of extrinsic reward), and a great respect for the thing-in-itself (as opposed to the ethos of success which encourages a nihilistically reductive preoccupation with the "cash value" of all things). To acquire even a small measure of independent critical judgment is to understand that "successful" does not necessarily mean "good" and that "good" does not necessarily mean "successful." From there it is but a short step, the shortest step in the world, to the ardent conclusion that the two can *never* go together, particularly in America and particularly in the arts.

But there are other, more strictly sociological, reasons for the connection. In the first place, a young man who studies literature is in effect electing to join a kind of political party within the American cultural order: the party of opposition to the presumed values of the business world. A negative attitude toward success is a requirement of membership in this party, and it will be strengthened by much of the new recruit's reading in the social and literary criticism of the past hundred years which, unlike the literary tradition itself, definitely does inculcate such an attitude.

A second reason, flowing from the first, is that a young man who studies literature is doing something which has at best a modest market value. He may—he almost invariably will—have fantasies of becoming a great writer himself, thereby at least achieving fame (the ambition for which has always enjoyed a better reputation among moralists than the ambition for wealth or power). But he is also sensible enough to know that in electing to pursue a literary career, which for all practical purposes means teaching in a college, he can probably look forward only to a life of relatively modest means on the periphery of American society. Most young men who make this choice make it with the greatest enthusiasm, imagining that they are entering an existence rich in spiritual satisfaction and turning their backs on one that has nothing to offer but empty material comforts. Naturally high-minded anyway, the young find it difficult to appreciate the value of these "empty" comforts; being human, they are quick to denigrate what they have not learned to appreciate; and being inexperienced, they are slow to understand that making a living in the academic world has more in common with making a living in the business world than a superficial glance at either would reveal.

All this clashed sharply with the direct and simple belief in the desirability of success I had absorbed at home, and especially from my mother. But that did not prevent the new attitude from taking a powerful hold over me. It did not, to be specific, prevent it from leading me (with a prodding assist from my Columbia friends) to the miserable speculation that my success at Columbia, far from being a confirmation of my worth and a certification of my promise as a future critic of literature, might in reality be a sign that, like a best-selling author, I was corrupt, opportunistic, and ultimately incapable of serious work.

It was at Columbia, then, that I was introduced to the ethos—destined to grow more and more powerful in the ensuing years—in which success was replacing sex as the major "dirty little secret" of the age. By the values of this ethos, the hunger for sex was a natural and indeed an admirable passion, whereas the hunger for worldly success was regarded as low, ignoble, ugly: something to be concealed from others and preferably even from oneself, something to be ashamed of and guilty about. My own conversion to such values was yet another sign that the first lap in the long, blind journey I was making from Brooklyn to Manhattan had at last been completed.

III   A critic with a very good pair of ears once wrote
that he could hear in some of my essays "the tones of a
young man who expects others to be just a little too
happy with his early eminence." Pleased though I was by
the implications of so casual a reference to my eminence,
the observation as a whole hurt. I knew that it must be
true, because the weakness to which it pointed was one I
had been struggling to overcome for many years and
thought I had overcome. Obviously, however, so far was
I still from overcoming it that I could not even prevent it
from showing itself in my published work. Was it possible
that it still showed in my life as well, despite all the vigi-
lance against it I had so laboriously been cultivating
from the time I first became aware of its existence and
began to understand how much trouble it could cause me
if I let it have its way?

The naïve expectation that others will take one's
own good fortune as an occasion for rejoicing is, of
course, characteristic of adored and indulged children. I
can at least claim in my own defense, then, that I came
by this weakness honestly. As the younger of my parents'
two children and as their only son, I was quite blatantly
the favorite at home; as a precocious, eager, affectionate,
chattering child, I was also the special pet of numerous
relatives, neighbors, and teachers—so much so that if
not for my sister, my reality principle, I might well have

grown up believing that the universe was inhabited exclusively by people whose eyes had no other function but to light up at the sight of me. Of course I also had playmates who were somewhat less than enthusiastic about my presence on the earth and who supplied an added touch of the reality principle in my life. But the adult world, and especially the female part of it, was one vast congregation of worshipers at the shrine of my diminutive godhead. They praised, they kissed, they pinched, they pulled, they hugged, they smothered me in their bosoms. They marveled at the blue of my eyes, at the thick curliness of my hair, at the streak of gray on its side (proof, they said, echoing an ancient superstition, that I was among the elect). But most of all they marveled at my cleverness, quoting my bright sayings to one another and even back to me ("You remember what you said that time when I was here last? Let me hear you say it again."). They called me adorable, they called me delicious, they called me a genius, and predicted a great future for me: a doctor at the very least I would be.

Freud: "A man who has been the indisputable favorite of his mother keeps for life the feeling of a conqueror, that confidence of success which frequently induces real success." And so it was that I became from the very beginning a great winner of prizes—gold stars, perfect report cards, medals for this and honors for that (but, to my sorrow, neither the "this" nor the "that" ever included athletics in any shape or form). To be a prizewinner is a joyous enough fate in itself, but to be a prizewinner whose prizes are a source of unshadowed delight to the world in which one lives is possibly the true definition of happiness.

This is how it was for the most part with me, certainly where all the adults in my life were concerned, and even to a considerable extent with my contemporaries. Up to a certain age children are extremely realistic in their appraisal of one another's skills, and no matter how prone to jealousy they may be, or how lacking in generosity, they are curiously straightforward in their recognition of exactly how they rate in various areas of competition and coolly respectful of ability superior to their own. In every gang of boys, for example, the precise hierarchy of athletic skills is always perfectly clear; everyone knows who the best pitcher is, who the second-best set-shot is, who the third-best passer is. Similarly in school, and all the more so in my day because of the custom then of seating the children according to academic rank. Everyone knew that I was the smartest kid in the class; it was a fact that would no more have been questioned or resented, despite the enmity it caused, than Carl Brown's supremacy at the plate.

What I am saying is that children are jealous creatures but not envious ones, the difference between the two passions lying in this: that jealousy says, "I wish I were as good a pitcher as you," whereas envy says, "You're not really a good pitcher even though you've fooled everyone into thinking so; if they weren't all so dumb, and if I felt like it, I could show them what pitching is." Where a precise ranking of best and second-best is not significantly relevant—in, for instance, the area of money—jealousy would say, "I wish I had as much money as you, but I don't mind if you have it too," whereas envy would say, "I wish I were as rich as you and you were as poor as I." Jealousy is thus the covetous emotion appropriate to a situation of abundance, and envy the covetous emotion appropriate to a situation of scarcity. In the utopia envisaged by Lyndon B. Johnson —an economy of such great wealth that the pie would be big enough for all to have an adequate share without recourse to the redistribution of income—jealousy would presumably become the ruling social passion (an honor which Tocqueville accorded to envy in democratic societies).

Yet it may be doubted that envy really would disappear even in the Johnsonian utopia, for it is an imperialistic passion with an inherent tendency toward expansion into territories of the spirit that do not belong within its natural sphere of influence. And it is, in addition, an ultimately cannibalistic passion: it aims at the expropriation of the enemy's power and can conceive of no other way to get it than to destroy and then gobble him up. This perhaps explains why the idea of being envied is capable of inspiring such terror. To be pierced by an envious (or "evil") eye is to feel pins being stuck into the effigy of oneself that lives in the primitive reaches of one's being. If, therefore, people will go to great lengths to arouse envy, they will also go to great lengths to ward it off— often, like misers, denying themselves any pleasure in the things they have acquired or accomplished precisely in order to *be* envied.

In any event, while I myself from a very early age knew everything there was to know about jealousy, and from both sides of the fence, I knew almost nothing about envy, having experienced so little of it either as subject or object. Not only did I not recognize it when I saw it, I was scarcely aware that such a thing existed; and this remarkable obtuseness was of course compounded by my adored-child illusion that the world around me would declare a holiday whenever I won a prize. Hence my incredible stupidity in failing to anticipate that my friends at Columbia would be envious when, after absorbing the blow of the Kellett, they would also have to endure seeing me win the only Fulbright any of us was to get. Hence too my incredible insensitivity in expecting them to be happy for me and my amazement when I realized they were not. And hence, finally, my inability to understand the intention behind their effort to persuade me that glibness and an adaptability bespeaking flabbiness of soul, rather than any virtue of mind or character, accounted for my success. Not perceiving the envy in this assault—taking it, indeed, just as my friends themselves did, for the honesty of a courageous love (we were great believers in telling one another the "truth")—I was altogether helpless before it and before the guilt and self-doubt it aroused.

It was the first time I had ever experienced the poisoning of success by envy. Because it was the envy not of enemies but of friends, and because it came at me not naked and undisguised but posing as love and masked in ideologically plausible rationalizations, it was hard to identify as envy—and harder still because in my instinctive terror of becoming the object of this expropriating and cannibalistic passion, I was unwilling to admit to myself that it was in fact being directed against me. And no doubt in my terror of it, I was also trying to ward the envy off by allowing my friends to make me so miserable that they would finally have nothing to envy me for. Theirs the virtue of failure, mine the corruption of success: who then was the enviable one?

With all this, my introduction to the dirty little secret of our age was more or less complete. I was now ready to set sail for England and run that second lap.

3 The Second Lap Across the Sea

I had not, I think, realized how *foreign* England would be, imagining, as I recall, that it would look something like Boston, only older and more elegant. But it did not look like Boston at all, it looked like *Europe;* it did not look old, it looked ancient; and it did not look elegant, it looked by turns majestic to the point of awe and charming to the point of fantasy. The people were an even greater surprise. I had imagined them, in my ignorant Anglophilia, as looking like American patricians, only classier and more aloof. But almost everyone was shabbily dressed, almost everyone seemed to have bad teeth and an unhealthy complexion, and no one was in the least bit aloof.

And Cambridge: physically it resembled no university I had ever seen. There was, in the first place, no central campus but rather some two dozen individual colleges, each with its own walled-in grounds and its own architectural style. I knew next to nothing about architecture in those days, but it was not necessary to know anything in order to tell within five minutes of one's arrival in the town that the real thing was here, all around and wherever one turned, that stretching far back into the Middle Ages one century after another had left its physical presence in this place, each embodying, in houses where people still lived and gardens where people still walked, its own distinctive ideas of grace, of stateliness, of luxury, of ease. And with it all, the famous "backs"—those lawns, so green they seemed artificial, feeding from the rear of the oldest colleges down to the banks of the surprisingly narrow Cam and overlooked by several of the most beautiful buildings in the world.

One of those buildings was my own college, Clare, founded in 1326, but the present two-storied quadrangular structure, called Old Court, dating only from the mid-seventeenth century. On the far side of the river, connected to Old Court by the loveliest of the many bridges spanning the Cam, stood Clare New Court, built in the 1930's to accommodate an expanding number of students. Like all twentieth-century Cambridge architecture up to that time, it represented timidity in the face of the best modern styles and a misguided effort toward harmony with the older buildings around it (even though they themselves had been allowed in the past to vary according to period); the result was the standard two-storied quadrangular structure, but nondescript in character, texture, and line. On the other hand, New Court was equipped with modern plumbing, and perhaps it was just as well that they decided to put me there.

But the phrase "just as well" comes out of me as I now am, not as I then was, for nothing will ever seem so beautiful to me again as the sight of New Court in the brilliant September sun that was presciently shining over Cambridge on the day that I arrived. Like a character out of Odets, I had been praying only for a room of my own, a room all to myself, a room with a door that had not, like every door we had at home, been thickened by repeated paintings to the point where it could not close. But the porter, oddly calling me "Sir," showed me to a two-room suite, all paneled in wood and furnished in leather, and told me it was mine. A year earlier, on a weekend visit to a wealthy friend, I had been ushered into similarly appointed quarters for the night and had been amazed to find myself bursting into tears of self-pity over my own roomless condition the minute he left me alone—amazed because I had truly never realized that such things mattered to me. This time, when I found myself weeping over a room again, I was not amazed. The only thing that amazed me was my luck.

With the rooms, as I was immediately to discover, came a new status in life, the most dramatic symbol of which popped its head into the doorway a short while after my arrival to welcome me to Clare. He was, he said, Aubrey, my "gyp." Gyp? *"Servant,* sir." He laughed with good-natured amusement at American ignorance. Before the war, he explained in his thick East Anglian accent (which resembles cockney but is if anything even harder for an unaccustomed ear to understand), I would have had him all to myself, but times were harder now and to his regret I would have to share him with several other young gentlemen on the "staircase." I needn't worry, however; he could take good care of us all. He would bring my scuttles of coal, clean out the fireplace, light a new fire, tidy up my rooms, make my bed, shine my shoes, and wake me with a cup of tea in the morning at whatever time I said. What with eight young gentlemen to tend to, he would be unable to run errands in the town for me, but he would do his best to keep my rooms in order and comfortable and warm (this last being difficult, since there was no central heating and coal was still being rationed on a wartime basis).

Aubrey neither knew nor cared that I was a boy from the provinces of immigrant Brooklyn, a member of roughly the same social class to which he belonged. So far as he was concerned—so far, indeed, as the whole of England seemed to be concerned—I was a Clare man and therefore a "young gentleman" to whom amenities, privileges, and deference were owed as by natural right. The scholarship boys at Clare from Yorkshire grammar schools, and with accents to match, were only grudgingly accorded this status. But to English eyes in those days when, Labour Government or no Labour Government and loss of Empire or no loss of Empire, the traditional class structure was still very strong and the concomitantly undifferentiated attitude toward foreigners still very widespread—especially in beleaguered pockets of the past like Oxford and Cambridge—an American was simply an American. And this meant that the only relevant social identity I possessed was that of a student at Cambridge. If, to exaggerate slightly but not much more than that, I had been a Cabot or a Lodge, neither Aubrey nor England would have perceived the difference. As it was, I had been magically transformed overnight from a Brooklyn "barbarian" into "one of the young gentlemen from America."

It took me some time, of course, to adjust to the change, but not nearly so much as might be imagined, for there are few things in the world easier to get used to than having lots of space to live in and being called "Sir." It has been said that it takes three generations to make an aristocrat; my own experience would suggest that three weeks are about enough. That, at any rate, is approximately how long it took for all the anxieties I had brought to England with me over such matters as clothes, manners, and general social style to evaporate: poof and they were gone.

They evaporated because, as it astonishingly turned

out, "manners" were of absolutely no consequence in a traditionally structured class society. So long as one was a member of the upper class, one could behave as one damn well pleased without fear that one's patent of nobility would be taken away; and if one were not a member of the upper class, there was no way to behave that would bring one any of its benefits. I had thought of class as an abstraction before, having to do mainly with style, but now I understood what it meant as a concrete condition. It did not mean acting in accordance with the social standards of a particular group; it meant being served as against serving and being deferred to as against deferring. Privilege or the lack of it was what it meant. And as Lord Melbourne had said of the Order of the Garter, it involved "no damned nonsense about merit."

In America, it began to dawn upon me, the whole issue of class had been complicated by the fantastic heterogeneity of the society. In a country with a homogeneous population like England, there were the rich, the middling, and the poor, but in America this basic division had been criss-crossed and papered over by many others: regional, religious, ethnic, and racial, each a further source of privilege or the lack of it. And to make matters still more complicated, there was the ideology of egalitarianism which had not so much resulted in the destruction of class distinctions as in their concealment within a kind of secret social cipher. In other words, while class in America certainly had as much to do with money as in England, it also had to do—in a way for which England offered no parallel—with the question of whether or not one had been born white, Protestant, and of Anglo-Saxon ancestry, and had been raised, of course, accordingly.

One could, as I had already learned, become a facsimile WASP: that much open to talent the American upper class actually was and that far its egalitarianism clearly did extend. But unless one succeeded in turning oneself into such a person, one was unlikely to become eligible for a whole range of the powers and privileges America had to offer. For the American social contract—on which, as with the primordial social contract itself, the peace of so divided and fragmented a society rested—had been implicitly extended in the post-Civil War period to cover the problems presented by the influx of millions of immigrants with their strange tongues, their peasant customs, their "barbaric" and "uncivilized" ways. And the contract was this: to the degree that these people would submit to "Americanization"—which is to say, to the degree that they would learn and adopt the language, traditions, and customs of the oldest American group—to that degree would they be "accepted"—which is to say, freed from *some* of the many kinds of discrimination, gross and subtle, open and concealed, to which, in defiance of the strictly legal social contract, called the Constitution, that presumably governed the country, they were invariably and cruelly subjected. (Of course they fought back, getting qualifying clauses written into the contract, but that part of the story I did not learn until many years later, and will tell in its proper place.) Hence the importance of "manners" at an institution like Columbia and their converse lack of importance at Cambridge, product of an ethnically homogeneous country and a more straightforwardly class-bound society.

The differences between life at Columbia and life at Cambridge, however, were not only physical and social; they were academic as well. I had expected to do graduate work at Cambridge, but it turned out that the English universities did not recognize the American B.A. as equivalent to their own. The alternatives, then, were to forget about pursuing a degree altogether or to go for a B. A. Cantab., which, as a graduate of an American college, I could earn in two years instead of the normal three. I would, in common with all Cambridge undergraduates no matter what subject they "read," write a weekly essay for my college supervisor (the same person Oxford calls a tutor), and spend an hour discussing it with him. Like all other undergraduates too, I could attend or not, as I pleased, any of the lecture courses open to any member of the university regardless of college; but instead of being required, as undergraduates were, to take the series of university-wide examinations known collectively as the Tripos at the end of each year in my chosen subject (English, of course), I would be exempt from Part I and would have to pass only Part II at the end of the second year.

On the whole this seemed to me, as it did to most American students at Cambridge, a better idea than not matriculating at all. For one thing, the real life at Cambridge was the undergraduate life; to follow any other course was to miss the full flavor of the Cambridge experience. In addition to that, a Cambridge B.A. was a good investment for anyone who meant to pursue an academic career in America, not only because of the prestige attached to it, and not only because it automatically "matured" into an M.A. after a certain number of years, but also because having it would open the way to a Ph.D. at Cambridge, where the requirements were much less onerous than in America itself. It was said that Cambridge had decided to offer a Ph.D. in the first place only as a concession to foreign students—the English themselves seeing no particular point in the degree—and took a malicious delight in flunking them whenever they made the mistake of going after it. But a graduate of Cambridge was different. An American to whose name the title "B. A. Cantab." was appended could no longer be considered an opportunist looking for an easy way to win his "union card"; he was a member in good standing of the university community and would therefore be less likely to fail. Such, at any rate, was the myth which, fortunately for me, I bought.

For as becoming a "young gentleman" freed me from my social anxieties, becoming an undergraduate again freed me for a while at least from my anxieties over grades and results. Under the Cambridge system, one's supervisor had nothing to do with grading. The only grades one got were First-, Second-, or Third-Class Honors, and these were determined exclusively by one's performance on Part II of the Tripos, which was always read by examiners from other colleges. Hence it was that the only considerations which could enter into the relation between supervisor and pupil were personal and pedagogic. In my usual fashion I wanted my supervisor to have a good opinion of me, but apart from that there was nothing—nothing, that is to say, extrinsic to the work we did together—for which I could strive in my contact with him. He could neither give me a First if I impressed him nor withhold one from me if I did not.

Under the circumstances I found myself able to relax as never before in all my years in school, or, for that matter, anywhere else. And there was time, more time than I had ever had to myself before. Except for taking in an occasional lecture in the morning, I would sit in my study, with the firelight at once brightening and deepening the brown of the walls, and I would read—not, as in the past, in a frantic rush to finish and to formulate a view, but at a slow and easy pace, interrupting myself every so often to chew a passage over, or to think, or to dream, or simply to relish the positively erotic pleasure of a gorgeous and abundant solitude. There was time, there was time: to spend months on a single author, to learn French, to immerse myself in political theory, to have all-night bull sessions with my economist friend from Australia, to wander about the town, to laze around the backs. And with all that, there was still time—for sleeping late and for movie-going, and there was even time for girls.

Clare, then, meant a long reprieve from being tested by others; even better, it meant a reprieve from being tested by myself. The intellectual style of my supervisor, a young don all tweeds and mustache and pipe, was the best possible antidote I could have found to the frenetic pursuit of "brilliance" to which I had become habituated at Columbia and whose imperatives constituted a more fearful tyranny, being largely internal, than any that could conceivably have been imposed upon me from the outside. Taciturn, hard-headed, common-sensical, scholarly, and as English as empiricism itself, he was not in the least moved by those thrilling leaps of "insight" uninhibited by an excess of knowledge; those pseudo-Germanic syntheses undisturbed by mere detail; those wild perceptions into the secret pattern of things whose secrets were actually all on the surface; those daring analogies, the far-fetched the better since it took greater ingenuity to defend them; those fancy jargonistic formulations bespeaking a mastery of the concepts of modern criticism in all its chic varieties, those Eliotic pomposities, those

Blackmurian obscurities, those (Kenneth) Burkean pro-
fundities—all those habits of mind and language which,
mixed together in an improbable stew and seasoned with
the special pretentiousness of the sophomoric temperament, were what we meant at Columbia when we used
the word "brilliance": most coveted of epithets, most
honorific of honorifics, was life worth living unless one
knew oneself to be deserving of its sacred bestowal?

Having written such a "brilliant" essay for my supervisor, I would be quietly challenged to tell him what
it meant. But surely he was being pedagogically disin-
genuous, surely he understood what I was saying? No, he
didn't understand; could I please (puff-puff on the pipe)
translate it into English for him? Philistine, I thought,
dope. But not for long. Not after my overheated brain
and my overardent soul had begun to cool down in response to the Northern English chill of my supervisor's
mind: a mind as placid and skeptical as Cambridge itself, which for more than six centuries had seen them
come and seen them go while it went on forever. And this
was precisely the spirit of Clare where, as (incredibly)
Geoffrey Chaucer and (all too credibly) a thousand future bishops of the Church of England had done in their
days before me, I worked and slept and took my meals
and had most of my social life. Clare: most complacently
English of all the Cambridge colleges, keeper of the faith
in rugger, cricket, and the manly Christian virtues. Let
Kings College be fashionably arty and Trinity College

intellectually advanced. One did not make too much of things at Clare; not of things and certainly not of one-self.

Thus on the surface, at least, the atmosphere at Clare was not unlike the atmosphere surrounding those at Columbia who respected the code which governed the expression of ambitiousness. But if so, why should I have felt comfortable with it there when it had given me the shudders at Columbia? The answer, I think, is that the one was real and the other feigned. The typical student at Clare was not, in fact, ambition-ridden, while the typical student at Columbia, pretending not to be, in reality was; the typical student at Clare did not, in fact, make too much of things, while there was little in the world that did not present itself to the typical student at Columbia as a matter of life and death.

Here too, as I began to see, the difference could be traced to the effects of living in a traditionally class-bound society as compared with living in one that is, or appears to be, highly mobile and open. The former, seeming to set fairly predictable limits to a young man's future, discourages appetite and demand; the latter, seeming to set no limits at all, incites to restlessness and wild imaginings. The former, seeming to provide a man with a fairly clear social identity to begin with, relegates "great expectations" to the realm of fantasy and ro-mance; the latter, telling a man that his social identity is something to be earned, makes of such expectations the very driving-force of the will. The former, in short—especially when the economy is stagnant—undercuts and subverts ambitiousness, the latter—especially in times of economic growth—excites and stimulates it. (It was, perhaps, as much the American in T. S. Eliot striving to be English as it was the nonbeliever in him striving to be a Christian who wrote: "Teach us to care and not to care, / Teach us to sit still.")

Of course English society in the 1950's was moving in a more egalitarian direction, while America was entering a period when the young would notoriously be setting limits on themselves, on their hungers and on their expectations (David Riesman, indeed, had only recently announced the birth of just such a new American type, the "other-directed" man). But these changes had by no means yet matured on either side of the Atlantic. For the moment at least, Clare was a place which gave one the sense, as Columbia most emphatically had not, that life was a walk and not a race, and that nothing could result from running but a useless loss of breath.

II   Was it, then, the case that Cambridge, by turning me into a "young gentleman," postponing the question of external success for long enough to push it out of the center of my consciousness, calming my internal drive to convince myself of my own "brilliance," and putting me at ease in a noncompetitive atmosphere, had finished the job of "conversion" begun on me at Columbia? Not quite, for there was, as usual, another side to the story.

Worlds apart from the Cambridge of Clare was the Cambridge of Downing College, and if the fires within me were banked at Clare, to Downing I came, burning, burning, even more hotly than before: burning to learn, burning to impress, burning to succeed, burning, in sum, to test myself and be tested, to find out once and for all whether I was really any good. Downing was the college of F. R. Leavis, the greatest critic in England—greater, some said, than T. S. Eliot himself, an old ally turned adversary—and the editor of the country's most formidable critical review, the terrifying *Scrutiny:* graveyard of a thousand literary reputations, ancient as well as modern; incorruptible guardian of standards in a decadent culture; upholder of seriousness in a frivolous age. If not Leavis, then who in the world could finally give me the word—the word about literature and the word about myself?

There was no problem about getting permission to sit in on his biweekly classes at Downing, where supervisions were not, as at Clare, individual; and soon he was also inviting me, along with his other disciples, to the indoctrination sessions, thinly disguised as tea parties, which he and his wife Queenie, a famous critic in her own right, would hold on the lawn of their home every Saturday afternoon. The tea parties were Leavis talking about his grievances: how they had tried to get him out of

Cambridge, how T. S. Eliot had betrayed him ("public blackguardy and private apology"), how one *Scrutiny* colleague after another had gone over to the forces of evil, how the "metropolitan weeklies" were in a conspiracy to deprive him of the influence that was rightly his, and so on and so on literally into the night, the bitter lament of a soldier of the spirit struggling in proud isolation to save the soul of his country. It was, as even I in my infatuated state could see, more than a little paranoid, despite the fact that most of the grievances themselves were real enough. They *had* kept him from a university lectureship until he was well into his forties, they *had* preferred mediocrities over him. But of course there is such a thing as being paranoid in the midst of actual persecution, and that Leavis was.

In the supervisions, however, the Leavis of the tea parties gave way to Leavis the critic, Leavis on English literature; and Leavis the critic was another matter entirely. He devoted himself in those classes mainly to preparing his pupils for a section of Part II of the English Tripos which consisted of several short passages of untitled verse and prose that the student was expected to date within ten years or so, giving his reasons for the guess; occasionally, to make life more difficult, the examiners would choose a piece written in imitation of an earlier period—say a sonnet by Rupert Brooke that at first glance looked Elizabethan. To sit week after week and listen to Leavis inductively arrive at a judgment as to why a particular stanza or a particular paragraph containing no substantive clue to its date of composition could *only* have been written around 1730 or 1910 was an experience for which the word "intimidating" would be an approximate description if it were itself approximately a hundred times stronger. He brought to bear on these analyses a knowledge of the literary, cultural, and social history of England frightening in its intimacy, a sensitivity to the nuances of English style phenomenal in its range, and a sense of the relations between tradition and the individual talent—to use a phrase of the prelapsarian Eliot to which Leavis was very devoted—that was breath-taking in its inwardness. And no less impressive, if somewhat less intimidating, were his absolutely irresistible demonstrations of why the passages in question were good or bad, "realized" or "unrealized," worthy or unworthy expressions of the traditions to which they belonged.

But this in itself, after all, only represented a superior critical mind at work, and that I had seen before: in Andrew Chiappe's lectures on Shakespeare, in F. W. Dupee's classes on Joyce and Yeats and Proust, in Lionel Trilling's course on the Romantic poets and Victorian novelists. Trilling, indeed, had the same power Leavis displayed for exposing the filaments which connect a great work of literature to all the life around it, energizing and vitalizing it; and like Leavis, he understood literature as an act of the moral imagination and as an agent of social and political health.

Trilling, however, went no further than this. He did not feel, and he did not make his students feel, that literature was of the supremest importance. He did not feel that "the common pursuit of true judgment and the correction of taste"—to use another of Leavis's favorite phrases from Eliot-before-the-fall—was a sacred duty enjoined upon the critic and that to waver in its performance, let alone to depart from it altogether at the behest of other considerations, whether personal (to avoid causing hurt, to curry favor) or ideological (notions of the relativism of taste or of the primacy of nonliterary factors over the literary realm itself), was a sin as cardinal as adultery, as foul as idolatry. Trilling's eyes did not blaze with a fierce Calvinist light upon the written word; he did not erect the capacity for "true judgment" into the very principle of being; he did not conceive of criticism as the rod of the Lord's wrath. Yet it was precisely this quality of puritanical ferocity—the other side of the paranoid coin—informing the workings of an intelligence as powerful and a sensibility as exquisite as any I have ever encountered, which gave Leavis a hold over me such as no one had previously been able to exert or ever would again.

And so I arrived at the second stage in my conversion to "culture": I became a Leavisian—not, perhaps, the most ardent of his young epigoni at Cambridge, but, in all truth, the others being a singularly dreary and humorless lot, the most adept. I was no longer so unformed as to be capable of an effortless imitation of the master's style in the papers I wrote, but I was still open enough and impressionable enough to be capable of imitating his mode of operation in dating exercises and in the critical analysis of isolated passages. I listened to him, I watched him, I studied his books. I appropriated his opinions and made them mine, holding to them with an intensity commensurate in its youthfully earnest way with his own fanatical devotion. And though I never *sounded* like him when I wrote—if I sounded like anyone, it was Trilling —I did to a remarkable extent learn how to respond in terms of his temperament, to think in terms of his categories, to judge in terms of his values. As will happen with a true conversion, the whole thing reached so rapid and thorough a consummation that before the end of my first year at Cambridge, the master's ultimate accolade was bestowed upon me: he invited me to write for *Scrutiny.*

Thus it was that at the age of twenty-one and in the notoriously hardest to crack of all the magazines of its kind in the world, I made my first appearance in print as a professional literary critic. The article, written with an assurance I could not possibly have possessed at the time, and representing what I suppose was an attempt to reconcile the conflict of loyalties I felt toward my two godfathers in culture on either side of the Atlantic, portrayed Trilling as being in effect the Leavis of American letters, though it was Matthew Arnold and not Leavis to whom I actually compared him. Leavis read the piece when I brought it to him with a sour expression on his face, squirming at this, sighing at that, and wincing in pain at a paragraph, later cut, which contained a pious reference to Wordsworth's "Immortality Ode" (a poem which no one with "independent critical judgment" was supposed to admire). In the end, however, when all the squirming and sighing were done and the last page had been turned, Leavis pronounced the piece "intelligent" and declared that he would print it (but not before bidding me to take careful note of the fact that, his reputation as an intolerant dogmatist to the contrary notwithstanding, he was willing to publish an article with which he strongly disagreed).

I had come to Leavis burning for the word about literature and for the word about myself. Within a year he had given me both, and what more could I have wanted? Why, a First on the English Tripos, of course. And when, a year later, that came too, what more could I have wanted then? That this question kept presenting itself so insistently to me at Cambridge pointed, I think, to something more than the depressive letdown which had begun to show up as a regular feature of the aftermath of any success I happened to experience: a period characterized by a vague sense of guilt, an almost nihilistic compulsion to minimize the significance of the triumph I had just enjoyed, and a curious desire to apologize for it to everyone else in the world. "Use every man after his desert," said Hamlet, "and who should 'scape whipping?" Again I had 'scaped whipping, and again; and again I feared the envy of those still under the lash.

There was that in my depressions over the successes I achieved at Cambridge, but there was, I now suspect, also an element neither neurotic nor superstitious simmering in the same nasty brew. Something within me must have known that this life into which I was moving with such apparent ease, though surely a good life for someone, was not the life for me.

III Depressions and obscure messages from the depths of my soul apart, however, I had come to feel very much at home in England, to the point where I even began flirting at the end of my second year with the idea of staying there forever. With a Cambridge B.A. and a First, there seemed little question that I could eventually get a university appointment, meanwhile supporting myself by conducting supervisions at Clare (which, in fact, I started doing when I returned for a third year) and with the help of various grants which I had already been offered. Why not stay? It was so beautiful here and so easy, and what, after all, was America to me? My family was there, and Columbia, but nothing else to which I felt a really strong personal connection. How indeed, I asked myself, could any such attachments have developed? In England, when people talked about the Battle of Hastings, it was as though they themselves had been there; and, through their ancestors, in a sense of course they had. But I could feel no intimate relation even to so recent a major event in American history as the Civil War, let alone the Revolution; the earliest historical landmark having anything to do with *me*—because it was the earliest my own family had shared in—was, ridiculously, the Depression of the 1930's. Nor had I ever thought of myself as an American. I came from Brooklyn, and in Brooklyn there were no Americans; there were Jews and Negroes and Italians and Poles and Irishmen. Americans lived in New England, in the South, in the Midwest: alien people in alien places.

I had, to be sure, undergone a "conversion" at Columbia, but it had not been to Americanness or to Americanism. Though I no longer thought of myself simply as a Jew from Brooklyn, I could never have said, as many German Jews of the nineteenth century said when they, the first group of Jews in European history to do so, experienced a similar conversion to a culture not their own: that the purpose of their immersion in German culture was a "German national education." I did not think of culture as anything *national,* and in any case American culture had no real status in the eyes of anyone in the 1940's; even if it had, an immersion in it would have left me feeling more, not less, alienated from the national life than before—would have left me feeling, in fact, that the country was hopelessly in the grip of the forces of commerce and that there was no place in it for a man of sensibility and taste. In the context of the idea of Western Civilization to which I had been converted at Columbia—"Western," as I have already indicated, having for me the force of "universal"—America was definitely a minor province and definitely to be treated as such. Thus only one small survey course in American literature had been offered at Columbia when I was there, and I had not even taken it, thinking there were more important things to do. Nor had I taken a course in American history or American philosophy or in the sociology of American society. Why bother with things inferior, things parochial, when there was so much else of greater significance to learn?

All this on the one hand. On the other hand—for there was, of course, another hand and in this case it proved to be the upper one—it was impossible to live in England or visit any European country in the early 1950's without being forced into a constant awareness of oneself as an American, and an unproblematic awareness at that. With the Cambridge academic year consisting only of three eight-week terms and long vacations between, and with the value of my fellowships enhanced by favorable rates of exchange, I was able to do a lot of traveling, and as happened with so many of my contemporaries (updated Columbuses all), it was the American in myself I stumbled upon while trying to discover Europe. For protest as we all might, the whole world insisted on regarding us quite simply and unarguably as Americans: we spoke English with an American accent, we carried American passports and travelers checks from American Express, we were overawed by cathedrals, we were buoyant and wide-eyed and talkative, we had good teeth and smooth complexions, we complained about the absence of central heating in winter, we were accustomed to modern plumbing, we had a thing about dirt, we preferred showers to baths and took too many of both, we grew impatient at slow service in restaurants, and we drank water more happily than wine. In short, we were in a million small details marked off in their eyes as an identifiable national type.

And in our own eyes, after a while, as well. In those days before pop became fashionable we shared in a thousand guilty secret loves: The Shadow and the Green Hornet, Batman and Superman, James Cagney and Pat O'Brien, Harry James and Glenn Miller, "Did You Ever See a Dream Walking?" and "I Left My Heart at the Stage Door Canteen." *You too?* we would say delightedly to one another, after listening to initially sheepish confessions about the incorrigibility of our low American tastes, *you too?* And then purifying ourselves in orgies of authenticity after days, weeks, months of genuflection in cathedrals and galleries and museums and chateaux, we would vie with one another in expertise in the culture that was really in our bones, dredging up the lyrics of long-forgotten popular songs, advertising slogans, and movie plots that neither Michelangelo nor Chartres could ever drive from our minds; remembering how we had all drunk Ovaltine as children because of Little Orphan Annie and eaten Silvercup bread because of the Lone Ranger, and how our mothers had forced cod-liver oil down all our throats and oatmeal in the winter because it was supposed to stick to your ribs and how we had all cried over the lumps. *Isn't it funny?* we would say to one another on a chance encounter in Paris or Athens or Rome, *isn't it funny? I never thought of myself as an American before.*

A young Negro writer named James Baldwin, whom I met for the first time in Paris in 1951, said the same thing, only he didn't think it was funny. He had decided, he told me, to go back to the States; it was terrible there for a Negro, no one realized how terrible it was, but it was no good being an expatriate either, and after trying to live in Paris he had come to the distressing realization that he was an American: hopelessly, helplessly, ineluctably so. It was not, I thought, entirely that way with me, but I knew what he was talking about all right. Only too well did I know.

Politics played its part in all this too, for the sheer vulgarity of the anti-Americanism one came upon everywhere in Europe pushed many of us into the unaccustomed role of patriotic defenders. There was no way of resisting the invidious comparisons to the benefit of America which popped into one's head when a waiter in a Paris café sneered, *"Un Americain, sans doute,"* as one handed him a thousand-franc note, or when a particularly philistine Englishman made snooty references to American materialism. Time after time, one would find oneself protesting, "No, it isn't really like that in America, you've got it all wrong," and then rather to one's own astonishment one would hear oneself offering a spirited defense of this or that aspect of American life which one had never felt the slightest inclination to defend while at home. No, American men were not all dominated by their wives; no, American women were not all frigid; no, not all artists were condemned to starvation in America; yes, Americans did care for other things besides money; yes, it was possible to live in New York; yes, Alger Hiss had been a Communist; yes, civil liberties still existed in America despite McCarthy; no, the country was not going fascist.

My own political views having recently come under the influence of the intellectuals of the anti-Stalinist Left who wrote for *Partisan Review,* I had also picked up their contemptuous attitude toward liberals who were willing to apologize for the crimes of Stalin's regime, and were accustomed to falling back on a double standard of judgment in discussing the Soviet-American conflict. This entire habit of mind was if anything even more widespread among English liberals and radicals than in America—and of course almost universal in France, especially in the circle that revolved around Sartre—and it continually drove me, as it did others, into passionate overstatements of the case for American virtue (so far as the case against the Stalin regime was concerned, no overstatements were possible).

But the passion I felt was not so much political as intellectual: it was not primarily America that I and others like me were defending; it was the new way of looking at things which was being developed in so many different quarters during the early years of what Irving Howe was later to call "The Age of Conformity" and I myself—somewhat more accurately, as I still believe—called "The Age of Revisionist Liberalism." As the word revisionist suggests, the effort was to purge the liberal mentality of its endemically besetting illusions regarding the perfectibility of man and the perfectibility of society, and to purge it as well of the particular illusions regarding the Soviet Union to which so large a part of its constituency had fallen prey in the 1930's. In line with this effort a whole range of questions was reopened—questions which had been locked for many years into the airtight clichés that passed for political thinking among most Americans who saw themselves as decent, right-minded, enlightened, and progressive.

It is true that some revisionist liberals went so far as almost to forfeit any claim to the title liberal, and it is also true that revisionist liberalism eventually came to be in need of revision itself. But at the beginning, reading Trilling on the liberal imagination, Hook on Marxism, Hannah Arendt on totalitarianism, Niebuhr and Morgenthau and Kennan on political realism, Macdonald on Henry Wallace, Bell on ideology, Fiedler and Warshow on the thirties—while supplementing it all with English works of a similar spirit like Brogan on revolution and on the American political system, Orwell and Koestler on Communism, Popper on the open society, and Oakeshott on Hobbes—was as liberating in its own fashion to someone like me who had been raised politically on *PM* and the New York *Post* as the earlier discovery through "culture" that all the possible ways of looking at the world were not exhausted by the opinions and views of Brownsville. Indeed, perhaps the most exciting thing about revisionist liberalism was its smooth compatibility with certain of the attitudes I had absorbed through the study of literature. Thus, for example, the anti-utopianism of the revisionist liberals—their Niebuhrian stress on human imperfection as the major obstacle to the realization of huge political dreams—jibed beautifully with the "tragic sense of life" which, in common with all students of literature barely out of their diapers, I was certain I shared with Shakespeare.

Like most of the people I knew who were going through the same experience, I was still far too high-minded to recognize that political considerations of rather a more vulgar nature than these must also have been playing a part in our new and surprisingly happy consciousness of ourselves as Americans. Much as a Negro until very recently could go through school without ever being told that he existed as a factor in the history of America, I myself had spent six years at two major universities without ever finding out that America existed as a factor in the history of the West, that it was anything but an inferior and altogether uninteresting offshoot of European civilization: the raw, uncultivated scion of an aristocratic line who had betrayed his noble ancestry by going disgracefully into trade (but then, poor fellow, what else was he fit for?).

If, however, religion, as they say, follows the flag, how could cultural attitudes, which after all do not even have any pretensions to the status of eternal verities, possibly fail to lag behind? How, in other words, could the fact that the United States was now the major power on earth and as such beginning to command the respectful, if resentful, attention of everyone in the world, have failed to alter the direction and quality of our own attentions? Let a province become really powerful and it will immediately cease being regarded, either by itself or others, as a province. Its history will be studied, its opinions will be heeded, and its writers will be read and translated. And because any phenomenon has a way of acquiring value merely through the amount of attention paid to it, the culture of this ex-province will soon be discovered always to have contained an importance and a beauty previously invisible to the mind and the eye. Does Finland have a great literature? Does Afghanistan? Does Ecuador? Who knows or cares? But give Finland enough power and enough wealth, and there would soon be a Finnish department in every university in the world— just as, in the 1950's, departments of American Studies were suddenly being established in colleges where, only a few years earlier, it had scarcely occurred to anyone that there was anything American *to* study.

Magically deprovincialized, America was now The West itself. And since "Western" had always meant "universal" to me, I was for a time in some danger of jumping (as in fact others did) to the conclusion that the transcendent realm of spirit which I had once thought could be located in "culture" was actually embodied in, of all places, America. Leavis, however, inadvertently saved me from any such neo-Hegelian silliness (not that his own neo-Burkeanism was altogether lacking in silliness itself). For just as life in England was teaching me what class meant as a concrete condition, studying with Leavis was opening my eyes to the particularism and historicity of literature—and, by extension, of culture in general.

The more I listened to him and the more I read him, the more uneasily aware I became of the Englishness of English literature, and the more I studied that literature itself, the more unfamiliar it paradoxically came to seem.

Obviously its greatest figures were "universal" in some sense, at least some of the time; obviously too one could delight in a lyric by Herrick without having grown up in London. But I was not a casual reader to be content with delight, I was a young man in the process of committing his life to the study of English literature, and it was therefore of no small consequence to me to discover how large a part of what I was planning to give myself to was in the nature of an entailed national inheritance carefully fenced around by its own inherent limitations—that is, its own untranscended parochialism and provinciality— against trespassers from outside the family. But if this was true of English literature, it must also be true of all other literatures, the American most emphatically included: an occasional Keats and a multitude of Crabbes. No more, it appeared, than there existed a socially neutral ground on which to stand did there exist a nationally neutral realm of culture in which to live. There was no such thing, I was beginning to see, as Culture in the abstract; there was only a multiplicity of cultures, each the patrimonial spiritual estate of a particular group of people, some no doubt richer and more valuable on the whole than others, some more accessible to visiting tourists than others, but every one of them in any case national to the core.

Where, exactly, all this left *me*, as a problematic American and an even more problematic Jew, I had no idea. But this much I knew: the notion I had been flirting with of staying in England forever was out. And if not forever, then why delay another year? Precipitously I applied for a graduate fellowship to Harvard. If it came through, I told myself, I would take it; if not, I would return to Cambridge after a visit with my parents and get my Ph.D. there.

By the time I heard from Harvard, I had convinced myself that I desperately wanted to go there, and yet when the fellowship did come through, I fell into a vicious funk. Interpreting this odd response as stemming from a reluctance to leave Cambridge so soon, I shrugged it off as best I could and packed my bags. What was the matter with me anyway? Would I never grow up? I did not know, and would not realize for some time, that what was troubling me had less to do with Cambridge than with my new feelings about America, about literature, and about culture. I can see now that I had, in my usual blind fashion, already decided against getting a Ph.D. and pursuing an academic career.

IV   It was a bad summer back in Brooklyn. I felt almost totally estranged from my parents, and the strain between us was intensified practically beyond endurance by their suspicion that I was planning to marry a non-Jewish English girl—a suspicion which, parental Jewish apprehensions on this particular score, if not on so many others, being rooted in sound empirical data, was thoroughly justified. No doubt they imagined the girl in question as the archetypical blond *shiksa* who once troubled the sleep of all Jewish mothers: the beautiful young siren luring innocent Jewish boys into her embraces with secret sexual wiles known only to the Gentile world. In fact, however, though my fiancée *was* blonde, she was not a beautiful young siren but a ripened and somewhat dowdy woman of twenty-eight, and so extraordinary a person that to this day I feel proud of myself for having had enough sense at the age of twenty-one to fall in love with her. In the end—luckily, as it turned out for both of us—we never did marry, and while she does not strictly belong to the story I am trying to tell in this book, I have brought her in because it was she who supplied the pretext for my sudden decision in the fall to skip Harvard and return to Cambridge after all.

Two things happened that summer which, I think, actually accounted for the decision. One of them was a visit to Westport, Connecticut, where Lionel and Diana Trilling were vacationing, and the other was a visit to the offices of *Commentary,* where I got my first glimpse of what the world of the nonacademic New York intellectual was like.

Trilling, of course, I knew from Columbia and we had corresponded during the past two years, but I had never been in his home before; nor had I ever met his wife. Riding up on the train through one fashionable suburban town after another, my so recently acquired

English poise quickly revealed itself as stubbornly un-transplantable to American soil; I had only to look out of the window for all my old anxieties about "manners" to come rushing back. I was wearing a cheap nylon cord summer suit which I had bought since coming home, a white shirt, and a tie, and as the train pulled into the Westport station, it suddenly occurred to me that I was overdressed for a Sunday visit to a smart seaside town. Why hadn't I worn something more suitably sporty? Should I perhaps take off my tie, or would that only make it worse?

But I had both Westport and the Trillings all wrong. Knowing literally nothing about money, and still thinking of it, if at all, in Brownsville terms (where two dollars an hour was considered a very high wage), I had imagined that a full professor at Columbia who also wrote books must be at least a moderately rich man. Yet there were the Trillings living not in a grand mansion overlooking Long Island Sound, but in a small bungalow a few blocks from the beach. Everything there was easy and informal—even, I thought, rather surprisingly bohemian—and no one seemed to care whether my tie was on or off. It was an atmosphere in which I could loosen up, and after a swim and several martinis, I began talking my head off about Cambridge, about Leavis, about Europe, and even, finally, about my secret uncertainties. My still inchoate but nevertheless clearly heretical sentiments about literature and my incipient rebellion against the academic life had been causing me a good deal of anxiety—was I turning into a "sellout"?—and I had feared that they might shock Trilling, who had, after all, followed the very course I was half-consciously proposing to desert on the ground—was it a rationalization?—that there was something false in such a life for someone like me.

But again I had him wrong. Yes, of course, he said, he understood exactly what I meant, and proceeded—with a witchlike precision which the hesitant style of his speech and the diffidently soft quality of his voice left one unprepared for and somehow surprised by, even though one knew he was Lionel Trilling and one of the most intelligent men in the world—to tell me what it was I had been trying to say. When he had finished, he asked me what I really wanted to do with myself, what kind of power I was after, thus ensuring that if anyone was to be shocked that afternoon, it would be me. Power? Who ever said anything about power? What did I have to do with power, or it with me? "Don't be silly," he said, "everyone wants power. The only question is what kind. What kind do you want?" Well, I asked slyly, what kinds were there to choose from? Money, he said, was a form of power, so was fame, so was eminence in a given profession. Oh in *that* case, I replied, greatly relieved, the answer was fame, no doubt about it; I wanted to be a famous critic.

At that point Mrs. Trilling, who, as I was all too uncomfortably aware, had been measuring me all afternoon with a pair of fierce brown eyes, broke into the conversation: "Have you ever considered going to law school?" she demanded. Again it was my turn to be shocked. Law school? Why on earth would I want to go to law school? Hadn't I, she countered, just said that I didn't really want to teach English? Yes, I had. And hadn't I also said that my ambition was to be a famous critic? Yes, I had. But didn't I realize that it was impossible to write criticism for a living, and that for all practical purposes it was also pretty well impossible to be a critic in America outside the academy? Yes, I supposed that I did. Well, then, why remain fixated on the idea of writing literary criticism? There were other things in the world to do, and law school was a perfect path to a thousand different careers, valuable careers, exciting careers. With my talent, there was no telling how far I might go; and being a lawyer needn't even prevent me from writing.

I was so outraged and humiliated by this suggestion —apart from everything else, I was sure I was too *old* to start on a new career—that the only alternative to losing my temper was to promise politely that I would think the idea over. Later, however, I found myself feeling strangely liberated by the speech she had made me. *There were other things in the world to do:* no one, it seemed, had ever told me that before; all anyone had ever told me, it seemed, was that there was almost *nothing* in the world worth doing. It didn't matter that I had no conception for the moment of what these other things, these other careers, to which she had referred might be; it was enough to be shocked for the first time since adolescence into the realization that the narrowness of the alternatives before me was a reflection not of reality but of the timidity of my own imagination, the scantiness of my own experience, and the lingering effects of a childhood among the poor.

It is hard for the poor to make demands, for they know the demands will not be met and they learn to avoid the added bitterness of unnecessary disappointment by settling for whatever the world in its arbitrary way pleases to let them have. Yet it is this habit of mind —a habit I had not even begun to rid myself of at twenty-two—that also helps to keep them poor, for the plain truth is that while those who demand do not always get what they want, those who fail to demand almost always get nothing. So it was with me, not in relation to actual poverty but in relation to the possibilities the world might have to offer. If such possibilities had not existed, of course, I could not have brought them into being by my demands, any more than an unskilled worker can get a job in a time of mass unemployment. But the fact is that possibilities *did* exist for the likes of me in the America of 1952; the fact is that it was *not* necessary for me or anyone else similarly situated to settle for the academic life merely on the assumption that teaching was the only career in America in which a serious man with intellectual interests could maintain his pride and his integrity. Was this assumption, then, only the defeated voice of Brownsville with its accent changed, warning me once again that if I took any chances I would most assuredly wind up in the street?

It was while questions and intuitions of this nature were floating around inside me that I received a call from the late Elliot Cohen, the editor of *Commentary*, who having heard about me from Trilling and having read my piece in *Scrutiny*, wanted me to come up to his office for a talk. I was not at the time intimately familiar with *Commentary*, though I had seen it often enough during its seven years of publication to be puzzled by the idea of a Jewish magazine in which the same kind of people who wrote for *Partisan Review* and the other quarterlies regularly appeared—people like Harold Rosenberg, Hannah Arendt, Leslie Fiedler, Sidney Hook, Alfred Kazin, Saul Bellow, Isaac Rosenfeld, Mary McCarthy, Trilling himself, and a dozen others. Two writers whose names I associated with *Partisan Review*, Robert Warshow and Clement Greenberg, were even listed as editors of *Commentary*—indicating, apparently, that it was possible to be an avant-garde intellectual and at the same time to be interested in things Jewish. Odd; very odd, considering how radically opposed I had always imagined the Jewish and "general" worlds of culture to be.

When I mentioned this to Cohen, a mischievous glint came into his eye: "The main difference between *Parti-*

san Review and *Commentary*," he said, "is that we admit to being a Jewish magazine and they don't." But the Jewish and general worlds were evidently not the only worlds which to me seemed radically opposed and which Cohen saw as naturally related. In that first hour I spent with him he jumped from literary criticism to politics, from politics to Jewish scholarship, from Jewish scholarship to the movies, from the movies to sports, and indeed spent a good deal of time trying to find out how much I knew about baseball. I did, as it happened (a Brownsville legacy), know rather a lot, if not as much as he, but I found it difficult to understand why it seemed so important to him.

Sensing this, he interrupted himself in the midst of a highly intricate analysis of Casey Stengel's managerial style and turned his famous smile on me, full force. What was the matter, didn't I think that Casey Stengel was an interesting phenomenon of American life? I said that I had never thought of him in quite that way. Well, did I think that Stengel was a worthy object for the critical intelligence to dwell upon, or did I perhaps think that the critical intelligence should be reserved exclusively for Henry James? His tone was ironic and his eyes had that mischievous glint in them again, but he was obviously doing something more than teasing—just what, I wasn't yet sure, except that the same exhilarated feeling of liberation, the same sense of a world of abundant possibility which had come over me after my visit to the Trillings now began coming over me again: *if there were other things to do, there were also other things to think about.*

Abruptly he handed me a book. It was a review copy of a first novel, *The Natural,* by a writer named Bernard Malamud, whose stories Cohen had been publishing. "Well," he said, "you seem to know something about novels, you know something about symbolism, you know something about Jews, and you know something about baseball. Here's a symbolic novel by a Jewish writer about a baseball player. I guess you're qualified to review it."

The *Commentary* offices were then located in a loft in the garment center which had been crudely partitioned into cubicles. There was no air-conditioning and the summer sun beat down mercilessly on the skylight, making it almost impossible for the editors to work. In one of those cubicles, his bald head sweating profusely, sat the senior member of the staff, Clement Greenberg, the most influential art critic in America, and opposite him the late Robert Warshow, at thirty-four already one of the best essayists in the English language and then, as now, one of the least appreciated. The other cubicle was shared by Nathan Glazer, the brilliant young sociologist (he was close to thirty but looked sixteen and was forever being mistaken for the office boy by visiting writers) who had collaborated with David Riesman on *The Lonely Crowd,* and Irving Kristol (also about thirty and looking twenty) whose notorious recent article on civil

liberties and the Communists in *Commentary* had made
him for a while the most controversial figure in New
York and who was soon to move to London to start a new
magazine called *Encounter*. I would at that moment
have given my life to be accepted as one of them, and
when Warshow called me a day or so later for lunch, I
felt as a girl with a secret infatuation must feel when
the boy she has been mooning over asks her for a date.
Despite the discrepancy in our ages, Warshow and I were
to become close friends in the short time he had left—a
friendship based on my great admiration for him, the delight he took in tampering spiritually with the young,
and the delight I took in all the attention he was willing
to pay me. He was to act not only as my mentor when I
began writing for *Commentary* and *Partisan Review* but
also as a guide on my first brief safari into the wilds of
New York literary society.

But that safari was still a year off. Shortly after
meeting Warshow and only a few days before I was
scheduled to check in at Harvard, I suddenly decided to
return to England, telling myself that I had to see my
fiancée again before making up my mind not to get married, and that I was really going back to Cambridge,
England in order to avoid going up to Cambridge, Massachusetts. I think I must have half-suspected that my
intentions as a graduate student were by now no more
honorable than my intentions as a lover, and I must have
figured that Cambridge was a better place in which to

mark time than Harvard would be. At any rate, just when I was supposed to be thinking about a doctoral dissertation, all I could think of was what I would find to say about the novel Elliot Cohen had given me to review.

V   Cambridge wasn't the same. As a graduate student, I was no longer entitled to rooms in college and I lived instead in "digs" on Kings Parade where I had a bedroom of my own but shared a sitting room with an acquaintance from Clare. We had a magnificent view of Kings College across the road, with its sixteenth-century English-perpendicular chapel blending in a parity of diverse perfections with the eighteenth-century palladian Gibbs Building to the left. And yet I soon came to feel oppressed by it all, even affronted; the eternal calm exuded by all that eternal beauty began to seem smug, like the whole of England itself: that "fen of stagnant waters," as Wordsworth had said, exactly expressing my own sentiments in the jumpy mood I was in all that year —my heart lusting for publication and for very little else and hot to get in on all the jittery excitement that I was now finding in the pages of *Commentary*. What I had so loved about Cambridge before, its easy ancient pace, now threw me into fits of insane irritation: how stupid and dull the place was, really, how unimaginative, how utterly oblivious to everything that was going on, that mattered. Did Cambridge care about the nature of totalitarianism? Did it understand the problem of popular culture? Did it know what a middlebrow was? Did it concern itself with the meaning of suburbanization? Did it have any conception of the possibilities of an affluent industrial economy? Had it ever heard of Robert Warshow?

In this mood, of course, I could as easily have done research on Marston or Milton or Meredith as take orders in the Church of England. Still, I was there, I thought I wanted a Ph.D. (in case), and I had no desire to waste my time. The subject I hit upon for my thesis was the novels of Disraeli, to whom I daresay I was attracted because he was a Jew, of a sort anyway, who had made it to "the top of the greasy pole" (his phrase), and because working on him would give me an opportunity to learn something about politics—a field in which, thanks to *Commentary*, I was growing more and more interested.

I read voraciously: Disraeli himself and everything ever written about him (ironically, or perhaps symbolically, the best single interpretation of his character and career I found was in a back issue of *Commentary*), nineteenth-century history, Victorian novels and memoirs. Meanwhile I also conducted supervisions at Clare, preparing my pupils for the examination on "The English Moralists and Their Background" (background meaning Plato, Aristotle, and Saint Augustine, among others) they would have to take as part of the English Tripos. It was better, given the state I was in, than a more strictly literary course of study would have been, but hard as I worked and fascinated as I was by Disraeli himself, my heart was never really in it. What I cared about, to put it mildly, was writing for *Commentary*. The review of Malamud turned out to be an awkward job, for I was straining too hard, as inexperienced writers always do, and I lacked the skill to set my critique of the book into the twin contexts of contemporary American fiction and the contemporary American situation, about neither of which, interestingly, I knew nearly as much as I did about Victorian life and letters. Warshow nevertheless cleaned the piece up and *Commentary* not only published it but asked me to do another. I had passed the test; I was on my way.

As for Disraeli, I got far enough to write a long essay on him as a political novelist which I submitted to *Scrutiny*. But Leavis thought it insufficiently "inward" in its understanding of Victorian society (the particularism of culture again), and rejected it with a letter acid enough to dissolve whatever lingering impulses I may have had to stay on another year and finish the degree. The Korean War having recently ended, but with conscription still in effect, I knew that I was certain to be drafted if I went home without registering in graduate school, but things had come to such a pass in my spirit by then that even the army seemed preferable to an extended tour of duty in the academic world.

Yet in stating it in this entirely negative way, I am

being less than fully honest, for I was by no means averse to going into the army. Like most American kids who had been old enough at the time to be aware of World War II but too young to fight in it, I had a kind of yearning to see what the army would be like, to share in an experience so universal in our day that one felt somehow incomplete without it; and indeed, people who had never been in uniform tended to be ashamed of the fact. To most of us, moreover, the army was a test of masculinity —something like a delayed puberty rite.

Vietnam, of course, later changed all that, but there was no opposition to speak of to the Korean War, certainly not a vocal one; on the contrary, American foreign policy was generally regarded as right and the Korean War as just, and I myself strongly held to that view. But the holding of it, I suppose, was also another of the many signs—along with my feelings of alienation from the English literary heritage, my impatience with England itself, my growing boredom with academic life, and my concomitantly growing fascination with the contemporary scene as I saw it being discussed month after month in *Commentary*—that I had finally arrived at the third (and final?) stage of my conversion: I had become a New York literary intellectual.

Part II

MOVING INTO MANHATTAN

4 The Family Tree

About ten years after I first set an eager foot into it, the New York literary world began to acquire a recognizable identity in the (more or less) popular mind and even to be spoken of as an Establishment, which no doubt it would have been had it still been in existence. By the mid-1960's, however, it had all but completely disintegrated, its cohesiveness destroyed in the third generation (mine) by the inexorable processes of acculturation. To that extent it resembles many other Jewish families in America, and indeed, anyone who wishes to understand that world would do well to pick up Murray Kempton's clue and to think of it as a Jewish family. Neither the rival idea of a clique nor the posthumous idea of an Establishment can convey so accurately the true flavor of how it operated or can account for its characteristic qualities, its strengths and its weaknesses.

Of course the metaphor of a Jewish family runs into certain difficulties of its own, for several core members (Dwight Macdonald, Mary McCarthy, F. W. Dupee, William Barrett, Elizabeth Hardwick, John Thompson, James Baldwin, and the late Richard Chase) and a few kissing cousins (Robert Lowell, Ralph Ellison, John Berryman, Kempton himself, Michael Harrington, Robert Gorham Davis, the late James Agee, and the late William Troy) were not Jewish at all. Nevertheless, the term "Jewish" can be allowed to stand by clear majority rule and by various peculiarities of temper I shall try to describe; and the term "family" by the fact that these were people who by virtue of their tastes, ideas, and general concerns found themselves stuck with one another against the rest of the world whether they liked it or not (and most did not), preoccupied with one another to the point of obsession, and intense in their attachments and hostilities as only a family is capable of being.

The designation "literary world," on the other hand, is more misleading, for only a very few core members (Saul Bellow, the late Delmore Schwartz, perhaps the late Isaac Rosenfeld, perhaps James Baldwin, and perhaps Mary McCarthy) were known primarily as poets or novelists; and although most of the others were always much interested in literature and habitually wrote about it, at least seven (Meyer Schapiro, Harold Rosenberg,

Dwight Macdonald, Paul Goodman, Clement Greenberg, the late Robert Warshow, and David Bazelon) mainly wrote about painting or films or social problems, and at least six more (Sidney Hook, the late Elliot Cohen, Hannah Arendt, Daniel Bell, Nathan Glazer, and Irving Kristol) could hardly be said to have had literary interests at all. A more embracing, if more confusing, term than "literary," then, might be "intellectual," for Jewish or not, literary or not, everyone who ever belonged to the family was unquestionably an intellectual in a very distinct tradition and of a very passionate kind.

At the point when it adopted me and I embraced it for my own, the family spanned two generations, separated by a period of ten to fifteen years; and those few of us who were to make up the third and last generation were separated from the second by a roughly equivalent gap in age. The Founding Fathers, born around 1905, included a few (Philip Rahv and Meyer Schapiro) who had been brought over to America from Russia or Lithuania as children and who continued to speak with noticeably foreign accents all their lives. Most of the other members of the founding generation, however (Trilling, Hook, Rosenberg, Goodman, Greenberg, and Lionel Abel), were born in New York of immigrant Jewish parents from Eastern Europe, or at least raised in New York. Of the rest, Macdonald came from a prosperous (Protestant) Brooklyn family and was educated at Exeter and Yale, and Dupee, of midwestern Protestant background, also went to Yale where he and Macdonald were classmates and close friends.

With the exception of Hook, who wanted to be a philosopher, Schapiro, who probably wanted to be a scholar, and Greenberg, who probably wanted to be a painter, they all as young men had literary ambitions and dabbled, some of them even giftedly, in poetry and fiction. Only Goodman, however, was to make any kind of real stir in the thirties with anything but criticism of one variety or another. Criticism was the mode they all excelled in, all of them being not only marvelously intelligent and learned (in some cases in a style one associates with autodidacts of a particularly maniacal type), but also madly in love with ideas, and (Trilling and Dupee excepted this time) by nature pugnaciously polemical in argument. Insofar as they were formed by native American influences of the immediate past, it was by the Greenwich Village rebels of the teens and twenties, the battlers against philistinism, commercialism, and bourgeois values—writers like Edmund Wilson and Van Wyck Brooks, and the "red-ink boys," as Mencken called them, around the old *Masses,* John Reed, Max Eastman, and Floyd Dell—and also by the expatriate novelists and poets of the period like Pound, Eliot, Hemingway, Anderson, and Dos Passos.

But this particular American ethos was perhaps the least important element of the tradition which they were later to make their own. To describe it in the most general way, that tradition grew out of an effort to forge an alliance between avant-gardism (which is to say, the movement of formal experimentation) in the arts, and radicalism (specifically, Marxist revolutionary socialism) in politics. Probably all the members of the founding generation had been socialists (unless Goodman sprang a communitarian anarchist from the cradle) as well as "modernists" in the twenties, and several of them became Communists while—and this was the unusual twist—remaining modernists in the early thirties. *Partisan Review,* which was of course to be the main family magazine, began publication in 1934 as the organ of the John Reed Clubs, a Communist Party youth group, and then broke about two years later not over politics as such but over literature—Phillips and Rahv, out of the good modernist belief in the autonomy of art, refusing to countenance bureaucratic dictation of their literary tastes and refusing to accept the Stalinist dogma that experimental poets of politically conservative bent like T. S. Eliot were to be attacked as decadent while tenth-rate proletarian novelists like Jack Conroy were to be promoted as great. When Phillips and Rahv, with the help of Macdonald and Dupee (and later Greenberg), resumed publication of the magazine in 1936, it was with the same modernist sympathies and the same belief in the autonomy of art but with a changed political orientation. Still preaching revolutionary socialism, of a vaguely Trotskyite brand, *Partisan Review* was now violently anti-Stalinist, and would continue to be long after the revolutionary socialism had gone the usual way of youthful revolutionary ardors.

This combination of a commitment to left-wing anti-Stalinism and a commitment to avant-gardism became the distinguishing family trait. To be sure, one or two writers in America outside the family (the name of Edmund Wilson comes to mind) were similarly marked off, but not many more than one or two. The great majority of American literary people in the thirties were Stalinist in their political sympathies as well as "middlebrow" in their literary tastes (that is, uneasy with or downright hostile to the modernist movement and much happier with the naturalistic tradition as represented most powerfully at that moment by Theodore Dreiser). Stalinism, of course, did not necessarily entail middlebrowism, for there were some "highbrows" (that is, friends of modernism), like Malcolm Cowley and Kenneth Burke, who were with the Stalinists (Burke even making use of his acrobatic ingenuity to write a defense of the Moscow Trials); nor, as the example of Eastman indicates, did anti-Stalinism always consort with a friendliness toward modernism. Finally, there were the Southerners like John Crowe Ransom, Allen Tate, and Robert Penn Warren who had their own distinguishing family trait: like Eliot and Yeats and Joyce themselves, they were modernists and at the same time avowed political conservatives.

It was because the political-literary position they held was so unusual that the Founding Fathers, in the highly charged polemical atmosphere of the thirties when friendships and marriages were made and broken on the basis of political views alone, got stuck with one another like a family against the rest of the world. But there was more to it than the word "position" suggests, for out of that position developed an intellectual style which for a long while was almost unique to *Partisan Review,* and which eventually came of its own force to be identified in the eyes of many with the quality of intellectuality itself.

The elements were these: out of the experience of the break with Stalinism, independence of mind—meaning a mind dictated to by nothing but its own sense of reality, and highly skeptical, even suspicious, of other senses of reality; out of the schooling in Marxism, a tendency to view all phenomena, including the arts, in their historical and social context; *but,* out of the schooling in modernism, a simultaneous belief in the irreducible status and freedom of a work of art; out of the schooling in modernism too, a passionate interest in the great masters of that movement and a contemptuous distaste for their "middlebrow" enemies and for the "philistine" critical rhetoric typically employed by such; out of the feeling of beleaguered isolation shared with the masters of the modernist movement themselves, elitism—the conviction that *others* were not worth taking into consideration except to attack, and need not be addressed in one's writing; out of that feeling as well, a sense of hope-lessness as to the fate of American culture at large and the correlative conviction that integrity and standards were only possible among "us." The style, then, was characteristically hypercritical, learned, allusive; it took its bearings not from any American tradition of letters (as, for example, Wilson's at least partly did) but from heavier modes of critical discourse which could be traced to France or Germany or Russia.

And, indeed, it was mainly on Europe that the fam-ily had its eyes. There were so many people there who would in the coming years be revealed as relatives—Or-well, Koestler, Spender, Merleau-Ponty, Silone, and a dozen others—and so few outside the family proper in America itself. The terms in which the family discussed things, the language it spoke, was a language that seemed to make more sense to European than to American ears; the books which were the family's touchstones and the issues it considered relevant all had greater currency in Europe than in America; and the ideas and tastes to which the family was attached constituted an ambience suggesting Paris rather more than it did New York (New York, appropriately enough, was the *New Yorker* crowd at the Algonquin Round Table, with one foot on Broad-way and another on the best-seller lists). Thus, when the family spoke of itself or was spoken of as "alienated," the reference might be to any number of things, but the deepest thing of all was this: *They did not feel that they belonged to America or that America belonged to them.*

Here we have the final element which distinguished their intellectual style from all others then current, giving it a tone of disinterestedness—as of a man who has nothing to gain and nothing to lose—in relation to social, political, and even cultural problems, and rooting it in considerations not of the practical or the viable but of the despairingly moral.

Of course there were many disinterested and moral critics outside the family who felt that America did not belong to them either—that it belonged rather to the businessmen and the philistines—but such nonfamily critics differed from those within the family in believing that they *did* belong to America, that it indeed rightfully belonged to them, and that it might perhaps even belong to them again some day as it had belonged to their grandfathers before being stolen away by the forces of mammon in the wicked Gilded Age. This had been the message of Van Wyck Brooks in his younger days, and it was the message of Edmund Wilson even after he had temporarily become sympathetic to Communism; and the sense of rootedness gave a certain music to their work, whose self-possessed melodies never entered into the family's prose. The family's prose had verve, vitality, wit, texture, and above all brilliance, but rarely did it exhibit a complete sureness of touch; it tended instead to be overly assertive or overly lyrical or overly refined or overly clever—and even on an amazing occasion or two overly diffident.

How could it have been otherwise? Far from entertaining the notion that its work was part of a battle for the soul of America which had a chance of eventually being won, the family thanked God (as it were) that it was surviving at all in so inhospitable a climate, and devoted much of its energy to protecting itself against contaminating influences from the surrounding American world: from *Kitsch,* from middlebrowism, from commercialism, from mass culture, from academicism, from populism, from liberalism, from Stalinism; from Louis B. Mayer, from John Steinbeck, from George S. Kaufman, from J. Donald Adams, from Archibald MacLeish, from Irving Babbitt, from Franklin Delano Roosevelt.

But if not to America, then to what did the family think it belonged? Not, certainly, to the Jewish people. They, of course, were universal men. As good Marxists, they regarded Zionism as yet another form of bourgeois nationalism, they considered the "Jewish question" a minor aspect of the crisis in capitalism, and they looked forward with great equanimity to the disappearance under socialism of the Jews as a distinct people, seeing no point in their survival.

So little point did the family see in Jewish survival that the threat being posed even at that moment by Hitler to the actual physical survival of Jewish men, women, and children did not, to judge by the files of *Partisan Review,* seem a matter of urgent concern. Clement Greenberg showed himself superlatively well qualified for the article on Jewish self-hatred he was to write a decade later in *Commentary* by arguing now, in 1940 (echoing Trotsky, also a Jew), that World War II—the war against *Hitler*—did not merit "our" support; Macdonald, who at least had the excuse of not being Jewish, agreed with Greenberg in crying a plague on both warring houses, resigned from *Partisan Review,* and went on to found his own magazine, *Politics.* There his Trotskyism cheerfully gave way to anarchism and pacifism, a shift which for a time brought him into alliance with Goodman, who, like Rosenberg, had earlier broken with the family for reasons that were partly personal and partly political (Goodman as an anarchist found their Marxism uncongenial—also "they wouldn't print my pieces"—and Rosenberg found it shallow). Phillips and Rahv, with the blunt good sense that always saved both of them from the more egregious potentialities for political stupidity inherent in the radical position, made a hash of the anti-war argument, and Greenberg too resigned (though continuing as a contributor), leaving *Partisan Review* completely in their control. Among the other casualties of World War II would be their revolutionary socialism.

To compensate for the weakening of the family in consequence of these defections and schismatic happenings, the second generation was by now heaving into view. It was truly a second generation in that the Founding Fathers had exerted a formative influence upon its members, helping to shape their ideas, their tastes, their prose, and in general their conception of the nature of true intellectuality and of the intellectual life itself. In the case of the older or more precocious members of the second generation—Mary McCarthy (who possibly even belongs among the first), Delmore Schwartz, William Barrett, Saul Bellow, Isaac Rosenfeld, Richard Chase, and Alfred Kazin—it was perhaps not so much a question of having been formed by the first as of having discovered in themselves a natural affinity with the family style. This may also have been the case to a lesser degree with those members of the second generation who came into visibility a little later, toward the end of the war and right after it: Leslie Fiedler, Irving Howe, Elizabeth Hardwick, Daniel Bell, James Baldwin, David Bazelon, Robert Warshow, Nathan Glazer, and Irving Kristol (the last three, of course, all joining the editorial staff of *Commentary,* which, founded in 1945, was to become along with *Partisan Review* the other main second-generation center). Politically, all were anti-Stalinist, many of them not via a prior period of Stalinism but through Trotskyism or democratic socialism, and those who were literary were strongly committed to modernism (which, with Schwartz and Barrett, who joined Phillips and Rahv on the staff of *Partisan Review*, amounted almost to a religion).

Still, as might be expected, important differences showed up between the two generations. The second, for example, was much less Marxist in its thinking than the first, though equally given to the seeing of things in historical and social context, and far more Freudian, though equally disinclined to make explicit use of psychoanalytic concepts in critical discourse. The second generation also wrote, or at any rate published, much more fiction and poetry than the first, though everyone in the second wrote literary or social criticism as well. And finally, while the second generation was even more attached to the idea of its own alienation than the first, in reality it felt somewhat more at home in America than the first, just as those who were Jewish tended to be more comfortable with that fact than their elders had been.

Marxism, the creation of a baptized German Jew, issues the command: "Transcend yourself and join in the universal struggle to bring about the self-transcendence of all men!" Psychoanalysis, the creation of an acculturated German Jew who never underwent baptism, demands by contrast: "Accept yourself for what you are and make use of it!" It is accordingly no accident, as disciples of both schools of thought once liked to say, that Jews have been among the most eager listeners to these calls, many of them responding first to one and then to the other at different periods of their lives. Thus it was with the second generation: from Marx to Freud, from self-transcendence to self-acceptance. Schwartz, Bellow, Rosenfeld, Kazin, Fiedler, and Howe—products every one of Yiddish-speaking households—all proclaimed their Jewishness, took relish in it, wrote stories, poems, and articles about it; and so, at the same time, did several members of the first generation, like Rosenberg and Goodman, begin to do. Of course more was involved here than the influence of Freud: Hitler's altogether irrefutable demonstration of the inescapability of Jewishness was no doubt an even more important factor in the emergence of this new attitude.

As with Jewishness, so with Americanness. But here the case is more complicated. Both Schwartz and Rosenfeld (whom Schwartz once jokingly called "the Jewish Franz Kafka") said in a 1944 symposium that Jewishness was not only a joy to them but a valuable asset in that it rendered them doubly alienated from American society. Yet nothing could have been clearer about those two extravagantly endowed young men, neither of whom the gods would ever allow to grow old—one from New York and the other from Chicago, and each in his own ebullient way embodying all the nervous energy, the quick brilliance, and the boisterousness of spirit of the American big city itself—than the easy relation they had to the national culture, both "high" and "low": Hawthorne as well as Hollywood, the New England transcendentalists as well as the New York Giants. And much the same could be said of the whole second generation. The problem of how to reconcile the man in him who loved Hollywood westerns and the man who loved Henry James became the leading theme of Warshow's work, and less explicitly of Bellow's and Fiedler's; it was not a problem which had interested the first generation, and it would never become a problem for them either.

When Rahv, of the first generation, wrote about American literature—and he did so with originality and depth in several seminal essays—it was with the eye of the learned outsider. When the twenty-five-year-old Kazin, of the second generation, turned his amazingly precocious attention on the same subject in *On Native Grounds,* it was with the aggressive conviction that this literature was *his*. The story, in fact, is told of Kazin's extreme irritation with another member of the family (second-generation) who once teased him about a phrase he had used in a piece on Parkman's *Oregon Trail* in *Partisan Review: "Our* forests, Alfred?"—which suggests that not everyone of the second generation, not even Kazin himself, had so assured a feeling of at-homeness in America. The nuances of individual feeling aside, however, a tendency to adopt a more benign attitude toward American society certainly was discernible within the family, first generation as well as second, throughout the postwar years.

Thus *Partisan Review,* which since the late forties

had been in what was to prove the greatest period of its glorious history, published a symposium in 1951 astonishingly entitled "Our Country and Our Culture," the pronoun by itself being as telling as anything the participants had to say. And indeed why *not* "our" this time? They had, as Mary McCarthy later said, just gone through a war and discovered that they had, whatever ideology might dictate, a personal stake in the victory of America. Besides, the depression was over, the war was over, there was more money around, there were teaching jobs and grants and fellowships to be had, and the big publishers were at last becoming aware of the family's existence (whereas before only a very few had been: Rosenfeld's first collection of stories, to take only one example of many, had to go begging to a tiny and unknown firm in Minneapolis).

Then too, of course, there was politics. As anti-Stalinists who could no longer entertain the hope, if they ever really had, that a true socialist revolution was in the offing, the family was naturally driven to support America as the main defense against the Soviet threat. But if in what was just then beginning to be called the cold war they were all on the side of America, they held differing views of what being on the side of America entailed. Because America was better than Russia, did that mean that America was good, and if so, how good? Because Stalinism was an international menace, did that mean that it was also a domestic threat—greater, say, than Mc-

Carthyism? As the 1950's wore on, as Eisenhower followed Truman, as the Oppenheimer case followed the Hiss case, as McCarthy followed McCarran, and as Khrushchev followed Stalin, these two questions were to become a major source of trouble to the family, leading to bitter personal disputes, shifting hostile alliances, and a general weakening of ties.

Hints of all this trouble had already begun to appear by the time I arrived on the scene in 1953, but the crisis was still a long way off. Meanwhile, the main element in the intellectual atmosphere of those years—years which were later to be lumped vulgarly and indiscriminately with the latter part of the decade as the dull fifties—was an exhilaration at the sudden and overwhelming appearance of new possibilities, in life as in consciousness. There was a world out there which no one, it seemed, had bothered to look at before, and everyone, happily shedding his Marxist blinkers, went rushing out to look. At what? Why, at America, of course—"America the Beautiful," as Mary McCarthy called it, by no means altogether ironically, in an article in *Commentary*.

In this atmosphere, Trilling, who had never been completely at ease with the spirit of the first generation (even falling under Rahv's glowering but thoroughly justified suspicion as early as the mid-thirties of having more Freud in his system than Marx), began to emerge as the natural leader of the second (though falling now under Delmore Schwartz's unjustified but even darker suspicion of the secret heresy of not really liking modernist literature). Trilling became, in fact, the family's single most influential member in the 1950's, the only one for a time whose influence actually extended far beyond the confines of the family proper.

Why this should have happened is easy enough to see, for in addition to being a critic and writer of the very first rank with a body of work that offered its own intrinsic delights to the mind, Trilling was exactly in tune with the temper of a period which found Tocqueville a more reliable guide than Marx to the American reality and whose cultural home was moving from Greenwich Village to an address as yet unspecified but definitely to the north of Fourteenth Street. Trilling's own rather anthropological interest in American culture, moreover, had not only long been intense but had yielded many extraordinarily rich ideas which others were to mine and exploit more systematically than he himself ever bothered doing. "Who among us intellectuals," he demanded of the rest of the family in the *Partisan Review* symposium, with all the authority of *The Liberal Imagination* behind him, "really knows what is being taught in the great teachers' colleges?" But it was not *Partisan Review* itself, it was *Commentary* which took up the job of finding out what was really being taught in the great teachers' colleges— and also in Hollywood and also in Washington and also in Harlem and also in the suburbs and also in the unions. And looking at all this ("O my America, my Newfoundland!"), *Commentary* on the whole liked what it saw and saw that it was good.

Mary McCarthy had been launched on her spectacular career as a theater critic when the editors of *Partisan Review,* wanting to make use of her wicked pen but not believing that a Vassar girl, and a very pretty one at that, could possibly be equipped to write about serious things, decided that only a trivial matter like the Broadway stage could be safely entrusted to her care. This was not the spirit in which Elliot Cohen edited *Commentary.* There was nothing, absolutely nothing, which he thought intrinsically trivial. He had, Trilling said of him after his death in 1959, a "sense of the subtle interrelations that exist between the seemingly disparate parts of a culture, and between the commonplaces of daily life and the most highly developed works of the human mind," and out of this sense of things—not to mention the sheer editorial genius Trilling also rightly credited him with—Cohen created the anomaly that was *Commentary.*

Unlike *Partisan Review, Commentary* was not a literary magazine. It was founded right after the war by the American Jewish Committee—an organization which had been set up in 1906 by a group of wealthy and prominent Jews of German origin to fight discrimination and which still had perhaps the classiest tone of any Jewish organization—with the idea that the need existed just then for a monthly journal of opinion that would devote itself primarily though not exclusively to a running critical examination of problems of Jewish concern. With a perspicacity rare in voluntary organizations, Jewish or otherwise, the AJC understood that unless the editor of the new magazine were given a free hand and protected from any pressures to conform to the Committee's own line, the result would be a pretentious house organ and nothing more.

What the AJC probably envisaged was a kind of Jewish *Harper's,* only more scholarly. But Cohen had other ideas. A prodigy from Mobile, Alabama, he had graduated from Yale at the age of eighteen and by the age of twenty-five had become managing editor of the *Menorah Journal,* a magazine whose aim was to explore the Jewish cultural heritage for the purpose, one might say, of proving to the world that there really *was* such a thing as a respectable (by the genteel standards of Harvard University) Jewish culture. In the *Menorah Journal* under the young Cohen appeared the first published works of such writers as Trilling, Clifton Fadiman, and Herbert Solow, and there too Cohen began to develop his special editorial style, pouring out endless, and endlessly detailed, suggestions for pieces to people who would then be coerced by endlessly detailed criticism into as many revisions of the manuscript as he could badger them into making before he himself took over for a final go. To write a piece for Cohen was an ordeal which not everyone was willing to suffer, but it was also, and especially for novices, an education in the impossibly difficult art of effective exposition.

After a few years on the *Menorah Journal,* Cohen had a falling-out with its editor-in-chief, Henry Hurwitz, and left. But there was nowhere else to go. A very bad writer himself, he published nothing but an obscure little pamphlet on yellow-dog contracts during an inevitable fling with Stalinism in the thirties, earning his living until *Commentary* came along as a fund-raiser for a Jewish organization. The misery he must have endured during those dark days is gruesome to contemplate, and when, at the age of forty-five, he was once again given an opportunity to get his hands on a magazine, to make up those fifteen lost years, he went at it with the compulsiveness and drive of a much younger man (incidentally taking a big cut in salary).

In one of my first meetings with Clement Greenberg, he startled me out of my wits by referring contemptuously to *Commentary,* of which he himself had been an editor from the very beginning, as a middlebrow magazine. Quite apart from my puzzlement over what he thought such a statement implied about him and his relation to the magazine, I was bewildered by this application of the term to so intellectually stylish, so (to me) obviously highbrow a phenomenon. But coming from the man who had written that famous essay on "Avant-Garde and Kitsch" and who in addition had discovered

Jackson Pollock, the charge had to be taken seriously.

I no longer recall exactly what he said in justification of it, but I think I know what he must have meant. He meant that Cohen was a believer in popularization—popularization at a very high level, to be sure, but popularization nevertheless. This, of course, was true. Unlike the indubitably highbrow *Partisan Review*, which was addressed exclusively to the family and to anyone else who had read enough to be able to eavesdrop on conversations in the allusive language the family habitually used, *Commentary* was edited by Cohen with his eye on a more diverse and more far-flung audience. Or, to put the point in a slightly different context, whereas *Partisan Review* might be said to have been a magazine for "producers" of ideas, *Commentary* was a magazine for "consumers." Yet even as such, it still bore a closer resemblance to *Partisan Review* than it did, say, to *Harper's*. The upshot was that *Commentary* simply defied accurate characterization in terms of the highbrow-middlebrow concept. And this was because it was already registering and reflecting the very changes in the cultural condition of America which were to rob that concept of the relevance it had once unquestionably possessed.

If, in fact, we take "avant-garde" to mean merely "in advance of the times" (though, of course, it means more than that), we can say that Cohen's *Commentary* was curiously avant-garde. In this sense: that it anticipated a cultural situation which would more nearly resemble that of the premodernist period, when the only relevant distinction was between those who had an interest in the life of the mind and spirit and those who had none (and that is precisely how Van Wyck Brooks used the terms "highbrow" and "lowbrow" when he coined them in 1914, there existing as yet no phenomenon in need of the name "middlebrow"), than it would approximate the situation of the postmodernist decades, when a serious split occurred among the culturally involved. Out of that split emerged two antagonistic publics, the smaller one supporting modernism and everything in the way of sensibility and attitude which modernism implied (avant-gardism in art, "alienation" in social philosophy, antiliberalism of either the Right or the Left in politics), the larger opposing modernism and taking its stand instead on the traditions of realism or naturalism in the arts, genteel belle-lettrism or populist rhetorizing in critical discourse, and a liberalism in politics which in the days of the Popular Front often melted smoothly into Stalinism.

Many forces were responsible for the eventual truce to this battle—and I have admittedly made the split sound more rigidly schematic than it actually was—but the most important of them was the triumph of modernism and its absorption by a once-hostile world (a parallel development was the absorption of many radical ideas by the liberal community—the "dishing," as it were, of the Socialists by the Democrats). And what happened to the artists also happened to the intellectuals who were their partisans and were marked off thereby as an identifiable faction in the politics of contemporary culture. The subfaction known as the New Critics became firmly established in the universities, while the subfaction I have been calling the family began in the fifties to find the world more and more hospitable to its writings and its ideas. What then could have been more natural than for it to respond by acting more politely toward the world, agreeing, that is, to speak to it in places other than the family magazines and in a somewhat less allusive style (by which I do *not* mean vulgarized or watered-down) than it had been accustomed to using when only relatives were willing to listen? On top of everything else, one got *paid* for speaking to the world, which was more than could be said of internal family talk.

But all this, which more than anything else would be responsible ultimately for the dissolution of the family as a family, was only just making a very dim appearance on the horizon when I returned to America in the summer of 1953—unless one regards Cohen's *Commentary* itself not as a family magazine, strictly speaking, but as the ground on which a hesitant first introduction was arranged between the family and a "consumer" world rapidly becoming "post-middlebrow." Whether or not that image would be able to withstand close historical scrutiny—and probably it would not, for it leaves out of account all the writing the family did for *The Nation* when

Margaret Marshall ran the back of the book—Cohen assuredly did arrange for certain members of the family to shake hands in public with their own Jewishness for the first time in their lives.

The American Jewish Committee's mandate to Cohen had been to produce "a journal of opinion on Jewish affairs and contemporary issues" that would be nonpartisan with regard to the complicated and often bitter politics of the Jewish community but that would also square with "the Committee's own program to fight bigotry, protect human rights, and promote Jewish cultural interest and creative achievement in America." But to ask Elliot Cohen, a born position-taker if there ever was one, to be nonpartisan about anything was like asking Harry Truman to campaign for Thomas E. Dewey. Thus, until the establishment of the State of Israel, he echoed the AJC's line on Zionism, which was not exactly anti (like the American Council for Judaism's) but was far from being pro.

Commentary's "non-Zionism" certainly contributed to the magazine's unpopularity with the overwhelmingly pro-Zionist organized Jewish community, but what was really bothering *Commentary*'s Jewish critics was the general tone of detachment in which things Jewish were customarily discussed in its pages (though not always: the department called "From the American Scene" specialized in Jewish-Americana which was rarely free of a distressingly vulgar coziness). This tone was, of course, the family tone, and if it repelled public-relations-minded Jewish readers who were used to something more hortatory and self-congratulatory, it attracted intellectuals to whom the idea had never before occurred that things Jewish could be talked about with the same disinterestedness, the same candor, the same range of reference, and the same resonance as any serious subject. Cohen thus helped to make an interest in things Jewish intellectually and culturally respectable within the family (even Trilling was discovered writing a piece on "Wordsworth and the Rabbis"), and at a time when this was so little taken for granted in America that the very notion seemed a self-contradiction to many.

So much for the "Jewish affairs" clause in Cohen's mandate. As to the "contemporary issues" clause, Cohen enthusiastically interpreted it as a license to go hunting far beyond the boundaries of the Jewish reservation, and he printed at least three or four pieces in every issue of *Commentary* having no apparent relation to "Jewish affairs" or to "Jewish cultural interest and creative achievement in America." Yet, as I have already indicated, Cohen was a man who saw relations which were invisible to other eyes: it was one of the qualities which made him a great editor until it went out of control after ten years at *Commentary* and literally drove him mad. Thus the increasingly hard-line articles he regularly published on Communism and the Soviet Union, while reflecting his own extreme anti-Stalinism, were also part of a secret program to demonstrate that not all Jews were Communists—even though, as all the world knew but as *Commentary* would have folded before admitting, Jews were disproportionately represented in the American Communist Party. But this secret program was itself part of a larger program, a Grand Design whose precise details were known only to Cohen, though guessed at accurately enough by others, to lead the family out of the desert of alienation in which it had been wandering for so long and into the promised land of democratic, pluralistic, prosperous America where it would live as blessedly in its Jewishness as in its Americanness, safe and sound and forevermore, amen.

Whatever Cohen did with *Commentary* he did in the service of the Grand Design. (It explains, for example, why he encouraged young writers, including me, to deal seriously and sympathetically with popular culture, and yet turned down a masterpiece like Warshow's article on Chaplin, with an explanation that was devious even for him: the real reason was that no fellow-traveler of Stalinism, genius or not, was going to be praised in *his* magazine.) A crippling rigidity would later set in, but in the early fifties the Grand Design was working at least to the extent of generating the unique excitement that comes to a magazine when with a certain air of secretiveness it communicates the sense that everything in it is somehow hooked into everything else and refers conspiratorially to some purpose, some Meaning, larger than itself.

It also worked to the extent of provoking opposition, in the form of a new second-generation family magazine which Irving Howe, ever loyal to the socialism of his youth and disturbed by the new "conformity" he saw developing within the family, began bringing out in 1954 under the title *Dissent*. At the same time, the Congress for Cultural Freedom, an organization made up largely of foreign relatives of the family, was planning to bring Irving Kristol to London to collaborate with Stephen Spender in starting *Encounter*. Very few members of the family who participated in the activities of the Congress for Cultural Freedom knew for certain, if at all, that it was being covertly supported by the CIA. But the fact that the CIA knew about *them* was itself a measure of how far, for better or worse, they had already traveled from their monastic confines of the thirties.

Scarcely aware of any of this long history, I returned to America from England at the age of twenty-three to discover that I had through some mysterious process been created by it. What remained for me to discover was that I was also destined to play a part in many of its future unfoldings. To call my adoption into the family the third stage in my conversion to "culture" is therefore accurate, but largely in the sense that a Marrano may be said to have converted to Judaism when he returns to the open practice of it after having practiced it before only in the secrecy of his cellar and in the deeper secrecy of his own mind.

5 Making a Start

Impatient, as always, to get everything over with, I had been planning to enlist in the army immediately upon my return to America, but it turned out that enlisting meant spending three years in uniform instead of the two required by the draft. A two-year period seeming in itself far in excess of the time required by the internal draft of my own curiosity about military service, I reported in to the local board, took twelve seconds or so to set my highly complicated affairs in order, and prepared my soul (grown monumentally anxious now that the army was about to be transformed from an interesting abstraction into a living condition) for immediate induction. Since there were virtually no limits to my naïveté at that age about things much closer to home, there is no cause for surprise in the fact that I should have had so meager an understanding of the pace at which armies and all institutions connected with them operate. For five months I waited, expecting each day to be the last—and, of course, experiencing an immense shock when the summons finally arrived to present myself for induction on December 15, 1953.

Still, I do wrong to complain of the lack of urgency the draft board showed about making a soldier out of me, for they were exquisite, those five months of suspension between a set of onerous obligations I had just renounced and a set of delicious fantasies for the (post-army) future. It is like a very long voyage, to be suspended in that way, a true vacation to the spirit. No one expects anything of you and you expect nothing of yourself. You sleep late, you loaf, you languidly watch television for hours on end—all without reproach, all without guilt. And if you happen to be suspended because you are waiting to be drafted, you will find an added pleasure in the clucks of commiseration that will deliciously fill your ears wherever you go.

It has been said of me, however, that I have "a super-ego like a horse," which is, I suppose, one of the three reasons why I was not content to avail myself of the pleasures of suspension alone during those five luscious months—the other two reasons being greed and ambition. Greed for the pleasures of publication; ambition for the pleasures of success. The way to satisfy all three was of course to write. And so I wrote, six pieces in all, which seemed at the time no great rate of production but which at other periods of my life would strike me as so herculean that I could not even imagine, let alone get myself into, the state of mind and spirit that would make it possible for me to write that much in that span of time again.

Writing is among the most mysterious of human activities. No one, least of all the psychoanalysts, knows the laws by which it moves or refuses to move. And yet the whole phenomenon obviously falls within the domain of psychoanalytic theory. The poem, the story, the essay, and even something so apparently inconsequential as a book review (I mean one which is approached with seriousness), is already *there,* much in the way that Socrates said mathematical knowledge was already there, before a word is ever put to paper; and the act of writing is the act of finding the magical key that will unlock the floodgates and let the flow begin.

As every writer can testify, the Muses once invoked by poets are a reality, except that the ancients were probably wrong in thinking that they reside in the heavens. More likely they are located in reaches of the mind which are accessible or not according to their own sweet volition. Unless he is writing mechanically, the writer does not experience his writing as an act of creation; he experiences it as an act of discovery: it *comes* or *happens* or is *given* to him, and when it does, he recognizes it at

139

once for his own. It is not within the power of his will to summon it forth if it refuses to come; nor is he capable of resisting it for long when it starts to demand release. What, according to Saint Augustine, the penis is to the body—he said it was the only limb or "member" which defied the control of the will, which, that is, actually had a will of its own, rising and falling of its own accord and not, like the arms or the legs, at the dictates of the "owner's" will—the act of writing is to the mind. In fact, so closely connected in some obscure way are the two phenomena, with the ability to write resembling the feeling of a ready sexual potency and the inability to write resembling the experience of sexual impotence, that many men have a strong impulse to masturbate when they are about to start on a piece of writing, as though to persuade themselves that they *are* in control, that they can get it up and make it come.

But if the act of writing cannot be controlled by the will, it can be controlled by that magical key of which I have already spoken. The key, I believe, is literally a key in that it is musical (which, if I may indulge in a bit of fanciful etymologizing à la Heidegger, is perhaps why it was to the *Muses* that the ancient poets appealed): it is the tone of voice, the only tone of voice, in which this particular piece of writing will permit itself to be written. To find that tone is to unlock the floodgates. Yet the unconscious, or the Muse, or whatever it is, often exacts a sacrifice from the writer before it will allow him to hit upon the right tone, the key. It may specify a certain number of hours or days or months of agony so intense that fantasies of suicide inevitably arise. (Conrad's wife used to lock him in a room to write; he would writhe on the floor and bang on the door, begging to be let out.) It may, on the other hand, decide to give him a break, possibly because he has accumulated a large enough balance of suffering to entitle him temporarily to a free ride.

In that blessed case, the writer will enter into a state of bliss such as exists nowhere else on earth, and probably not in heaven either. He will be in touch with himself and in command of all his powers to a degree that would gratify the greatest narcissist (and being a writer he will invariably be a greater narcissist than anyone except singers and actors) while paradoxically freeing him from self-preoccupation (the disease D. H. Lawrence described as "falling from the hands of God") to a degree that would gratify the most ambitious saint. In this beatific condition, he will sit with a pen or at a typewriter and watch, in delight and amazement, sentences mysteriously shaping themselves into rhythms he *knows* to be right and then giving birth by parthenogenesis to successive generations of sentences which flow into paragraphs which in turn by seamless transition flow gently into other paragraphs which in their turn begin to shape themselves into an organically coherent pattern that miraculously corresponds—only better, much better—to the dim vision he had had of it and which had driven him in the first place to the desk. He will find that he has not only been permitted to uncover things he did not know he knew, but that he has also been allowed for the first time to say many things he knew he knew and had never been able to get onto a page because they never *fitted* anywhere and only what fits is allowed.

Finished, he will be exhausted and exhilarated, all anxieties gone; he will feel that everything in the world makes sense after all, that there is an order to things, and that he himself is part of that order. For that, at bottom, is what he wants—coherence and order, coherence with himself and order in the world. (Not for nothing, then, do writers slip so easily into paranoia. The paranoid fantasy, a drama in which the minutest details all hang together in a perfect fit, with oneself as the menaced hero, would naturally be the occupational hazard of a narcissist questing for order.)

I have, of course, been describing the process as it must look in an ideal state—with Shakespeare, say, who according to Ben Jonson "never blotted a line," or with Mozart, who could write a whole symphony while riding in a carriage along a bumpy road. The reality with lesser mortals is likely, as usual, to fall considerably short. Thus even when the flow is true, when the piece is writing itself, it may not be entirely true, and the writer's will then has to intervene to blot a line or two or ten or a hundred: to correct, to polish, to reorganize, to perfect. At this point exhilaration often gives way to self-doubt.

Was the whole thing, now beyond reach and the flood-gates slammed shut, an illusion? Sometimes the doubt is justified: it may be, flow or not, that what the writer had to say was not especially worth saying, what he had to do not especially worth doing.

But even if it was not an illusion, even if he has just produced a masterpiece, the writer may find himself full of loathing for it. Instead of being better than his original dim vision, it is, he is certain, a betrayal of it and defective past redemption. So, for example, T. E. Lawrence, after finishing *The Seven Pillars of Wisdom*, very nearly burned the manuscript, explaining to George Bernard Shaw: "There's a lot of half-baked thinking, some cheap disgust and complaint . . . : in fact, the sham stuff you have spent your life trying to prick. . . . My own disgust with it is so great that I no longer believe it worth trying to improve (or possible to improve)."

In other less-than-ideal instances, the writer may have been driven by desperation into the delusion that he has found the key, and he may in that case force something onto paper that a perceptive critic can recognize as "willed." Or the flow, having truly started, may suddenly decide to stop, and the writer may nevertheless push desperately ahead with a willed pen, refusing to acknowledge his loss of the flow. Yet even here the matter is not so simple. The Augustinian analogy to a willed piece of writing would be an orgasm achieved by masturbation, and just as masturbation does in fact produce an orgasm (a point which puritans invariably forget to mention), so force-fed writing can sometimes work a momentary opening of the floodgates: a minute ago the mind was dead and all at once it comes alive, only to die again a minute later. This kind of writing (which is very precisely described in Dan Jacobson's novel, *The Beginners*) the critic will recognize as "uneven" or "unrealized." It differs from mechanical or hack writing in deriving from the ambition to attain to the real thing, and from the real or "realized" thing in not attaining to that quality of organic coherence which Coleridge rightly identified as the mark of a living work of the Imagination (his upper case, not mine).

Where all the Coleridgeans among us go wrong, I think, is in their assumption that this quality of Imagination can exist only in poems or stories. The truth is that it can and does exist, demonstrably so, in any form of writing, however humble or trivial that form may be by the evanescent or even the legitimate standards of a given moment. Writing always involves a man sitting with an implement and an inchoate idea before a blank sheet of paper and in terror at the answering blankness of his own mind. Consequently, if one is speaking of the experience of being a writer, the only defensible distinction is between writers who are willing to accept the risks of suffering entailed by the effort to tap their inner potentialities of organic coherence, and those who are unable or unwilling to take such risks.

Because misunderstanding on the point is very widespread indeed, it is important to stress that a writer's motives are relevant to the quality of his work *only* to the extent that they relate to this willingness or the lack of it. "No man but a blockhead ever wrote except for money," said Dr. Johnson. Well, he was wrong, but not in the way the kind of purists he was trying to shock by the statement are pleased to think. There are other forms of worldly currency, such as attention, admiration, and fame, for which men have always written, and there cannot have been many men in history who have written in total disregard of these things. But the issue of motives is simply irrelevant, having arisen in the first place from a confusion between art and religion and a misguided consequent campaign to erect the artist into a substitute for the saint. It may well be true of the saint that he not only refrains from physically committing adultery but also refrains from lusting after his neighbor's wife in his heart; or, to extend the Pauline image, he not only refrains from devoting himself to the pursuit of worldly goods but transcends his natural desire for them. But artists have rarely if ever been notable for transcending the desire for worldly goods. There is indeed no reason why they should cultivate this curious ambition unless conditions absolutely force them into it (which, of course, conditions in the modern world have frequently enough done), and many reasons, directly affecting the vitality of their work, why they should not.

A writer, it seems necessary to say in the face of his mistaken romantic identity as a saint, is a man, and being such his motives, in writing as in everything else, are likely to be mixed.

More than that, even, the narcissism which is an invariable and indispensable element of his very being as a writer is bound to leave him with an unusually strong appetite for success, and as many forms of it as he can get. So long, however, as his aim in the *act* of writing is to find the key to the quality of organic coherence locked within the reaches of his mind—and this, to put it with maximum plainness, is what "giving his all" really means —he must be deemed a serious writer, whether he is writing "for" money, sex, invitations to parties, or any other unseemly objective.

I thought my own objectives very unseemly indeed when I began writing a piece a month for *Commentary* in the fall of 1953. Money was not one of them, and in any case *Commentary* paid next to nothing (though still much more than *Partisan Review*) in those days, my fees ranging from thirty-five to one hundred and fifty dollars, depending upon the length of each piece. Nor did I care much about parties (*that* was to come later). What I wanted was to see my name in print, to be praised, and above all to attract attention.

Any praise I got and any attention I could attract would be all to the good, but it was the attention of the family I most dreamed of arousing. There was no doubt in my mind any longer that it was *my* family, for reading its writings was like hearing a call from the depths of my very soul, and there was nothing I loved better than to sit around with Warshow or Greenberg and listen (my wide-eyed worshipful fascination egging them on) to tales of the patriarchal past: how "Mary" had left "Philip" to marry Edmund Wilson (no relative he, to have his first name taken in vain), how "Dwight" had once organized nude swimming parties on the Cape, how "William" really felt about "Delmore," and how "Isaac" really felt about "Saul." Oh to be granted the right to say "William" and "Philip" and "Dwight," as I could already say "Bob" and "Clem" and "Nat."

But as I was learning from Warshow, the mere fact that a man wrote for *Commentary* or even *Partisan Review* did not necessarily mean that the family would accept him as one of its own. He himself, he said (another great puzzlement to me, like Greenberg's "middlebrow" charge against *Commentary*), was not a full-fledged member, though he wrote for both magazines. He was not considered serious enough and his work, dealing mainly as it did with the movies, was regarded as pleasant but unimportant. This was why, he explained, he never got invited to participate in *Partisan Review* symposia. Being a man who took it totally for granted that everyone was ambitious for success, he had no compunction whatever about complaining bitterly over the lack of recognition the family (which in 1953 still for all practical purposes meant "the world" where the work of a literary intellectual like Warshow was concerned) accorded him. He knew he wanted recognition, he thought he deserved it, and he suffered, though resignedly, over seeing it withheld.

"Haven't you ever known anyone older who seemed to be everything you wanted to be?" says a character in a Dorothy Baker novel. I certainly have, several, and Warshow was one of them. As a type, he resembled one of my earlier heroes, Moses Hadas, in being a man who combined great coldness of mind with great warmth of heart. Like Hadas, too, he genuinely loved the young (no easy thing to do, as I was subsequently to find). Neither man felt that hungry generations were treading *him* down, or that he was in any danger of being eaten up alive (which, in actual fact, they both were) by the pesty voraciousness characteristic of youthful demands upon sympathetically inclined adults. But then both men were humanists in the most literal sense of that word: human nature charmed, amused, delighted them, and where better to see it nakedly exposed than among the relatively unguarded young? (Perhaps the humanism accounts for another peculiarity they had in common: a positively Voltairean hatred of clergymen of any and all denominations—and yet Hadas was himself, as I mentioned earlier, a lapsed ordained rabbi.) And from each man, one of whom gave me my first martini and the other my first New York "author's lunch," I learned the same lesson:

that it was possible to achieve cultivation without losing touch with oneself, without doing violence to one's true feelings, without becoming pompous, pretentious, affected, or false to the realities of one's own experience —without, in short, becoming a facsimile WASP.

It was said of Hadas after his death in 1966 that his greatest quality as a teacher was his power to make the classics come alive. Indeed he could, because unlike most professional scholars he never forgot that the classics were *books*, books written by *men* who were much like men have always been, only graced with a gift for showing what they were on paper. "Here was a man," he would say in beginning a freshman class at Columbia about Aristotle's *Ethics* (Aristotle a *man?* one would think, startled), "who took it into his head to cut up a fish because he wanted to see how it was made; nobody ever thought of doing that before." Or, in starting a discussion of *The Iliad,* a poem which is by no means easy for moderns to make sense of, his eyes would twinkle, a small smile would play around his beautiful bearded face, and his Georgia accent would grow ever so slightly more pronounced as he called wickedly on a Roman Catholic student to ask: "Mr. Sullivan, what kind of gods are these who like to screw mortal women?"

This was Warshow too, though in an altogether different style. As Hadas strove to keep his "low" self alive in his scholarly commerce with the Greeks (and, incidentally, his "vulgar" Jewish self alive in his com-

merce with Columbia gentility), Warshow was determined to guard the integrity of his feelings, whatever
they might be, against the assaults of moral or cultural
piety. He would not pretend to like what he had no taste
for or to dislike what the pieties insisted he condemn;
and if his experience belied an accepted "truth," it was
the experience he held onto and the "truth" that had to
go. There are not many absolutely convinced atheists in
the world, but Warshow was one of them, and his un-
wavering reliance for knowledge on his own experience
may perhaps have been made possible by his atheism: if
there is nothing beyond human life, then there is nothing
beyond experience, and to deny one's own experience is
the surest form of spiritual suicide.

In any case, it was the principle of fidelity to his
own experience, to his own tastes, to his own responses—
together with a certain intellectual diffidence—which,
Warshow told me, led him to write movie criticism. But
it was movie criticism with a difference. "A man watches
a movie," he once wrote, "and the critic must acknowledge that he is that man." The critic is not, in other
words, a sociologist studying the fantasies embedded in
American popular culture or a highbrow going slumming.
He is a man watching a movie and being affected by it
like everyone else in the audience, even if he is also a
man who loves Henry James. Was this simultaneous love
of Henry James and of Hollywood Westerns a contradiction, Warshow wanted to know? He did not believe that

it was, and he found a kind of double-vision way of writing about the movies that resulted in essays of a beauty and a wealth of implication which scarcely have their equal in the whole of American literature.

That Warshow was not appreciated by the family at his proper worth was, oddly enough, one of the signs that it *was* a (Jewish) family. Years later, William Phillips, preparing for a course in modern literary criticism he was about to teach as a guest professor at NYU, said to me that he had discovered why "we" were on the whole so much less successful in the world than the New Critics of *Kenyon Review* and *Sewanee Review:* "I've been re-reading their books; all they ever do is praise and promote one another, and all we ever do is attack one another." While not totally true, this observation came pretty close. In the fall of 1953 I had not yet learned, but I would very soon, that although the family paid virtually no heed to anyone outside it except kissing cousins, it had no mercy whatever on anyone inside it. To be adopted into the family was a mark of great distinction: it meant you were good enough, that you *existed* as a writer and an intellectual. But once adopted, you could expect to be spoken of by many (not all) of your relatives in the most terrifyingly cruel terms. They would rarely have even a grudging good word to say for anything you wrote, though they would at least always read it, and they would attribute the basest motives to your every action. Transposed into a different key, it was the

Jewish self-hatred that has always been the other side of
the coin of Jewish self-love and which found its classic
formulation in Groucho Marx's immortal crack: "I
wouldn't join a club that would have me for a member."

This was not Warshow's view of the matter, however. All he knew was that he enjoyed a rather low standing within the family. And because I shared in his sense
of injustice over that fact, I reacted to the signs that I
was beginning to attract the family's notice with more
trepidation, less delight, and considerably more guilt
than I would otherwise have felt. It was Warshow himself who kept a fascinated, paternally proud, and frankly
envious eye on the accumulation of these signs, reporting
each one to me as it appeared like a broker ticking off the
latest stock-market reports. Clement Greenberg, who
was not always to be so generous in his estimate of me,
had said that I was a "natural," like the hero of the
Malamud novel I had reviewed; Philip Rahv had been
asking people who I was and what I was like; Irving
Howe had been expressing concern over the neo-
conservatism of the younger generation on the basis of
one of my reviews ("Shoot as soon as you see the whites
of their eyes," Warshow said; "Irving has seen the
whites of your eyes"); and most thrilling of all, Elliot
Cohen had been throwing out hints of an intention to
offer me a job on the staff of *Commentary* to replace the
recently departed Irving Kristol.

I have often wondered why those early pieces of mine, which for all their showy intellectual precocity are so gauche and callow that they make me writhe with embarrassment when I look at them today, created as much stir as they did. Yet if I bring myself to look at them with the eye of the editor I now am and as the work of a twenty-three-year-old, I begin to understand what it was about them that attracted attention. Warshow had taught me to think of book reviewing, in the way the whole family did, as *writing,* as an art, and although I was still a million miles from the mastery of this art, I was already practicing it, the first young man in many years to do so with any authority, squarely within the family tradition.

Authority in writing need not be accompanied by consummate skill or any other virtue of craft or mind, for like the personal self-confidence of which it is the literary reflection, it is a quality in its own irreducible right, and one that always elicits an immediate response —just as a certain diffidence of tone and hesitancy of manner account for the puzzling failure of many otherwise superior writers to attract the attention they merit. Wherever it came from (the habit of writing A+ papers?), those early pieces of mine unquestionably had authority—while those of my friend and rival Steven Marcus, which were better in many ways, did not—and this in itself instantly turned them into a kind of application for a position which happened at that moment, when the second generation was maturing and the time had clearly arrived for a third generation, to be open.

In the 1960's, Susan Sontag, the youngest member of the third generation and one of the most highly talented, was to make an even more rapid rise to attention than mine had been, at first within what was left of the family and then, the sociology of American culture having changed radically by this time, almost immediately far beyond it. Her talent explains the rise itself, but the *rapidity* with which it was accomplished must be attributed to the coincidental availability of a vacant position in the culture. That position—for which, by virtue of their unmistakable authority, her early pieces constituted an implicit, though of course not intentional, application —was Dark Lady of American Letters, a position that had originally been carved out by Mary McCarthy in the thirties and forties. But Miss McCarthy no longer occupied it, having recently been promoted to the more dignified status of *Grande Dame* as a reward for her long years of brilliant service. The next Dark Lady would have to be, like her, clever, learned, good-looking, capable of writing family-type criticism as well as fiction with a strong trace of naughtiness. But the ante on naughtiness having gone up by the 1960's, it was not nearly enough by the new standards for a bluestocking to confess to having slept with The Man in the Brooks Brothers Shirt; in an era of what Sherry Abel has called the "fishnet bluestocking," hints of perversion and orgies had to be there.

I do not in any way mean to imply that there was anything calculated about Miss Sontag's work or even that she had Mary McCarthy in mind as a model. On the contrary, though her figure mystically resembled that of the young Mary McCarthy and she had the same rich black hair, her literary style and her preoccupations were both very different. If it had been otherwise or if there had been calculation (as was the case with a score of other applicants who had already been turned down), no one would have paid the slightest mind to Miss Sontag's work; and it would have lacked authority. It is simply that a public existed when she arrived on the scene which was searching for a new Dark Lady, and she was so obviously right that a spontaneous decision was made on all sides to cast her for the role—exactly as I in my time had been chosen for a role I seemed practically born to play.

What clinched it for me was a long review of Saul Bellow's *The Adventures of Augie March*. In giving me the book Warshow explained that *Commentary* had decided to assign it to me because almost every other possible reviewer they could think of was either a friend of Bellow or had read the novel in manuscript and praised it privately to him. (*Advice to Young Authors:* if you want to prevent someone from writing an unfavorable review of your book, send it to him in manuscript with a note humbly requesting his criticisms. Even if he doesn't read it, he will feel flattered by your note and therefore queasy about attacking the book. If he does read it, chances are that he will say something nice to you out of politeness or laziness and will therefore not wish to change his line in public; if, in addition, he makes a few criticisms as well and you gratefully take them into account, or even pretend to do so, in revising the draft, you have at worst neutralized him and at best committed him. Of course you may also have cut down on the number of reviews you will get.)

Bellow, Warshow continued, was a contributor to *Commentary*. The staff admired him and was entirely in sympathy with what they took him to be trying to do in this new book, which was to break through the constrictions of the well-made novel and moreover to express a new, post-thirties sense of American life very much in tune with the general intentions of *Commentary* itself. But they did not want to "set up" a review, and they had chosen me as a disinterested party (which, in truth, I was, my only impression of Bellow having come from a respectful reading of *The Victim* some years back and the knowledge that he was the family's White Hope, as it were, in fiction). Warshow instructed me to trace Bellow's development through his first two novels to *Augie March* and to measure *Augie* itself by how well its various intentions had been carried out.

Taking this assignment with great solemnity, I carefully read *Dangling Man* (it was, by the way, out of print) for the first time and *The Victim* for the second before going on to *Augie,* which I had every expectation of admiring. But to my dismay, the further I got into it, the less I liked it: it seemed forced, strained, shrill, and finally even tiresome. Was I wrong? I must be wrong. Warshow had told me that Trilling, who I knew was far from promiscuous in distributing praise, thought it an extraordinary novel, and everyone else I respected was reportedly overwhelmed. Really worried, I read it once again—and liked it even less. What to do now?

There is, I will admit, a certain plausibility in the idea that young critics characteristically lash into things because they know that the best way to attract attention is to go on the attack. Yet try as I may and aware as I am of how hungry I was for attention, I can unearth no such motive in the piece I eventually wrote on *Augie March.* The most powerful impulse I remember having, in fact, was to fake the review or not to write it at all, for I was in terror of the scorn that might be heaped upon me for making a mistaken judgment (Dwight Macdonald, I had heard, was still being laughed at for a youthful attack on T. S. Eliot thirty years earlier).

It may be true that there is no disputing tastes, but it is also true that differences of opinion over taste are very often the source of bitter hatreds. As a critic, editor, and writer I have continually been struck by the sheer *violence* of response a strongly expressed judgment, especially a negative one, of a novel or a play almost always provokes: you would think that an issue of life and death was at stake in the decision to like or dislike a particular book. But that, it seems, is precisely how many people feel: threatened in their very being when a critic challenges their tastes, and wildly grateful, as though it were a sign of Calvinist grace, to be confirmed and justified.

When I sat down to write about *Augie March* I was not aware of the full dimensions this madness can assume, but it is impossible to go through a college like Columbia without learning that to dissent from the fashion in matters of taste can be a very expensive act of spirit; and I had, after all, sat for more than two years at the feet of F. R. Leavis himself. I would like to think that it was courage which carried me through in doing the review, but I know very well that it was the greater fear of losing Warshow's respect if I played false with my response to the book—the one unforgivable sin in his otherwise absolutely tolerant eyes—which conquered the lesser fear of being wrong. In any case, faking the review would have been impossible, lacking as I did the smooth professional skill that would have been necessary to compensate for the withholding of the "key." The alternatives, then, were either to say what I really thought and felt, or to funk the assignment—and that too I was afraid of doing, lest it damage my beautiful relations with *Commentary*.

Everyone at *Commentary* was much impressed with

the piece, and delighted by the fact that they would for a change be printing a review of a book in the same month the book itself was being published. Warshow, who actually liked *Augie March* and thought I had been too harsh on it, sent Bellow an advance proof of the review with a dissenting and mollifying covering letter. And then the storm broke—so wild a storm that it took even the weatherbeaten *Commentary* staff by surprise. Bellow's reply to Warshow, with carbon copies sent to a dozen or more people, ran to two single-spaced typewritten pages. "Your young Mr. P," he called me throughout, understandably not being able to bring himself to utter my despicable name; he said that I had charged his book with false spontaneity, but he himself, although only a graduate of the University of Chicago who had never enjoyed the advantages of so classy an education as I had had, *knew* this charge to be untrue. He had written the book and he knew. A writer knows these things and he knew. After repeating this point several more times, Bellow dismissed Warshow's avowal of admiration for the book, and ended the letter with an admonition from Cromwell: "I beseech you in the bowels of Christ, think it possible you may be mistaken" (an appeal, incidentally, which I have always found curious coming from Cromwell of all men).

In itself, the letter was nothing more unusual than a sensitive writer's outburst against a critic, but Bellow was (and is) rather more than usually sensitive to criti-

cism. Learning that I had a connection with Trilling, he
decided that Trilling had for some dark purpose been
completely insincere in his own glowing review of *Augie
March*, which appeared about the same time as mine
and was in perfect harmony with a virtually unanimous
chorus of hosannahs for the book all over the country;
then, in collusion with the editors of *Commentary*, he
had put me up to writing a piece which represented what
they all really thought about *Augie* but were afraid to
come out and say. Not only did Bellow apparently believe in this fantasy; he actually persuaded many of his
friends that it was true. (About three years later, someone I had never seen before and who turned out to be one
of America's most eminent poets, staggered over to me at
a party and drunkenly declared: "We'll get you for that
review if it takes ten years." *I* should only have such
friends.)

The net effect of Bellow's campaign to discredit me,
of course, was to make me for a while a favorite subject
of gossip throughout the whole family. Attention I had
wanted? Attention I was getting. But I was nevertheless
unsettled by the particular form it was taking. It had not
occurred to me in my incredible naiveté that Bellow
himself would take any notice of what an unknown
young critic thought of his book when everyone who was
anyone had been celebrating his emergence as a major
American novelist (Delmore Schwartz even went so far
as to say in *Partisan Review* that *Augie* was a greater

novel than *Huckleberry Finn*). What I had been worried about was what such members of the family as might read my review would think of me. But I need not, as it developed, have worried on that score, for there was some foundation to Bellow's suspicion that the family actually felt somewhat less enthusiastic about *Augie* than his famous touchiness, and their genuine desire to see one of their own make it as an important American novelist, had bullied them into pretending to feel. This desire was not, I think, fully conscious, but it was there and it was genuine enough to overcome their normal lack of generosity about one another's work.

But something else of a more subtle nature was there as well. Bellow was not one of the family's own only because he was a Jewish intellectual; he also spoke for and embodied the impulse which had been growing among all the members of the second generation (and which was the animating principle of Elliot Cohen's Grand Design), to lay a serious claim to their identity as Americans and to their right to play a more than marginal role in the literary culture of the country. Both the claim and the right were a decade later to be taken so entirely for granted that one is in danger of forgetting how tenuous they seemed to all concerned even as late as the year 1953—how widespread, still, and not least among Jews, was the association of Jewishness with vulgarity and lack of cultivation. To write fiction out of the experience of big-city immigrant Jewish life was to feel oneself, and to be felt by others, to be writing exotica at best; nor did there exist a respectably certified narrative style in English which was anything but facsimile WASP. Writing was hard enough, but to have to write with *only* that part of one's being which had been formed by the acculturation-minded public schools and by the blindly ethnicizing English departments of the colleges was like being asked to compete in a race with a leg cut off at the thigh. What was one to do with that other part of one's being, the lower-class, urban, East European Jewish part? Kill it off in order to be accepted as a writer of centrality, as one had to kill it off in order to be accepted as a full-fledged American?

A man of great intelligence, Bellow had been aware of this problem from the beginning—the problem, as we might call it, of literary pluralism—and his struggles with it were made if anything more urgent by the ideal of wholeness and spontaneity he got, apparently, from Wilhelm Reich. After "dangling" in his first novel between the family world of alienation and the vision of a life of larger possibility, after being "victimized" in his second novel by the spiritual timidity he found in his own Jewishness—both books already revealing his impatience with the facsimile-WASP style in which they were largely written—Bellow, in his third novel, boldly hit upon the idea of following the example of a book which had found the solution to the problem of literary pluralism at a time when regional cultures stood in the same "colonial" relation to the genteel tradition of the East as ethnic cultures later came to do. Mark Twain in *Huckleberry Finn* had crossed the regnant "high" literary language with the "low" frontier vulgate, and Bellow now similarly crossed it with American-Jewish colloquial, thus asserting in the idiom of the novel itself what its opening sentence, in full awareness of what it is saying, makes altogether explicit: "I am an American, Chicago-born. . . ."

That is what Bellow the man says. What Bellow the writer is saying is this: I am an American *novelist*, born into a Yiddish-speaking household and also educated to use fancy English with the best of them, and the way I speak as a result of these two facts, the way I *really* speak when I am being myself and horsing around with Isaac Rosenfeld, is a fully legitimate literary language. To appreciate the force of this assertion, we need only remind ourselves that fifty years earlier Henry James had come away from a tour of the Jewish ghetto on the Lower East Side wondering what would become of the knightly and embattled English language when the children and grandchildren of these people came into possession of it. "Whatever we shall know it for," said James, "we shall not know it for English." Saul Bellow to Henry James: Up yours, buddy.

So far, so good. The trouble arose from a misunderstanding on Bellow's part as to the source of the problem which has occupied him so obsessively throughout his career. For if he was telling off Henry James in *Augie March,* he was telling off his elders in the family—and beyond and behind them everyone who had ever counseled alienation and withdrawal as the proper strategy for surviving in the "waste land" of the modern world— even more passionately. It was *their* fault that the world had rejected them; had they not prissily rejected the world?

This view of the matter, which Bellow would reiterate with increasing hysteria in the 1960's, was oddly reminiscent of the thinking of some of the earliest leaders of the nineteenth-century Jewish Enlightenment who believed that of the two ghettos cutting the Jews off from the surrounding European environment, the one inside themselves was the more crucial. Accept the modern world, cried these leaders, and it will respond by accepting you; deghettoize yourselves, and the walls of your physical ghetto will crumble like the walls of Jericho at the trumpet-sound of your own willingness to embrace the modern world. There was some truth in this, to be sure, but not enough to make it stick. For the real problem, as the Jews of Germany and indeed all Europe were to discover a century later, was unfortunately on the other foot: it was not a question of whether the Jews would accept the world, it was a question of whether the world would accept them. And similarly with Bellow (in this representing the early-fifties mood of most of the family) in relation to America.

In a long essay on Bellow written a few years and a few novels after *Augie March,* I said, in a sentence he subsequently parodied in *Herzog,* that there was a sense in which the validity of a whole phase of American experience was felt to hang on the question of whether or not he would turn out to be a great novelist. The phase to which I was referring—obscurely, because I was too timid then to come completely clean—was this turn toward the acceptance of America by the family in the second generation, the turn away from "alienation" and toward . . . what? The answer was never clear, and from that lack of clarity arose the other trouble with *Augie:* the quality of a willed and empty affirmation which showed itself in the forced spontaneity of the prose (for I was right about that in my review). The family's "pro-Americanism"—as Philip Rahv called it, making as usual no bones about things—in the early fifties was beset by too much doubt, hesitation, and uncertainty to yield much more than a willed and empty affirmation; and all this *Augie* reflected; and in reflecting it exposed how long a way the family still had to travel to reach that hoped-for, yearned-for, oh-so-impossible-she of a condition which a critic was to sum up descriptively in the phrase "beyond alienation."

When I wrote my review of *Augie,* I had a dim intuition of all this, but dim was better than nothing, and some members, at least, of the family found their doubts about the book confirmed by it. These doubts, as I have been trying to make clear, involved far more than strictly literary considerations. There is a mystique according to which the "true" or "real" consciousness of an age, and therefore the truth about its life and experience, is to be found in the art it produces—in the deficiencies of its art no less than in its strengths. *Augie* could thus be seen as an acting out of the new attitudes and feelings and ideas with which the family had been experimenting, and its aesthetic failings could be understood as a partial refutation of the proposition "I am an American" that the book itself was attempting to "prove."

That I was virtually the only reviewer of the book who was able to see and understand it, even if very imperfectly, in this way settled the issue of my adoption into the family for good. For some it made me an object of bitter personal attack, itself a sign of family membership, and for others it made me a personage to be reckoned with. Warshow, still with his nose firmly to the ground of my career, told me that this was now definitely the case, but even if he had not, I would have known it by the fact that in the midst of the storm my review had kicked up I received a phone call from one of the two Patriarchs, summoning me to what, looking back upon it, I think might fairly be described as a bar mitzvah ceremony which signified, like that ancient Jewish rite itself, that I had finally come of age.

Kissing-cousin Robert Lowell refers in one of his poems to the night he and his second-generation core-member wife, Elizabeth Hardwick, "outdrank the Rahvs" (that is, Philip and his then-wife Nathalie). I can understand why Lowell made such a proud point of that feat, and it also helps indirectly to explain why my memory of the bar mitzvah ceremony in the Greenwich Village apartment of the Rahvs is so hazy. I was not in those days as experienced a drinker as I would, alas, later become, and it was therefore unfortunate for me that Nathalie Rahv was so scrupulously attentive a hostess, refilling my glass to the top the instant I had, in my fear of being thought unsophisticated, emptied it in two or three rapid gulps. I remember, before the whole world started to swim, Rahv saying ("Today you are a man") that he wanted me to write for *Partisan Review*. I also remember him gruffly replying in that absolutely brutal style of his when I asked him what *he* thought of *Augie March* (a book I was beginning to feel I owned): "It doesn't have a plot. A novel has to have a plot." This statement very simply left me with nothing further to say. For the rest, I remember hearing my voice pronounce an incredulous, "You mean Alfred *Kazin?*" or "You mean Dwight *Macdonald?*" or "You mean Mary *McCarthy?*" as Rahv and a woman who was present treated me to my first horrified experience of true family-style gossip.

About one o'clock in the morning, I staggered through the door with the other guest and after a perfunctory and fortunately abortive pass at her, I made my dizzy way toward the subway station on Sixth Avenue where the bourbon and the gossip and everything else my stomach was still too young to digest came pouring out in great retching heaves. And yet in the very midst of all that misery, I knew that I had never been so happy in my life.

But my cup of regurgitable bourbon had not really run over, and more was yet to be poured into it. Of all the members of the first generation, the one who was probably the most generous about other people's work was Dwight Macdonald, who had by this time given up his magazine *Politics* (and the anarchism and pacifism, though not the anti-Stalinism, that went with it) to become a staff writer at the *New Yorker*. As it happened, Macdonald agreed with my estimate of the literary quality of *Augie March*, and he not only sent me an admiring note about the review but called it to the attention of William Shawn, who had recently succeeded the late Harold Ross as editor of the *New Yorker*, with a recommendation that I be asked to review some books for them. And this was how I became the first and possibly the only young literary man ever to be invited to write both for *Partisan Review* and the *New Yorker* in the course of a single week.

It may come as a surprise when I say that the invitation from the *New Yorker* aroused more anxiety in me than joy. Yet that was precisely the case, and the reasons were more than merely neurotic. Even ten years later, when it was already more or less commonplace for writers who had once been thought of as pure "*Partisan Review* types" to publish in the *New Yorker*, J. D. Salinger could still suggest that *New Yorker* people and *Partisan Review* people were able to read each other's magazines only after covering them in plain brown wrappers. This joke no longer applied when Salinger made it, but in the early fifties, the antagonism between the two magazines, and more importantly between the two worlds of sensibility they represented, was much too great to have been comprehended by so bland a comment.

The *New Yorker* under its founding editor Harold Ross was never exactly a middlebrow magazine, for it had its roots in, and was perhaps the only remaining literary exemplar of, the cultural traditions of the premodernist period—the period, that is, before the highbrow-middlebrow split occurred. Modernism and its attendant issues were of little concern to the *New Yorker* under Ross; no doubt Max Beerbohm's crack, "How I wish I could keep up with these fashions as they pass by me into oblivion" might have served as a fair statement of the magazine's attitude toward the whole sorry business. Nevertheless, on the principle of those-who-are-not-with-me-are-against-me, the *New Yorker* was almost universally taken by highbrows as the quintessence of commercialism (all those ads) and middlebrow philistinism—a reputation which, ironically, Dwight Macdonald himself had in the thirties done much to establish by his famous attack on it in (where else?) *Partisan Review.* For its part, the *New Yorker* responded with an aloof disdain which, as is often the case with disdain, concealed a considerable degree of unease and an even greater degree of vindictive anger. (After I had begun writing for it, my editor at the *New Yorker* once asked me in the dryest possible way whether they had special typewriters in the *Partisan Review* office with entire words like "alienation" stamped on each key.)

Because it had its roots in the cultural traditions of the premodernist period, the *New Yorker* was able, despite its hostility to highbrowism, to accommodate highbrows like Edmund Wilson, Alfred Kazin, and Dwight Macdonald whose *style,* if not their cultural loyalties, came out of the same traditions. Wilson, of course, had always been a skilled professional journalist, Macdonald had started as a writer for *Fortune* before undergoing a conversion to Trotskyism, and Kazin (differing in this from most of his contemporaries within the family) had from the beginning possessed the unusual knack of writing as comfortably for a large and diverse audience as for a small and highly informed one.

The literary and intellectual credentials of all three were, moreover, so impeccable that their association with the *New Yorker* could not, despite a few efforts in that direction, be held against them in the highbrow world, any more than their surprising presence in its pages could do anything to affect its reputation in that world. It was simply assumed, when the matter was thought about at all, that the *New Yorker* had chosen to publish them for reasons of its own and that they had chosen to write for it because of the money. Even Macdonald was forgiven for what might easily, in view of his past opinions of the *New Yorker*, have been condemned as a "sellout" to the enemy. But he had, after all, a long history of just such shifting alliances, and yet, Luce-man today, Trotskyite tomorrow, pacifist the day after that, he always unfailingly, unmistakably, and good-naturedly managed to remain the same Dwight Macdonald. How could writing for the *New Yorker* change the man who had quoted Trotsky's remark, "Everyone has a right to be stupid, but Comrade Macdonald abuses the privilege," against himself?

As I all too keenly understood, no similar dispensation was available to me when I was asked to write for the *New Yorker*. My own attitude toward it was the standard highbrow one, which is why the call I got from the book-review editor left me feeling less flattered than worried. And lest I not be worried enough on my own, my old friends from Columbia were there to make sure that I would become fully aware of the possibly sinister implications of this latest triumph of mine which they were being forced to endure.

Except for Steven Marcus, who was in Cambridge that year working on a Ph.D. and had also begun to publish in *Commentary,* no one in the old Columbia crowd was doing very well. Most, on the contrary, were caught in that niggardly and lugubrious style of life so characteristic of the first postwar decade and which Philip Roth was to evoke so cruelly in *Letting Go*—the life of the married graduate student dragging his slow length along the endless road to a Ph.D. with an increasingly resentful wife working as a typist to support a makeshift household containing one Herman Miller chair, the reward of heroic self-deprivations, set incongruously down amid the foamland benches and the door-store tables and the glass-brick bookcases. Still laboring under my ancient stupidity about envy and my somewhat younger terror of it, I did not realize how the life I myself was beginning to lead must have looked to them. I was making it and they were not; perhaps they never would; perhaps they would remain buried forever in that tunnel of five-by-seven index cards; or perhaps they would crash through it only to find themselves with no other honorable place to go.

Did other honorable places even exist? They had never thought so, and yet there was I hanging around with Philip Rahv and Robert Warshow, writing, publishing, attracting attention, and now even being given an opportunity to move in on The Big Money. More bitter still, there was Jason Epstein, who had been associated with a rival faction at Columbia which our crowd had considered "unserious," working in publishing, already planning what was soon to become known as the paperback revolution, living romantically with his new wife in the Village, and throwing parties to which, it was said, famous writers always came, including (incredibly) W. H. Auden himself. Why me? Why him?

I did not realize that this was how they felt, and just as I had done in college over my A+'s and my fellowships, I took their tongue-clucking and their head-wagging over the fact that the *New Yorker* wanted me to write for it, not for the envy it was but as a disinterested and indeed loving concern for my ever-threatened integrity. They had always known that I would turn out to be another Clifton Fadiman. It had been joked about even in college, for Fadiman had gone to the same high school as I, had won the same scholarship to Columbia, and had as an undergraduate enjoyed a reputation similar to mine. Was it then not altogether fitting that I should wind up, as he had, a *New Yorker* critic and a middlebrow star?

Fortunately for me, Warshow thought otherwise—and so, to my surprise (for I was always getting him wrong), did Trilling. No sooner had I hung up after the call from the *New Yorker* than the phone rang again. Warshow's absurdly thin voice sounded, in his excitement, even thinner and higher than usual. "Did they ask you to write for them?" he demanded. He had known they were going to call me because, having searched in vain for my name in the Manhattan phone book and never thinking that a writer the *New Yorker* might wish to use could possibly be living in Brooklyn with his parents, they had finally—unheard of, unprecedented event —requested my number of the *Commentary* office. "You lucky bastard," he said, "I wish they would ask me" (they were to decide to do just that the day before he died).

Warshow's excitement seemed a bit odd to me, considering some of the things he had written about middlebrowism, but not nearly so odd as Trilling's pleasure when I told him about the invitation in the expectation that he would advise me, as my Columbia friends all had, against accepting it. Like Warshow, however, Trilling regarded this invitation as an extraordinary event—a kind of confirmation, I think, of his ideas as to the nature of the changes which were obviously beginning to take place in the American cultural situation. That the first son born to the family in the third generation should be someone capable of straddling the once absolutely antagonistic worlds of *Partisan Review* and the *New Yorker* suggested (as of course many other signs did too) that a different and perhaps healthier cultural situation was in the making than the one which had come definitely into being in the early thirties. If this was so, it was foolish to refuse the opportunity to reach out beyond the family for fear of being "corrupted." Thus, roughly paraphrased, Trilling. And Warshow, commenting on my worries over how writing for the *New Yorker* would affect my reputation within the family, chuckled gleefully and assured me that they would all envy me at least as much as he did.

Before I had a chance to take an assignment from the *New Yorker,* but not before I had written my first piece for *Partisan Review,* my draft notice finally arrived, perfectly timed to coincide with the disappearance of the last shred of the curiosity I had felt a mere six months earlier about military service. At the sight of that cursed envelope in the mailbox, brightness fell from the air: everything would have to be postponed for an interminable two years. Now they were beginning to know who I was; would they still remember two years later? Would I have to start all over again?

Elliot Cohen (of blessed memory to me for this among many reasons) said that I would not. If I were willing to commit myself to coming to work for *Commentary* as an editor when I got out of the army, he would hold Irving Kristol's job open for me, filling it meanwhile with a temporary person. *Willing?* As a man is to embrace his destiny if he is lucky enough to find it.

The staff gave a small farewell party for me at the *Commentary* offices the day before I left, and understanding—with the sweetest unconscious perception of which I have ever been the object—that my bar mitzvah ceremony at the Rahvs had been incomplete in one important detail, presented me with the most traditional of bar mitzvah gifts: a fountain pen. Now did my cup truly run over. Today, as bar mitzvah boys always say, I was indeed a man: I had a family, I had a name, and I had a place in the world. Twenty-four hours later, it took the army a mere fifteen minutes to fix all that—to empty my cup and to grind it, as it seemed for a while, totally and forever to dust.

6 In and Out of Nihilism (and Uniform)

I would not have missed the excitement and joy of those five months in New York for anything, but when the bill was presented on December 15, 1953, they turned out to have been a very expensive time—more expensive than I could comfortably afford. The life of an army recruit would have been difficult for me to bear under any circumstances, as it is difficult for everyone to bear, and certainly if I had been plummeted from the condition of young-gentlemanhood I had enjoyed at Cambridge directly into the subhuman servitude which is for all practical purposes the condition of the military trainee, I would have suffered torment enough. At Cambridge I had had a somewhat adulterated taste of what the class system was like at the top; now I got an entirely unadulterated taste of what it was like at the bottom. What it was like down there was, not to put too fine a point on it, pure hell. It was a place where you were pushed around every minute of the day, forced to do backbreaking menial work, denied any physical comfort or liberty of movement, deprived of individuality, and treated with contempt. All this, as I say, would have been bad enough under any circumstances, but going into the army out of a condition of budding literary fame and growing self-confidence—the condition, in short, of being a *somebody*—made the experience as nearly unendurable as anything I have ever undergone.

All through the first freezing weeks I spent in the bleak wastes of Fort Dix, New Jersey—always hungry because there was never enough to eat, always exhausted because there was never enough sleep, badly constipated because there was never enough time to use the toilet properly, even after one had become relatively accustomed to sitting on it in an open row along with five other grunting men—I would marvel to myself at how easily and swiftly life could strip you down to nothingness, how it could rob you in a mere instant not only of everything you had but of everything you were. I had begun to acquire a name and overnight, literally overnight, they had taken it away and given me a number. I had finally found a world in which I knew how to move about with a bit of skill and grace, and they had seized me by the throat early one dark winter morning and hurled me into a world which in every detail seemed to have been constructed for the express purpose of rendering me inept: a world built to all my weaknesses and not a single one of my strengths. I was in a righteous, self-pitying rage with life for being able to do such a thing, to get away with it, and in a fury too with every veteran I had ever talked to, every book I had ever read about the army, and every movie I had ever seen. Why had they lied? Why did they always make a joke out of it? Why hadn't they told what it was really like?

In my hysteria I thought it was really like a concentration camp, and while slogging with burning breath on a march through the snow or shivering at attention with open collar on a below-zero day or standing rigid with terror in front of my bunk as an inspection team approached, I would take an odd comfort in adding to my secret inventory of the parallels between Basic Training and the Nazi camps as Hannah Arendt had described them in *The Origins of Totalitarianism*.

The camps, she had said, served as a laboratory in which experiments in domination were performed; in them the true nature of totalitarianism stood nakedly exposed. Just so, I thought, with the army, where the true nature of organized social life itself was nakedly exposed. For here was a heterogeneous mass of men rudely tossed together against their will, and out of them a viable society had to be formed. The techniques by which it could successfully be formed had been developed and refined over the centuries; collectively they constituted the system of military discipline common to all armies, and the secret of this system was a minutely articulated, perfectly defined, and absolutely visible hierarchical structure. On what was the structure based? On power, of course. And what was power? Nothing, clearly, inherent in the personality. *Power was position,* for did not the army teach that one saluted the uniform and not the man? I was in a miserable rapture of revelation. What children we all were! We prated solemnly and stupidly about Identity in all our novels and all our talk; we went searching for ourselves within ourselves, when the only "identity" that mattered was in the insignia we wore on our "uniforms": insignia which were as visible in their way to the world's eyes as the bars on an officer's shoulders or the blankness on a private's sleeve.

As the interminable weeks of Basic Training crawled by, however, a new revelation began taking hold of me and self-pity then gave way to a self-hatred of very impressive dimensions. This revelation was triggered by the arrival one morning in the mail of an issue of *Partisan Review* containing the piece I had written, as it seemed, at least a century before, and it took the form of a weird question which popped into my head at the sight of my name on the cover: *How come I had to go from there to here, when they never have to go from here to there?*

The "they" I had in mind were the platoon sergeants who were in charge of our training and who were everything a soldier was supposed to be: tough, erect, competent, and above all physically strong. They could stand in the freezing wind without even wearing a field jacket; they could double-time forever without so much as a pant; they could do a hundred pushups without showing the strain; and they all wore the proud badge of the veteran combat infantryman. I had come to feel infinitely humble before these men, and very jealous of those of my fellow-recruits who were able to take and even to thrive on all the physical punishment we had to endure when I was always an inch away from total collapse. I had been angry with myself from the very start over my ineptitude with equipment; as a civilian, I had regarded such ineptitude as charming and perhaps even as a sign of spiritual superiority, but now there was nothing charming in it at all, and if it was a sign of anything, it was a sign of dependency and of my inability to manage the world like a man.

I was supposed to be endowed with exceptional intelligence, and yet it took me hours to learn how to lace my new combat boots efficiently, it took me days to learn how to reassemble my rifle in the required time, and I never learned how to adjust a gas mask properly. What was my kind of intelligence worth then? What good did it do me that I knew long stretches of Shakespeare by heart or that I could understand Hegel? Did these things help me bear the cold? Did they comfort me in the

shame I felt at falling behind on a march for shortness
of breath and weakness of leg?

Still, I could tell myself that this was not, after all,
my element: would my platoon sergeant look good if he
were forcibly transferred to an English class at Columbia? But then that issue of *Partisan Review* arrived, and
it occurred to me in a hideous flash that there was no
conscription into English classes at Columbia, there was
only conscription into armies—and into prisons, and into
exiles: places and conditions where survival depended
upon physical stamina, competence, and strength. My
platoon sergeant would never have to prove himself in
my element as I was now being forced, and might be
again at any moment in the future, to prove myself in
his. Therefore—the logic seemed inexorable—his element, being of the body, was bedrock and real, and mine,
being of the mind, was the vain illusion of a privileged
and protected few.

Basic Training, however, is not the army; it is only
the infantry as seen in an ideal or nightmare state. Its
function, even in wartime, is not primarily to teach the
skills of war: has anyone ever really learned how to
handle a machine gun or disarm a mine in Basic Training? The real purpose is to turn civilians into soldiers,
and that means not only breaking down all resistance to
the rules of the military community but affecting the
personality in such a way as to make a man easily capable of violating his natural instincts by rushing into dan-

ger and possible death simply at the sound of a command. Obviously, or there would be no wars, the system works brilliantly, representing the collective wisdom of the race on this matter, and it works mainly by eliciting the collusion of its victims through the principle of collective reward and punishment, which ensures that the subjugated group itself will enforce discipline upon recalcitrant or rebellious members, and through the calculated reduction of each individual to complete dependency upon its pleasure. The trainee is put into a child's relation to power and authority: he eats, defecates, and sleeps at the will of authority, and the result is to activate the obedient and fearful child who remains forever alive in most of us. (According to Selma Fraiberg, Chinese brainwashing represents the ultimate refinement of just such a technique for reawakening infantile dependency.) Since, moreover, the authority figure in this case, the platoon sergeant, does everything his "children" are required to do, with the important exception of menial chores (from which they too are promised exemption when and if they ever "grow up"), and does it infinitely better, he becomes within the tightly sealed-off world of the training camp almost literally a figure of omnipotence, to be feared for his superior strength and finally even worshiped.

All this was operating on me throughout my first three months in the army, but Basic Training did not last long enough to make it stick and to convert me, as it had threatened to do, entirely away from "culture" and to the reductionist nihilism which lies behind the worship of power and physical strength (and which, of course, is the animating principle of fascism). After it was over, I found myself for the remainder of my two years of military service back in a more normal and benevolent world —one, that is, where my kind of intelligence turned out to count for a great deal after all, and where the hierarchical structure, though very much there, was less rigidly observed than it had been at Fort Dix and could even be circumvented. In consequence of a fortunate clerical error, I was sent up to learn some of the lower-level mysteries of communications intelligence at the Army Security Agency School at Fort Devens, Massachusetts, where I spent four delightful months earning three-day passes every weekend for being the star pupil on the post, an achievement which also earned me (there being no noncoms in the school) an appointment as honorary sergeant of a platoon and thereby the sure knowledge of how much more pleasant it is to issue commands than to be issued them.

Graduation came all too soon, to be followed by a year in Germany, where I was quickly relieved of the job I had been trained at great expense to do at Devens, and ordered by my commanding officer to take over the compulsory lecture program on "Democracy *vs.* Communism" which, he had decided, none of the officers in the company was so properly qualified to handle as "a graduate of Harvard and Oxford" (it had been a few days since he had looked up my record, and if he had mixed up the details in memory, he had nevertheless held on to the essential point).

We were stationed at the time near Kassel, in a *Kasserne* which had in days past quartered a detachment of Luftwaffe officers, and even by civilian standards it was luxurious. KP and other menial chores were done by hired German help, and enlisted men slept comfortably two or three to a large room. Altogether, life in the company was easygoing and informal, discipline was lax, and passes were abundant. As acting Information-and-Education Officer, I was my own boss now, keeping regular office hours and no longer even vulnerable to the sergeant who had previously used me, albeit good-naturedly, as an object-lesson in the realities of power for new arrivals to the company whenever he suspected them of having been insufficiently educated in those realities before: "You see that guy there?" he would say pointing to me. "He got about ten degrees from all kinds of fancy colleges all over the place, but when I say 'Shit!' he shits."

The truth was that this sergeant—like almost everyone, regular or conscript, officer or enlisted man, I met in the army after Basic Training—was as humble before people better educated than he as I had felt in relation to the platoon sergeants at Fort Dix: in a subtle spiritual sense, there was, after all, such a thing as conscription into English classes at Columbia. The only instances of that famous American "anti-intellectualism" I ever came upon in the army were either justified in being directed against college graduates who affected a prissy superiority but were in reality neither intelligent nor good for *anything,* or else derived from feelings of intimidation toward the idea of education so touchingly great as to border on superstition. The more common response was a frank and self-abasing respect. Thus everywhere I went in the army I would find myself being treated with deference and becoming the barracks adviser on everything from sex to religion.

Usually my closest friends were back-country Southern boys, real rednecks, with whom, rather to my liberal surprise, I always seemed to get along very well. Besides being a great comfort to have around in belligerent small-town bars, they were a type I found attractive much in the way I had found the platoon sergeants in Basic Training attractive: brave, proud, and unstintingly loyal once they had decided to befriend you. There was the time, for example, that I was drinking beer in a *Gasthaus* in Frankfurt with a hillbilly buddy and a German tried to engage us in conversation. I always tried to avoid these confrontations because I simply did not know how, as a Jew, I was supposed to behave toward Germans, and so I tried to shake him off. Refusing to be rebuffed, however, he drunkenly confided to me (in German, which my friend could not understand) that he too had been a soldier, a member of the SS. My heart sank: what was I to do now? *"Ich bin ein Jude,"* I said to him, hoping he would go away, but instead of being crushed, he threw his arms around me and shouted that he had been in the *Waffen* SS and anyway those stories about the Jews were all British propaganda.

Thoroughly disgusted with my inadequacy before the situation, I pushed him away and told my glowering friend, who had not the slightest idea of what was happening but was of course ready at a word from me to take on the entire bar and the whole town of Frankfurt too if need be, that we had better leave. When we got outside and I started to explain the incident to him, I discovered to my amazement that he knew next to nothing about the Germans and the Jews and that he had not even realized before that I myself was Jewish. He was both fascinated and shocked, but it took him exactly one second to recover. "Let's go back in there and kill the dirty kraut bastard," he said. I managed, not without miserable misgivings, to persuade him against it.

Though I understood very well why I admired such Southern boys, I was puzzled as to what they saw in me, and my curiosity drove me once to ask one of them why he liked me. "Because," he answered in a thick Mississippi drawl, "you *talk* so good"—a remark which not only did much to restore my confidence in the validity of my own "element," but also made me regret the jeer I had directed in *Partisan Review* a year earlier at the contention that Southerners have a more sensitive feel for the language than other Americans.

Whether or not this humility in the face of education was a response to the changing conditions which were soon to give intellectuals a greater degree of status and power than they had enjoyed in America for at least a century, I cannot say. But new or not, it was certainly real. It would in any case have been easy for me to get along socially in the army, for the world of the barracks was a world much like the one I had grown up in on the streets of Brownsville: its culture was the universally American culture of "the boys," and I needed only to turn a switch in my personality to feel completely at home within its terms. There was one difference, however, and it worked to my advantage. In Brownsville I could never have been looked up to as a leader, for being good in school and mediocre at athletics made one's manliness suspect to "the boys," whereas in the army no one seemed to assume that manliness was compromised by education or even cultivation (no doubt my conversational habit of liberally mixing obscenities with the big words did something to help this assumption along).

Was I not learning, then, that the other revelation I had been vouchsafed in Basic Training had also come from the Devil? Was I not learning, in other words, that power was not wholly consonant with position, that it could inhere in the personality, and that identity was not merely given in the insignia of rank on the uniform?

Not quite. For I was very conscious of the fact that the power I myself was able to acquire in the army had little if anything to do with any intrinsic virtues with which I might be endowed (except perhaps for the energy I inherited from my mother: energy possesses a charm of its own), and that it had everything to do with the insignia on my civilian "uniform." I was respected because I had gone to college, and not only one college but two, and not any two colleges but fancy ones both. Moreover, I was a writer who could get the things he wrote published—and that too amounted to a position, a rank. It was no tribute to *me* that my commanding officer in Kassel took me out of the category of enlisted man and gave me an officer's job along with many of the perquisites thereof: he did it because my record said that I was a graduate of "Harvard and Oxford" (the slip itself was significant) and because that fact alone, *even in the army*—even, by 1954, in the *American* army—meant that I properly belonged to the upper (i.e., officer) class. And so too with my fellow enlisted men.

It has been said that intelligence of the kind that lends itself to book-learning (for there are other kinds, some of them at least as beautiful) has become a form of capital in America because an overdeveloped technological society resembles an underdeveloped one in being heavily dependent on highly trained minds. I think this is true, but such intelligence is capital in more than the restricted sense that a person who possesses or acquires it can now invest it at a profitable return (i.e., get a higher-paying job than he would once have been able to do). Such intelligence is capital also in the sense that it gives its possessor, even its apparent possessor, a status in the eyes of others which only the possessors of literal capital —namely the rich—commanded in the past. I myself first became dimly aware of this situation in the army, both in consequence of the way I was treated and the way I responded to that treatment. Like an heiress who wants to be loved for herself alone, I worried constantly over whether I was being admired for the man I was, not wanting to be admired for *what* I was (that is, educated).

"Only God, my dear, could love you for yourself alone / And not your yellow hair," said Yeats; this curious anxiety of mine, taking the form of the assumption that my intelligence was somehow extraneous to my self, derived, I now believe, from the vague perception that intelligence had mysteriously become a kind of yellow hair in the eyes of the world—or more precisely, a kind of inherited wealth. This situation was to blossom fully out into the open during the Kennedy years and to make possible the emergence of something that for once in American history really deserved the title of an Establishment: that is, an alliance of the rich, the powerful, and the fashionable which allows entree to the talented (talent being measured by position in the worlds of intellect and art) on (almost) equal terms. And why indeed not, if intelligence has become by common agreement a kind of wealth itself?

Meanwhile, power or no power, I was still an Sp3 (the equivalent of corporal) and relatively pleasant or not, the army was still the army. I was itching to get out and throw myself full-force into the literary life of New York. There was enough leisure time between lectures for me to start writing again and I managed to get a few pieces done for *Commentary* while still in Germany— one of them an article on Faulkner taking off from *A Fable*, written originally on a commission from the *New Yorker* but turned down as "a good first try for us." After it had been published in *Commentary*, I received a bulletin from Warshow telling me that my less than reverential attitude toward Faulkner had provoked the pious ire of several members of the family, including one who had apparently forgotten about his own more disrespectful attitude toward the same writer in the past. *They're still talking about me*, I said to myself, *thank God*.

In the fall of 1955, an order came through from Washington under which I became eligible for discharge ninety days before the actual termination of my hitch. In great jubilation I boarded a military transport plane in Frankfurt, only to be informed when I arrived at Fort Dix that the order permitted the early discharge only of personnel who had returned from overseas with ninety days or less left to serve; like several others in the group,

I had landed on American soil with ninety-one. No threats of suicide and no amount of screaming, crying, or appealing to the Inspector General availed, despite the fact that no one at Fort Dix wanted us or knew what to do with us. I was destined, it seemed, to spend my last three months in the army in the same place I had spent the first three.

But it was not really the same place. After a couple of weeks as an unsupervised casual, I was given a nine-to-five job interviewing incoming recruits (poor bastards) for the purpose of making a preliminary determination as to the sort of work they should be doing when, and if, they managed to survive their Basic Training. It was all done strictly by the book, the book in this case being a microscopically detailed manual in which civilian qualifications were translated into potential military occupational specialties. I did not fail to notice during the ten weeks or so of my daily intimacy with this book that it was based on a very clear bias in favor of men with high IQ's and college degrees (especially, of course, in the sciences, but not in them alone), and that the infantry was considered by the army itself as the branch of military service fit only for those unfit by the exclusive testimony of their educational records and their short-answer test scores to perform less onerous and less physical duties. Insofar, then, as Basic Training instilled in one the idea that the only real soldier, and indeed the only worthwhile type of man, was a combat infantryman, it was a lie by the army's own lights. Farewell the worship of strength; farewell nihilism, a fond farewell.

December 14, 1955 dawned at last, as even a lustfully awaited day will eventually do, and I left Fort Dix for what I devoutly hoped was forever. Three days later I went to work at *Commentary*. By now, however, the office on Thirty-third Street was no more the same place I had left two years earlier than Fort Dix was when I returned, and the time I was to spend there would, to my astonishment, turn out to be considerably less pleasant, if rather more eventful, than most of the time I had spent in the uniform of an American soldier.

Part III

MAKING IT

MAKING IT

7 Working for a Living in New York

Only one member of the editorial staff I had known was still in the *Commentary* offices by the end of 1955. After nine years with the magazine, Nathan Glazer had left to join Jason Epstein at Anchor Books, then at the height of its fame as the series which had launched the quality paperback revolution in American publishing. Then, in the spring of 1955, disaster struck: first Robert Warshow died of a heart attack at the age of thirty-seven (his notorious and much-joked-about hypochondria had not, as an autopsy revealed, been hypochondria at all), and soon thereafter Elliot Cohen fell into a severe depression. Utterly paralyzed, he sat day after day in his office, unable to do anything but stare listlessly at the desk; finally, amid much Jewish hushing over the disgrace and in a screen of rumors about viral infections, he was sent to the Payne Whitney Clinic for treatment.

Until my appearance on the scene, this left only two editors to carry on alone: one a veteran member of the staff and the other a fairly recent arrival. These two men happened to be so closely related that they were able to act as one man after Cohen's departure, when they assumed de facto control of the magazine. Since they also behaved as one man toward me, and because of the form this behavior took, I will be doing no violence to the truth if I refer to them from now on in the singular, and as The Boss.

I said that in Cohen's absence and until my appearance, The Boss had to carry on at *Commentary* alone, but this was not entirely true, for Sherry Abel was also there. She had come to the magazine in 1950 as an editorial assistant whose job was mainly to style manuscripts for the printer, keep track of and proofread galleys, and screen unsolicited material, but it was only her determination to avoid too much responsibility that had prevented her from becoming an editor. If she had ever entertained any ambitions for herself in the working world, they had long ago been renounced or perhaps transferred to the men she admired.

Because she did no writing herself, the world had been deprived of one of the potentially great minor novelists of all time, for she was a compulsive *raconteuse* with an unmatchable gift for extracting fun and drama from the most trivial incident, whether a conversation with a cab-driver or a shopping expedition at Klein's. Her imagination, getting no rest, was constantly open and alive; her sense of things was at once as shrewd as a corporation lawyer's and as naïve as a romantic girl's; and her mind was as fast as her sensibility was subtle. All this, of course, made her a delight to have around in an office, but in addition to being a delight, she was possessed of a fanatical concern with the bone and sinew of the English language, and if there is such a thing as flawless taste in matters of style, tone, and rhetoric, she had it. It was, then, an invaluable and incomparable eye that she cast over the pieces she would be given to prepare for the printer after they had been worked upon by one of the senior editors.

I had met Sherry only briefly before, but it was clear from the first minute that we were destined to become close friends. The army had left me literally obsessed with privacy, and contrary to *Commentary* custom, I had immediately closed the door of my cubicle upon moving in; a minute later, there was a timid knock, and Sherry cautiously stuck her head in: "Are you at least picking your nose in there?" she giggled. But it was also clear from the first minute that my relations with The Boss were destined to be troubled. Except for Sherry, who wanted it that way, all the members of the editorial staff had for some years held the same rank, that of asso-

ciate editor, and the atmosphere had traditionally been
that of a society of colleagues and peers in which everyone had an equal voice and did the same work (though
Cohen, of course, as editor, had set the overall policy and
made the final decisions): commissioning and editing articles, dealing with writers, voting on manuscripts, and
participating in such technical operations as proofread-
ing, dummying, and composing authors' notes. Aware of
this tradition, I had taken it for granted that I would be
joining the staff as an associate editor too; in fact, this
had been the rank of the man Cohen had hired as a stop-
gap while waiting for me to return. Cohen and I had
never discussed salary—I was shy about money in those
days and also genuinely indifferent to it except insofar as
it symbolized status—but Warshow had given me to understand that I could expect to begin at approximately
seven thousand a year. Since this came out to more than
three dollars an hour, it sounded dignified to my proletarian ears, and it was, moreover, a high enough figure
to calm my mother's anxieties over my decision to take a
job in "journalism" and skip the Ph.D. She wanted me
to get it, she said, so that I "would always have something to fall back on," but her real reason was that she
wanted her son to be called "Doctor."

When, however, I came in during the fall on a pass
from Fort Dix to see The Boss, I immediately noticed
that the cordiality he had shown toward me in our earlier

encounters had for some mysterious reason turned to coldness; and even if I had not noticed it, the change would have been glaringly discernible in his announcement that, as a young and inexperienced man, I was to have the title of assistant editor, on a six-month trial basis and at a salary not of seven thousand but of fifty-five hundred. More surprised at first than indignant, I asked him whether Cohen had made this decision. He answered testily that Cohen was out of the picture and might never return to the magazine: the decision had been his and would stick. He was now The Boss.

Many scales dropped from my eyes as a result of that conversation, but my pride was too wounded, my feelings too hurt, and my beautiful vision of the future too nastily besmirched for me to realize it yet: was *this* what the glorious life of intellectual New York was going to be—army-style chicken-shit, trial periods, hostile and suspicious superiors, and a lousy hundred bucks a week? I thought for a while of turning the job down altogether, but that meant being shamed in the eyes of all the people to whom I had already bragged about *Commentary*. It also meant, or so I thought, going back to graduate school; and which of these two consequences I dreaded more, it would have taken a very nice calculation to determine. In the end, and against Trilling's advice (compromise on the money but don't compromise on the title, he had said), I went to work at *Commentary* as an assistant editor at a not-quite-face-saving salary of two hundred and fifty dollars more per year than The Boss had originally offered.

My negotiations with The Boss had taught me what anyone less retarded would have known by the time he was out of knee pants: that literary intellectuals are no different from other mortals when it comes to many of the things to which they themselves are often in the habit of pretending superiority. The occupational hazard of the literary intellectual is to believe that he is redeemed by consciousness. He knows, for example, what mean-spiritedness is, and he is, of course, against it; therefore, he need have no further worries about falling into it himself. He is opposed to all the vices and in favor of all the virtues; and this, of course, makes him a righteous man without further ado.

But besides being retarded, I was also very forgetful on certain matters, and I needed repeated drilling before the lesson of those negotiations could really sink in. I had gone back, as a good unmarried Jewish boy was expected to do, to live with my parents in Brownsville after being discharged from the army, and when I finally told them, in response to several worried queries, why I looked so unhappy whenever I came home from the office, my mother said very simply: "Of course. He wants everything for himself, so he's trying to cut you out." I treated this interpretation with the contempt I was so high-mindedly sure it deserved: maybe the kind of people *she* knew acted out of such low and vulgar motives, but not intellectuals like The Boss.

To be sure, my stubborn and stupid refusal to see what was happening to me from 9:30 to 5:30, and to call it by its proper name, had a strong assist from a subtle psychological mechanism which comes into play in an employee's soul whenever his boss manifests dissatisfaction with his work. Given the primitive dynamics of that relationship, it is very difficult for the employee to believe that the boss may be wrong. In certain jobs, notably of the bureaucratic type, the boss cannot be wrong by definition, since the only standard of satisfactory performance is the one he decides to set. Yet even at the other extreme, where a completely objective standard apparently exists—the volume of business a salesman does, let us say—it is still the boss who determines whether the employee is hustling enough or is breaking enough new ground; and it is still he who distributes the praise that is hungered for and the reproach that is feared.

At *Commentary*, there was the pretense of a more or less objective standard. We were presumably there to get out the best magazine we could, irrespective of circulation and advertising, within the limitations of the AJC charter and the budget allotted to us each year. "Best" may seem a subjective rather than an objective standard, but we were all agreed as to the rough criteria by which quality should be judged and the terms by which a judgment could be argued. Consequently, although even *I* knew after a few weeks in the office that The Boss was less than perfectly noble in his feelings about many things, I could not believe that he was anything but disinterestedly dedicated to the enterprise for which he was now responsible.

I was too young and too self-involved to realize—not that it would have mattered much to me if I had —that The Boss, being in reality only the "boss," was in an impossibly difficult position in trying to run a magazine over which he both did and did not possess authority, and that the strain was telling in the change he had undergone from the friendly personality I had known before to the grim and resentful bully I was getting to know now. I thought Lord Acton's maxim about power explained the change, but actually it was the absence of sufficient power rather than the possession of too much which caused the trouble in this particular case.

In any event, that The Boss felt I had moved up in the world too rapidly for anyone's good, and that he suspected me of being opportunistic and dangerously ambitious was clear. What was just as clear to everyone but me, however, was that these feelings and suspicions accounted for the attitude he took toward my work. When he ignored my comments on a manuscript, or when in violation of traditional *Commentary* practice I was suddenly presented with galleys of an article I had never been allowed to vote on, or when editorial conferences were held to which I was not invited, or when he would check over a piece I had edited and either say nothing or tell me coldly that it needed more work, or when his only reaction to a triumphant coup I had pulled off (like getting an article from Edmund Wilson) was to jeer to Sherry that I had put myself in charge of "the department of big names"—whenever, in short, he indicated that he did not consider me a good editor, I secretly believed that he must be right; and the first months of my life in the office became a misery such as I had not experienced since my first months in the army.

In some ways it was even worse than the army. For this was, after all, supposed to be my element, and they said I was swimming badly in it. If not here, where *did* I belong? And there was something else too. Almost any job above the purely mechanical involves the exposure of vanity, but vanity perhaps plays a greater role in the offices of a noncommercial magazine than it does on the premises of most other enterprises. Such a magazine, indeed, deals as much in vanity as in any other commodity: the vanity of authors, which is daily being wounded or soothed, and the vanity of editors, which is always at stake in the pronouncing of judgments. In the nature of things, nothing can be done about the former, but when personal relations among a group of editors are good, when they like and respect one another, conferences over manuscripts can get to be relatively free of anxiety and an exhilarating collaboration of minds can sometimes get set into motion which approximates T. S. Eliot's description of what a genuine critical community ought to be engaged in: "The common pursuit of true judgment and the correction of taste."

On the other hand, when there is hostility or rivalry or envy among a group of editors, disputes over judgment and taste (which, as a wag once said, are the only disputes worth having) often come to resemble those situations in which three little children are playing together and two of them sadistically gang up on the third. To voice a dissenting judgment in such an atmosphere is to feel with considerable justification that one is laying one's entire being on the line. And since no one, least of all a young man, not even one so fundamentally sure of himself as I was, ever feels completely secure about his judgment (I have known famous literary critics whose confidence in their own taste could be shaken by the merest display of assertive opposition), the results of disagreement are bound to be bruising to the vanity and bloody to the spirit.

Yet I *knew* I was a good editor. I knew it from Sherry's assurances, I knew it from the respect with which my suggestions and criticisms were treated by authors, I knew it from the surprising technical dexterity I, usually so incompetent in such things, instantly showed in the handling of galleys and page-proofs. But most of all I knew it from the experience of editing manuscripts. There were several reasons why manuscript editing had always been so important at *Commentary*. For one thing, as a magazine that ranged over a very wide variety of fields, *Commentary* necessarily had to rely on specialists who were often unskilled in the art of exposition or lacked a literary touch; many of its most valuable contributors in the early years, in fact, were recently arrived German Jews whose ignorance of English was matched only by their blandly arrogant assurance that they had already mastered what was, in their eyes, the language of an inferior culture. I once had occasion to correct an elementary grammatical error in a piece by one such contributor who insisted that his original formulation be restored; when I told him that his original formulation violated the rules of English grammar, he snapped back in a thick German accent, "How do *you* know?"

Beyond and behind the traditional *Commentary* insistence on clarity and concern for literary grace, however, lay Elliot Cohen's Grand Design, his dream of arranging a marriage between the intellectuals (that is, the family) and American culture, and at the same time a reconciliation between them and the Jewish community. I have already indicated what this dream entailed in the way of substantive editorial policies, but a certain conception of style also went along with it: a style of exposition which might, like the magazine itself, be called "post-middlebrow." The model for it Cohen found in the pre-middlebrow belle-lettristic mode of the teens and twenties, which was based on the existence, or perhaps presumed existence, of an audience made up of educated general readers, or, in eighteenth-century parlance, "common" readers. This audience was assumed to be intelligent, intellectually curious, and alive to the world around it, but it was not assumed to be intimately familiar with specialized materials—the arts definitely included. The writer who wished to address it therefore had to do much more explaining than would be necessary in talking to his fellow specialists. The trick was to do the explaining without patronizing or pontificating, and to make oneself simultaneously intelligible to the general reader, interesting to the specialized one, and pleasing to the best educated sensibility.

In trying, however, to reconstruct a mode of discourse which could serve as the medium of a new conversation between groups who had not for a long time been on speaking terms with each other, Cohen ran into the usual difficulties of those who take it upon themselves to promote the resumption of interrupted traditions. The habit of writing that way was no longer widespread in America (though still dominant in England), very few people had any desire to do it, while those who did have the desire and the ability were few in number or busy with projects of their own. There was no alternative, then, but to do it through editing: to create as far as possible the monthly illusion that the tradition was still alive, in the hope that the visible presence of the illusion in the world might lead to its gradual transformation into a reality.

Just how conscious I was of all this when I came to work at *Commentary* I cannot say, but there is no question that it was in my bones. The first manuscript I was given to edit was a totally disorganized piece on Spinoza and the Jews, written, inevitably, by a German Jew, and with equal inevitability in very bad English: it was, in short, what at *Commentary* was called a "typewriter job" (as opposed to manuscripts which required only a little touching up or the kind of tightening and polishing that could be managed with a pencil between the lines). No one (naturally) had told me what to do with this mess of an article, but while looking at it in a sick panic and under the microscope of an abnormally close reading, I suddenly *saw* what needed to be done—beyond, that is, correcting the grammar, straightening out the fearsomely twisted syntax, and lightening the gratuitously ponderous conceptual load under which all Germans seem doomed to travel whenever they venture forth into the realms of the mind. I saw how the piece had to be organized, how it had to begin, how it had to proceed, how it had to end, if it was really to say what the author was trying to say (which happened in that case not to be very much). I worked in an intoxicated fever, and the speed at which I went was a sure sign, as it had always been and would ever be with me, that I was working well, that my instinct for the job was sound and true. It was as though I had been editing manuscripts all my life in the *Commentary* way; it was as though the peculiar pleasure of getting inside someone else's mind, and yet managing to keep a firm enough hold on one's critical sense to prevent oneself from being swallowed up by that other mind once inside, had been a lifetime craving of my soul which had at long last found its object and been satisfied.

But the pleasure I derived from the actual work of editing was not enough for the first few months to still the self-doubt that The Boss had aroused in me; nor did my fascination with the whole enterprise of getting out the magazine cut significantly into the unhappiness his hostility caused me. And to make matters worse, he responded so coldly to the first few pieces I wrote for the magazine (on my own time) after joining the staff that I was quite unable to undertake any more. Why then did I stay? The reason, I told myself, was Elliot Cohen. No one was sure just how ill he was, but it had been communicated to me that he was counting on my presence in the office, so that there would be at least one friendly face to greet him upon his return. Having been hit very hard by Warshow's death, perhaps in some obscure way even feeling responsible for it, Cohen had apparently confused me in his periods of delusion with Warshow himself, and this had left him fixated on me as somehow essential to his salvation. He might, it was said, come back any day now; he was much better and the doctors were optimistic; surely I could stick it out a little while longer when I knew that the situation would change radically in a very short time?

And so I stayed, my misery growing worse as my self-doubt turned more and more into resentment both at the way The Boss was treating me and the moral pressures that were forcing me to go on taking it. I would come to the office every morning feeling slightly ill and leave it every evening in a frustrated rage, cursing The Boss, cursing Elliot Cohen, and cursing myself for a coward and a fool. Daily I swore that not one more slight to my bleeding pride would I endure. Did I owe Cohen *this* much? Was I his son, that I should have to suffer for his sins? Was this the army, that I couldn't get up, tell them all to go to hell, and walk out?

I have by now seen enough of the world of jobs to know that Elliot Cohen was only an accidental detail in my refusal to leave *Commentary;* if he had not existed I would undoubtedly have had to invent him. In a sense, indeed, I did invent him—by exaggerating both my debt and my importance to him—for lack of other plausible alibis. I was young, I was still unmarried, I had no financial obligations beyond a small weekly contribution to the parental household, and I even had a reputation which would have been negotiable on the job market. True, I had inherited the depression-type mentality which forever leaves a still small voice in the victim's spirit to whisper: "Jobs don't grow on trees. Don't be a wise guy. Nobody needs you, nobody wants you, stay where you are, be happy you've got what to eat." Even so, another voice, backed by more up-to-date evidence gathered from the affluent society, told me that if I were to quit *Commentary* I could easily find a higher-paying job in publishing—feelers, in fact, had already been put forward—or perhaps on another magazine; or as a last resort I could have gone back to graduate school on the G.I. Bill. Nevertheless I refused to quit a job that was low-paying, that was making me more unhappy than I had ever been in my life, and that—as Cohen's promised return began to seem about as imminent as the coming of the messiah—offered no prospect for the future but a continuation of the same wretched conditions. Why? What kept me from quitting?

One reason, no doubt, was a childish desire to make The Boss admit he was wrong about me: childish because, as I knew perfectly well, there was no possibility that he ever would. (Yet I have seen many people enslaved to jobs they hated by the same childish desire.) Another reason, no doubt, was fear: if working for an intellectual magazine was as bad as this, what must it be like elsewhere? (This too, with suitable modifications, explains the enslavement and exploitation of many.) A third reason was that in spite of everything, being at *Commentary* gave me an identity, in the old army sense of rank: it told people *who I was*. Of course my writing

for believing ~~~~
fashioned and more accurately sugg~~~~
"job"—at *Commentary* counted for a great deal. The
discovery that in certain circles it was considered very
bad manners to ask a man what he did for a living made
a powerful impression upon me. It meant that most people were ashamed of the jobs they held and did not wish
to be defined by them. I hated my job, but I was by no
means ashamed of it and by no means averse to being
defined by it. That was the main reason I felt so reluctant to quit.

The ironies here are so thick that I can hardly begin
sorting them out. Let me take it from the angle of the
people who were ashamed of their jobs. Many of them
were aspiring writers with half-finished novels on the
desk (a very small number of which would eventually
even get finished and be good) who worked in advertising agencies, public-relations firms, publishing houses,
television, or as speech-writers and publicity men in phil-
anthropic organizations. They were all cynical about the
enterprises through which they made a living and regarded themselves, without exception but not always
with justification, as superior to their jobs. (Richard
Yates's unfairly neglected novel, *Revolutionary Road*,
provides the best portrait of the type I have ever come
across.) That they were often—though again, not always

213

be sure of the relative weights, and there were grounds
contributed to this identity, this rank, but I could never
...ing that my "position"—to use a more impressive word than
...spondeds ... to use a more old-
... never

...ent" to

y jobs their training

...their number was and is legion

...dison Avenue, and every year thousands

upon thousands of them would pour forth from the colleges with their B.A.'s in English and a pair of starry eyes destined to grow bloodshot before long from three martinis at lunch and another three before taking the IRT or the New York Central at five.

The liberal-arts colleges did not, and do not, consider that a liberal-arts education had been so named in the first place because it had been designed for men at liberty—that is to say, men with an income who had no need to worry about making a living—and that the aristocratic bias built into it and strongly reinforced by the anti-bourgeois passions of the cultural Left, could only have the effect on such of the young *not* at liberty who were subjected to it of persuading them to despise the work they would almost certainly be forced to do unless they chose to teach or had a genuine artistic gift and enough luck to make it pay off in cash. When Henry David Aiken says in a beautiful passage that liberal education should concern itself with "the durable intrinsic interests of literature and philosophy themselves: with their power, that is, to delight the spirit, to enliven the imagination, to refine and clarify discourse, and to bring to the whole mind a fuller sense of its inventiveness, singularity, and freedom," one can only agree. Yet in relation to the realities of American society, such an education, *especially* at its best, translates into a hatred of Madison Avenue and all its works, in spite of the fact that those same realities have for all practical purposes turned that very education into a training course for—precisely—Madison Avenue and all its works. This may be humanities but it is not humane.

Within a few years, this schizophrenic situation was to issue in a variety of interesting consequences. On the one side, it was to result in the emergence of the Beat Generation, significantly enough led by Allen Ginsberg and Jack Kerouac, products both of Columbia College, the capital, as one might say, of American liberal-arts education and also, because of its proximity to Madison Avenue and Broadway, willy-nilly the most prominent embodiment of the contradiction I have been trying to describe. The message the Beats would come to deliver was very simple: they were going to solve the contradiction by refusing to go to work on Madison Avenue

Kerouac was to put it, with a touching faith in
ingness of the Angel of Death to stay away from
cker Street, would only wind them up in "those
ful cemetery cities beyond Long Island City." And
since they were unfitted by their education to work anywhere else, they were going to adopt the traditional
strategy of Bohemian poverty and not work at all.

This would be a logically consistent position to take
and for those few of the Beat *writers* who had any talent,
a possibly viable strategy. But "opting out of the system" would provide no solution for the kids they were to
influence who would not themselves be gifted in the arts:
these kids would simply be left with nothing whatever to
do and would inevitably be conscripted into the system
as they grew older and punished to boot with a lower
annual wage for having once temporarily dropped out. It
was therefore to be expected that sooner or later a political solution to the contradiction should be proposed, and
thus, midwived by the Negroes in the South, the New
Left was eventually born. The message the New Left
would come to deliver would be as simple as the message
of the Beats from which it was dialectically to derive:
they too would refuse to be "dehumanized"—as they
had been educated to think they would be—by going to
work on Madison Avenue, and since the system offered
no other possibilities for making a living, they were going
to adopt yet another traditional strategy, that of the

ascetic political revolutionary, and work to change the
system.

The Beats and the New Left were to get all the publicity, as dissenting movements usually do in contemporary America, but the intolerable contradiction between
liberal education and the vocational realities of the society would also generate an attempted solution from the
other side. This would be an accommodationist strategy
in the sense that those who were to adopt it would try to
make the best of a bad bargain by seeing how far Madison Avenue would allow them to use their educated fac-
ulties if they in turn agreed not to despise their jobs.
Among the most visible fruits of this strategy would be
the introduction of wit, style, and imagination into advertising, and the heightened literacy of several mass
magazines. But the pioneering step in this direction had
been taken as early as the early fifties by another product of Columbia College, my old friend Jason Epstein,
who had been driven to start Anchor Books at Doubleday precisely by his unhappiness with the kind of stuff
the firm regularly published and by the will to find a way
—a commercially viable way it had to be—of exploiting
his best "liberal-arts" talents. The brilliant solution he
hit upon could only have been arrived at by someone
whose spirit had been touched by the "durable intrinsic
interests of literature and philosophy themselves" but
whose mind had not at the same time fallen into a nihilis-

tic incapacity for the making of distinctions in the here and now (despite the fact that he was then and always would be incorrigibly fond of the rhetoric of nihilism). For this solution rested upon the perception that those ancient American enemies, commerce and culture, were on the way to being reconciled by social and economic changes; or, to put it more concretely, that the growing population of the colleges, which on the one side was creating so much dissatisfaction, was on the other side creating a profitable market for serious and difficult books.

Rather to our mutual surprise, Epstein and I began to become close friends almost as soon as I started working at *Commentary*. We had gone through Columbia together but had at that age, as I have already indicated, been temperamentally out of step: I had thought him and his friends frivolous and he had considered me and my friends a collection of boors. Now, however, we were each being victimized by the aggressive and whining treatment which is always reserved for the newly successful by their less fortunate old friends, and which more than anything accounts for the tendency of most people to associate only with their peers in status or wealth. One gets tired of feeling guilty and apologetic toward others to whom one is constantly forced to accord sympathy without the reciprocal entitlement to it. So it was with Epstein and me, and it drove us, at first reluctantly, together, as also did the fact that we were usually the only members of our own generation to be found at the family parties where we so frequently met—he after his own sardonic fashion having become a third-generation sibling.

Though I was getting to know him well, however, I did not fully understand the significance of what he was up to with Anchor Books, and my own view of the job world was still much the same as that of the people all around me who were ashamed of the jobs they held. Epstein had obviously beaten the problem, but that did not mean that I or anyone else could. It seemed better to stick with a job I hated but that I was not ashamed to hold than to admit defeat by going back into the academy, or to take another job that was disreputable in the eyes of the culture to which I had been so very carefully bred.

And here we come to the largest of the many ironies in which I was caught. My job was respectable in the eyes of this culture, and therefore in my own eyes as well, because *Commentary,* as a subsidized magazine, was obviously free of the taint of commercialism, and as an intellectual magazine was putatively run for no other purpose than to publish the best writing of a certain kind it could manage to get into type. Everyone, of course, understood that it might fail in this purpose for lack of the right editorship, but even if the results of the enterprise were judged harshly, the enterprise itself, like any cultural product of serious intent that lost money, was automatically given the benefit of the doubt, just as on the other side a best-selling book or a hit play or movie was automatically suspect of having been cynically tailored to the demands of the audience rather than created out of the best talents of the author. Without thinking about it very much, I myself shared in this conveniently tidy point of view—so fully and uncritically that it took me more than a year of working under The Boss at *Commentary* to realize that there were other ways of being impure than those marked out by the pursuit of monetary profit, and other reasons for submitting to the impertinently imagined demands of an audience than the elementary hunger for gold.

I had taken it for granted that we were there to get out the best "monthly journal of thought and opinion on Jewish affairs and contemporary issues" we possibly could—"best," as I have previously suggested, according to criteria on which we were all in rough agreement. When The Boss accepted some pieces I thought we should have rejected and turned down other pieces I thought we should have published, or when he encouraged certain writers who seemed worthless to me and put a ban on others I considered good, or when he insisted on "covering" issues that I felt sure were pseudo or trumped up while ignoring questions that I found interesting and urgent, my initial response was to worry about the soundness of my own judgment.

After a while, however, even someone far more neurotically uncertain of himself than I was would have been forced to recognize that many of the editorial decisions at *Commentary* were being made with an eye on considerations having little to do with the question of quality. I do not mean to imply that The Boss's judgments of quality were always wrong and that mine were always right; often enough, it pains me to admit, it was the other way around, and I did indeed, as he had charged, suffer from a tendency to confuse quality with reputation. Nevertheless, right or wrong in my particular judgments, and in spite of whatever faults of character or mind might have accounted for the mistakes I made, I always assumed that it was my job to think of quality, while The Boss, as he himself once exasperatedly told me, was also trying to be "responsible." Responsible? I asked innocently. To the Jewish community, he said, to the AJC. But *Commentary,* I answered, has editorial independence; the AJC isn't supposed to interfere or exert pressure. That doesn't, he shot back, mean we can do what we want; just remember it's their magazine, not ours.

This struck me as a strange interpretation of the concept of editorial independence, but it explained many things which had puzzled me before, especially the positions The Boss repeatedly took with reference to the magazine that completely contradicted everything he stood for in his own writing. The Boss was running *Commentary* not to please himself but to please the American

Jewish Committee—*his* Boss—and he was doing this not out of cynicism but out of a sense of responsibility. He had placed himself, then, in that special condition of unfreedom which is the fate of any employee who tries to second-guess the boss, who spends so much time and energy in figuring out what his immediate superior will or will not like that he becomes a slave to an unrealistically rigid notion of what is required of him. Bosses, because their power gives them a greater share of autonomy than most people are lucky enough to enjoy, are likely to be inconsistent, arbitrary, impulsive men: it is a perquisite of the freedom that comes with power to be able to indulge in a whim, take a plunge, reverse a course. Men like these can more easily be brought around by their subordinates than second-guessed by them. The second-guessers are thus not only invariably wrong in their guesses, but by imagining themselves to be less free than they actually are, they also deprive themselves in the end of any freedom at all.

Such was the case with The Boss, and it was all the more foolish for being based in this particular instance on a mirage. For *his* boss did not even exist in the sense he supposed him to exist: *his* boss was an organization embracing people of such diverse and heterogeneous tastes that with the best (or worst) will in the world, it would have been impossible to publish a magazine to please them all. Yet even if the American Jewish Committee *had* been a monolith with clearly identifiable and predictable demands, neither The Boss nor anyone else could have published a good magazine (for he did want it to be good as well as "responsible") by attending to those demands. I say this not out of piety, but because I believe it to be a practical condition, given in the very nature of things. No editor (or theatrical producer, as witness how many go broke) can really know what an audience wants for the simple reason that no audience ever knows what *it* wants until it has already had it. Consequently, any editor who operates by "feeling the pulse" of his readership is bound to make mistake after egregious mistake, whether the readership he is appealing to be large or small. All an editor can do is go, for better or worse, by his own personal lights. If those lights are bright enough, he will turn out a good magazine; if, in addition, he happens to be a man whose preoccupations are representative rather than idiosyncratic (and if he isn't such a man, he belongs in another business), he will find an answering response of greater or lesser magnitude in the world out there.

In its practical effects on the magazine, therefore, the "responsibility" of The Boss would have been hard to distinguish from the cynicism of the box-oriented producer. As for its effects upon me, they were at once comforting and traumatic. Comforting because I now knew that at least some of the trouble I had been having with The Boss was ascribable to the cross-purposes at which we had been operating and not to my own deficiencies as an editor; traumatic because it made me despair of the job world altogether. If this was how things were in what Terry Southern was later unforgettably to name, in the irreverent spirit of the sixties, "the quality lit. biz.," what must it be like elsewhere? I found it hard to believe that there were any other jobs around answering to what I was beginning to think must be an infantile demand for "purity." Not only that, but I was also finding it harder and harder to resist the conclusion that the whole of the job world was organized beneath its smiling exterior with quite as much reference to hierarchy, to superordination and subordination—to power, in short—as any army.

While in the army, I had imagined *Commentary* as a society of peers engaged in a collaborative process of mutual correction and refinement; and indeed, there had been a time when life on the magazine had seemed (no doubt falsely) to approximate that utopian dream. But that time was past and it did not appear likely to me that it would ever come again. Meanwhile, here I was once more at the bottom of a hierarchical heap. A different part of me was being kicked around, insulted, bullied, and run ragged than had been subjected to the same treatment in Basic Training, but it was still me, and a more important part of me at that. Was it only attributable to the personality of the boss I happened to have drawn? I strongly doubted it: did the personality of a platoon sergeant have anything to do with the way he treated his trainees?

It was life, it was people, it was Original Sin: it was Working for a Living.

Was there a way out? Obviously becoming a boss oneself was a way out, but even if I had been entertaining any such ambition—and I do not believe that I was —there would have been no chance of realizing it. I wanted to escape from the condition of subordination by becoming my own boss, not by acquiring the power to push other people around, and the one possibility of transporting myself into so blissful a state was to earn my living as a writer. Could I do it? The question was complicated by the fact that I had by this time acquired not only a wife but her two small daughters from a former marriage, and even with her working, I would need to earn at least eight thousand dollars a year merely to make ends meet. My salary at *Commentary* had automatically been raised after a year from fifty-seven hundred and fifty to six thousand dollars, and I was by now earning another two thousand or so from writing. Would I be able by writing full-time instead of just evenings and weekends to make up the six thousand I would lose if I were to quit my job? The indications were that I could. I had already done several long reviews for the *New Yorker* at what seemed the gigantic fee of two hundred and fifty dollars per piece (*Commentary* in those days paid as little as twenty-five dollars for a review and rarely more than fifty); the *New Yorker* would certainly go on giving me assignments, and my work was in demand by other well-paying magazines as well. Several publishers, moreover, had been after me for a book, so I knew I could also count on an advance. I was twenty-seven years old, I had a brown study at home in which to work, and I felt confident of my energies, if not of my ability to pay $165 in rent every month. With my wife's encouragement, I finally decided to take the risk.

One day shortly thereafter, triggered by a particularly nasty piece of provocation, the rage which had been choking me for over a year exploded in a voluptuous emission of obscene expletives shouted at The Boss in the highest register my cigarette-roughened vocal cords could attain, and I walked out of the *Commentary* offices with a sensation in my heart strangely and appropriately like the one that had been there on the day I had boarded the bus that was to take me home for a two-week leave after Basic Training was over. Indeed this was the completion of my Basic Training in the world of civilian work. But it was not to be my discharge from the service: not quite yet, and not until I had learned a few more lessons about power and my own relation to it.

Power, I had concluded in the army, was position, and my experience at *Commentary* had added confirming evidence for that conclusion from a setting which would have seemed a polar distance away from the military: as sergeants and officers had been to me in Basic Training, so The Boss had been to me at *Commentary*. Yet my experience at *Commentary* had also taught me—what I should already have known from all the reading in political philosophy I once had done—that there was another kind of power which had little connection with the state of being in a position to push subordinates around, and that was the power to do as one wished in the performance of an action. Power, then, was not only position, it was also sovereignty, autonomy, freedom. To the degree that one was answerable to oneself in the doing of a job, to that degree did one possess this second kind of power, and to that degree alone.

This second kind of power, unlike the army kind, the kind that came with position in a hierarchy, could not simply be conferred: it had to be wrested to be acquired and then asserted to be made real and effective. The AJC could appoint The Boss to a position of control over *Commentary,* but unless he took the risk of exercising the power implicit in that position, it would not be real. He chose not to take the risk, masking his choice with rationalizations about responsibility, and was therefore left only with the lesser power of lording it over his subordinates. This is what turned him into a bully.

As for me, I made the opposite mistake in my relations with him to the one he was making in his relations with the AJC. I had come to *Commentary* ingenuously thinking that power would be no issue in such a place. When The Boss informed me in no uncertain terms—the terms of rank and money—that it very definitely was an issue, I responded with shock and resentment, like a little child when the nature of reality is first borne in upon him in that most important of all the schools of infancy, the sand pile. Later, after submitting to the power of his position, I grew hurt and resentful again when it became clear to me that he had no intention of rewarding me with so much as an ounce of the other kind of power in exchange for my having agreed to acknowledge his (shaky) authority as The Boss. I thought I could wrest a bit of this other kind of power from an unwilling monopolist by winning his respect, but the harder I tried to do that, the worse the situation became. My efforts to win his respect looked like, and in fact were, expressions of weakness which could only have the effect, as in fact they did, of exciting his sadism to a still higher pitch. That there was no dignified or pretty means to the acquisition of any power under those circumstances, I could not or would not face.

But from what I did in the blind fashion so typical of all the actions I had ever taken under the aegis of ambition, it became obvious that my refusal to face the truth that the only path to an acquisition of power at *Commentary* would inevitably lead through ugliness, did not mean that my behavior would fail to be governed by an unconscious perception of this truth. After storming out of the *Commentary* offices that day, I went to the offices of The Boss's boss to announce my resignation, and in the course of explaining to the head of the AJC's personnel department why I was quitting, I heard myself saying things I had never had any conscious intention of saying. The Boss, I said, was running the magazine in a spirit altogether alien to the way in which it had been run by Cohen; worse, if Cohen ever came back The Boss was planning to make life so miserable for him that the return would last only long enough to induce a relapse and set the stage for a coup. I had, I said, nothing to gain from exposing this nefarious plot. I was doing it out of regard for Cohen and concern for the future of *Commentary*. I had no wish to return to the magazine myself; all I wanted to do was write.

In thus committing the prime crime of American boyhood, snitching to the authorities, did I feel guilty? A little, but mostly I felt pleased with myself for having acted so selflessly, so nobly. How fortunate for me that all I had been called upon to do in order to serve morality, justice, and truth was to wreak vengeance upon an enemy! I believed every word I had uttered about my own plans, and I still think that at least half of me really meant them. But the other half had committed us both to a power struggle whose seriousness and reality showed in nothing so clearly as in the dirtiness with which it had opened. One does not start such a fight without being forced to finish it: and that was another lesson I was to learn about power when, terrified that my action would be interpreted as self-interestedly ambitious, I tried to back out even before the first round had been fought. The AJC would not accept my resignation; an investigation was conducted, and after six weeks of enough intrigue to have launched the Russian Revolution itself, a hearing was held, complete with secret testimony from the entire staff and from every former editor who could be rounded up and persuaded to offer an opinion. The verdict in effect was to split the Boss, so to speak, in two, one of him to be retired from the field and the other retained but stripped of his bosshood. I was to be promoted to associate editor, given an equal share of power in the running of the magazine until Cohen's return, and a salary of seventy-five hundred dollars. To my surprise, the demoted demi-boss agreed to these conditions, but it did not, I imagine, surprise him that I agreed as well. We also both agreed on a third editor to be brought in as a buffer between us.

Not only had I won, but I had conducted the battle over a period of six weeks as skillfully as the most seasoned pro—lining up support and sympathy from all the right quarters and behaving myself with just the right combination of diffidence and fervor. Yet in the very midst of all this, I still refused to admit to myself that it was a struggle for *power* I was involved in. I was willing to call it anything but that: I was willing to say that I was acting out of vindictiveness, petulance, and spite toward The Boss while only pretending to a concern for Cohen; I was willing in certain moods to castigate myself for being a filthy squealer and a hypocrite. If anyone had hurled these charges against me, and worse, I would have meekly pleaded guilty. But the one charge that everyone was actually hurling against me—the charge of ruthless ambition—I indignantly repudiated and could not tolerate. To refute the charge, I determined not to return to *Commentary* even if they offered to make *me* the boss. But when, after causing so much trouble, I found myself unable to reject the AJC's offer, I childishly determined not to exercise the power I had wrested when I returned to the office: I would be so magnanimous in victory that not even my ex-demi-boss would be able to believe that I was the kind of man who cared about *power*.

I turned out to be neither magnanimous nor ruthless during the year the troika lasted at *Commentary*, the nature of a troika being to force compromises on its members. I was happy to have been sprung from the condition of subordination; if I still lacked the power to do with *Commentary* what I thought should be done with it, at least I had enough power to prevent certain things from being done that I thought should not be done. If I had no power over others, no one had any power over me, and that was what I had wanted. Thus for a brief time *Commentary* became what I had once dreamed it would be: a society of colleagues and peers (except that two of these colleagues in utopia were barely on speaking terms and had to communicate through the third) in which hierarchical power, the army kind of power, simply did not exist, and in which everyone enjoyed the autonomous kind in his day-to-day work to the same imperfect degree.

The trouble was that with hierarchical power abolished, a third kind, of whose importance I now got a glimpse, was unable to come into existence: the power to put autonomy to a truly creative use. The troika did reasonably well with the magazine, but it could not generate excitement or urgency. For that, an editor, a boss, with strong ideas and the willingness to put them into practice, was needed. If I had been in a wartime army, when all the discipline might have justified itself in combat, or if The Boss in the old days had done anything with his position at the top of the hierarchy but use it to inflict punishment on his subordinates, I would have made the acquaintance of this third principle of power at an earlier stage of my experience. I would have understood that hierarchies are essential to the world of jobs because nothing can move without them. But when nothing moves with them, when they exist only for the sake of perpetuating the structure of privilege embodied in them, they deserve, and occasionally even suffer, the fate that Tocqueville prescribed for aristocracies which have lost the function of rule.

I was looking forward, then, in a new way to the return of Elliot Cohen, but when he finally did return, it was as a shrunken, shaken man in his late fifties who was pitifully unsure of himself and obviously not in any shape to take the strain of running a magazine. Now the power situation shifted again, but not this time in my favor. Feeling guilty toward my ex-demi-boss who had kept the magazine going in his absence, Cohen began siding regularly with him on disputed questions, and after several such questions had been settled in what I considered a disastrously "responsible" way (commissioned articles by Hannah Arendt and Robert Graves, for example, were rejected on the basis of various high-sounding pretexts but actually because they were too controversial), I resolved to give up for good on *Commentary,* on jobs, and on the whole racket of power that inevitably went with them. This time I quit quietly, regretting that I had not held firm to my resignation the year before. I had been right in wanting to become my own boss, and right in thinking that writing was the only way in which that ambition could be realized, given the nature of the world of jobs and my disinclination to do the type of thing it was necessary to do in order to prevail in that world. I had no stomach for another power struggle. For I had waged a dirty fight and won, but I had also paid a price in opprobrium (the hideous reputation of ruthlessness would, I felt sure, cling to me forever) which had been higher than the victory turned out to be worth.

When I told Jason Epstein that I was going to leave *Commentary* and take a stab at earning my living as a writer, he suggested that I hedge the bet by going to work for him at Doubleday on a half-time basis. They would pay me five hundred dollars more than my full-time salary at *Commentary*, and I could still have four days a week to write. Here was a new idea, one that had not occurred to me before: a job that would pay a living wage and that I need not be ashamed of, but that at the same time would be sufficiently circumscribed in its design to prevent my ambitions from getting engaged in it. The trap, I suddenly saw, was to be too serious about a job, in the sense of wishing to make it into a complete definition of oneself. Because I had been serious in this way about *Commentary*, my job there had hooked itself into my natural ambitiousness. I had not wanted to become the boss, but I had wanted the magazine to reflect *me*, and this desire had ineluctably led to my ensnarement in the nasty networks of power. None of this need happen in a part-time job with Epstein. I would do my work honestly and conscientiously, but that was all. As for my ambitiousness, let it operate full steam in the domain where it really belonged anyway—the domain of my writing.

Alas, I was not given the chance to test this sensible compromise out. After what may well have been the shortest career in the history of American publishing, a mere three weeks, I was put by the then president of Doubleday into the position of either quitting along with Epstein, who had got entangled in a power struggle himself, and lost, or succeeding him as editor of Anchor Books. The salary offer was huge by my standards of those days (and—another lesson about the world of jobs

—vindictively higher than Epstein's had been). But having already betrayed an enemy, could I now betray a friend? If I had really wanted the job, no doubt I would have found, and believed, no end of plausible arguments for the superior morality of betrayal in such a complex situation. Fortunately for my soul, however, the last thing I was looking for at that moment was a big full-time job.

I left the offices of Doubleday without a penny in the bank, with a wife and (by now) three small children at home, and a stack of bills in the desk from stores I had once been too afraid even to enter. How I was going to manage, I had no idea. But except for a pang of regret over the loss of my deliciously air-conditioned and carpeted office, I felt good, very good, as a man always does when he realizes that an ancient fear—in this case, the fear of not being able to pay the rent—no longer is there to plague him. It was not I, of course, who had conquered this fear: the affluent society had killed what the depression in its day had created. For whatever else I had or had not learned in two and a half years of Working for a Living in New York, I knew for certain that there was money around in America—even for the likes of me.

Thus, appropriately enough, ended the third lap of my journey from Brooklyn to Manhattan.

8 Writing for a Living in America

One of the reasons I was so miserable at *Commentary* during my time there under The Boss was that it had become practically the only place in the world where the sun still failed to shine on my fortunate young head. The Boss made me doubt myself, but everywhere else I basked in smiles of love and bathed in admiring eyes. For I was just then entering that glistening phase of a successful literary career when the world decides that a young writer is a winner and everyone is on his side.

Later there will come a turn and he will pay for it all, but for the moment his lot is one huge whipped-cream cake of attention, praise, and flattery. He gets fan mail from strangers and invitations to glamorous parties;

publishers write him letters expressing the hope that he will consider signing up with them when he sets out to write a book, and they take him to lunch in expensive restaurants (by which, he resolves, he will some day learn to stop being frightened); magazine editors ask him to contribute and television producers ask him to appear; his pieces get reprinted in anthologies and colleges request him to lecture; his name begins to be mentioned in articles, always respectfully and sometimes more glowingly than that. At the publishers' cocktail parties, to which he is still new and green enough to want to go, he comes upon an increasing number of people who have read his work and who are only too happy to tell him how brilliant they think he is; and the girls at those parties—the secretaries, the readers, the publicity "gals," all of them, by an inexorable sociological law governing the publishing trade, exquisitely bred and expensively educated—begin looking at him in a way girls had not generally looked at him before. So it was with me, and if I wilted in self-doubt eight hours a day in the offices of *Commentary,* I blossomed into self-assurance under all the loving encouragement that enveloped me everywhere else.

It may seem strange that someone whose corpus of work consisted mainly of book reviews should have received this kind of treatment. There were, however, reasons. I will not be coyly modest and say that the particular qualities of my writing had nothing whatever to do with it, but I will not be foolish either and say that those qualities by themselves accounted for the reputation I was acquiring in New York. Much of it, I think, was attributable to the unusual set of certifications I carried. I was a *Partisan Review*-type intellectual and I was also the man the *New Yorker* was choosing to review such classy authors as Simone de Beauvoir, Camus, Nathanael West, and Faulkner. *Partisan Review* and the *New Yorker,* so opposed in most other respects, had one important thing in common: they were both magazines with a (justified) reputation for being very hard to crack. To write for *Partisan Review,* it was supposed, one had to be formidably intelligent, conversant with impossibly difficult books, and full of deep thought; to write for the *New Yorker,* it was conversely imagined, one had to be graceful, witty, and charmingly casual about one's learning. Each magazine represented the quintessence of a different species of sophistication: *Partisan Review* was the arbiter and embodiment of intellectual sophistication, and the *New Yorker* was the arbiter and embodiment of worldly sophistication. I was therefore presumed, even by people who had never read a word I had written, to be uniquely endowed with both— and the more so as I had with such rapidity and apparent ease moved into the pages of both magazines.

I had known how much power *Partisan Review* commanded in the literary world, despite its tiny circulation (then about seven or eight thousand). I knew, for

example, that no young novelist, whether successful elsewhere or not, could feel secure about his status as a serious writer until he had been favorably reviewed, or better still published, in *Partisan Review;* nor could a
young critic, whether in the academy or not, be altogether happy about his career until Phillips or Rahv had
conferred upon him the honor of an invitation to do
something for them. But I had not realized how very
powerful in *its* way the *New Yorker* was until I started
writing for it. No sooner had my first *New Yorker* piece
—a long review of Nelson Algren's novel, *A Walk on the
Wild Side*—been published than I found myself transformed overnight into a minor literary celebrity. Everyone, it seemed, read the magazine, including the most
unexpected people (for Warshow had been right in pre-
dicting that the family would be impressed, if somewhat
concerned, by my appearance in the *New Yorker*), and
the status a writer automatically acquired, especially in
publishing circles, from being one of the Sacred Few
who were permitted to adorn the *New Yorker's* exclusive
pages simply had to be experienced to be believed.
(Symbolically enough, the day the issue containing my
Algren review came out, I received a telegram inviting
me to a party on Sutton Place.)

But my dual certification from *Partisan Review* and
the *New Yorker,* while a necessary part of the explanation for the way I was being treated, was by no means
the whole story. I have already referred to the peculiarly

intense response which always seems to greet a strongly expressed negative judgment of a novel or play that has been widely praised, and I have also suggested that this is so because many people feel that they are exposing their very beings every time they form a like or dislike for a new work of art. "I don't know," they say, "there must be something wrong with me, I just can't read that book"; or they congratulate themselves on their discernment: "It's all marvelous, of course, but the *most* marvelous part is. . . ."

Scholars have told us that the vogue of sentimentalism in the eighteenth-century English novel was the creature of a debased and secularized Calvinism, the idea having arisen that the capacity to shed tears over the contemplation of certain situations was the "fruit" of the "right" feelings within and therefore a sign that one was not among the damned—in secularized terms, the hard of heart—but among the elect—in secularized terms, the spiritually refined. (Oscar Wilde's great quip, "It would take a heart of stone not to laugh aloud at the death of Little Nell," acquires an added dimension, as though it needed one, from this bit of cultural history.) It may well be that something of the same process was at work in establishing the curious tyranny that taste came at some point to exercise over the souls of educated Americans, leaving them with the uneasy conviction that by the fruits of their aesthetic sensibilities would they be known as saved (superior) or damned (crude and philistine)—known, that is, as much to themselves as others.

But whatever the roots of this tyranny may be, it appears to grow stronger in a politically quiescent period like the fifties, when taste tends to become a substitute for politics as an area for the testing of virtue, and to decline somewhat in a period like the sixties, when it is replaced by the need to show sufficient concern for the plight of Negroes and to express the proper degree of outrage over the war in Vietnam (both of which invariably seem to entail being in favor of books sharing the same political point of view: an easier and much less anxiety-making property to perceive than whether a book is good literature). Thus any critic of talent who devoted himself in the fifties to writing about ambitious current novels could expect to be read with far more attention and discussed with far more intensity than he would ten years later. In the early sixties, the *New York Review of Books,* after achieving a dramatically rapid success as a taste-maker, would probably have been unable to maintain its position if it had not shifted the center of its attention to politics. A devastating assault on James Gould Cozzens' *By Love Possessed* by Dwight Macdonald in the troika *Commentary* of the fifties, by contrast, probably did more to make Macdonald famous than all his past political writings put together.

Like those few members of the family who also wrote about current fiction fairly regularly, I reaped the benefits of this situation—the more so for being young and for being able to publish my reviews in a magazine whose audience was preponderantly made up of precisely the type of person to whom taste was of such overwhelming importance. Since, in addition, I took a highly irreverent stance toward several inflated literary reputations which had bullied large numbers of these people into worrying over the soundness of their taste, I came to be held by some in almost priestly regard. By the same token I made enemies, but enemies are all to the good at an early stage of a critic's career, helping as they do to spread his name around.

Finally, there was the kind of review I wrote. My pieces were all in the family tradition in the sense that they attempted to relate an aesthetic judgment of the book to some social or cultural or literary issue outside the book itself—the strengths and deficiencies of the work being assumed to mean something more than that the author was operating at the top of his bent here and nodding, as even Homer occasionally does, there. This made it possible for me to use the book review in true family style as a vehicle for all my ideas about the subject in question: to show off, in short, how much I knew about this, that, and the other thing. But if the form and approach of my reviews were solidly in the family tradition, their style was less allusive and more explanatory than family writing had traditionally been, and they were thus more accessible to readers outside the family.

I had very little time to write while working at *Commentary,* but late into the night and on weekends I wrote nevertheless, carried along by the endless energy which comes to a young man on the make when he knows that the world is with him, and driven by an ambition for fame which, unlike my ambition for power, was self-acknowledged, unashamed, and altogether uninhibited.

There was nothing peculiar to me in these contrasting sets of feeling toward power and fame, for of the three main goals of worldly ambition (money, of course, being the third—and about that I still had no feelings at all), fame has always been the only one to enjoy a decent moral reputation. Efforts, to be sure, have been made to bring it under the rule of the dirty little secret into which success has been turned in our time—like the campaign to establish a prissy distinction between fame (good, but impossible to attain by pursuing it) and something called celebrityhood (bad, and only attainable by actions that distract a man from selflessly doing the work which alone can bring him fame, preferably after the grave has carried him beyond the reach of corruption). This campaign, however, itself testifies to the enduring reputation of fame as the only worthy object of noble ambition.

My allusion in that last sentence to Milton's much-quoted lines—

> *Fame is the spur that the clear spirit doth raise*
> *(That last infirmity of Noble mind)*
> *To scorn delights and live laborious dayes;*

—was intended to suggest one of the reasons why fame should have been granted an exemption from the moral disapproval that seems always to have surrounded money and power: because it is what the most highly articulate class of people in the world, the poets, have been most ambitious for, it has received the kind of press over the centuries that the rich and powerful have been unable to arrange for the respective objects of their own ambitiousness. As they say on Madison Avenue, you can't buy that kind of publicity; and indeed the rich have no more succeeded in buying it than the powerful, as witness the sorry effusions of poets laureate throughout the ages, have been able to coerce it.

Milton, who besides being a very great poet was also a very intelligent Puritan, qualified his praise of fame by calling it (in parentheses that give away the character of the idea as an afterthought) an "infirmity"—the last weakness to go in a noble mind (meaning his own, of course); in addition to this, he made sure to praise it for its effectiveness in getting a man to despise pleasure and devote himself entirely to work. It is not recorded that Milton ever praised the pursuit of wealth or the pursuit of power, even though they are perhaps even more effective in achieving the same puritanically satisfactory results. Almost every other poet in history has contributed his bit to the pro-fame propaganda, most of them not bothering with any Miltonic qualifications, but rather emphasizing the connection of fame with immortality (spiritual, therefore good), while also doing their spiteful best to blacken the names of wealth and power (mortal, therefore merely of the flesh, therefore bad).

There is, however, this much validly to be said in favor of fame as against power and money. Power is inevitably the power to coerce, hurt, kill, and thus the ambition to achieve it is rightly suspect as the ambition to give vent to aggression. Money is the essence and most brilliant servant of the principle of the extrinsic, and so imperialistic in its nature that it tends toward the abolition of all intrinsic standards, setting itself up as a measure of things it lacks the capacity to measure; money is therefore rightly suspect as a destroyer of other unquantifiable values, not to mention the unlovely traits of character which have so often been brought to the fore through its pursuit, acquisition, and possession. Fame, on the other hand, does no one any direct harm; it cannot be transferred or inherited and can therefore be thought to inhere in the person, and the hope of it has encouraged and sustained many people, in addition to the poets, to work at things for which they were being rewarded in no other worldly currency.

There is a fourth object of worldly ambition, social position, that also does no one any harm, but its reputation has nevertheless always been very low, perhaps because the passion for it has largely, and unfairly, been associated with women. If I had been asked at the age of twenty-six whether I cared about social position, I would have laughed at the ludicrousness of the suggestion, but only because I would have taken "social position" to mean hanging around with the upper class and the (Gentile) rich. I knew a few people, including to my puzzlement Mary McCarthy, who did seem to have a thing about titled Europeans and Americans with historically resonant surnames, and who loved going to places like Newport where they could mingle with the fashionable rich. I had no such emotions, but I did care terribly about my social position—though the term would not have entered my head in this connection—within the family. I wanted to be able to invite the family to the parties I was beginning to throw without having to feel presumptuous, and I wanted to be invited to all the parties at which the family periodically reaffirmed itself as a family: the ones William Phillips was always giving on behalf of *Partisan Review* for famous European writers who rarely seemed able to speak any language but French; the ones Daniel Bell was always giving on behalf of the Congress for Cultural Freedom for visiting Indian writers of whom no one had ever heard and to whom few of the guests would bother to speak; the ones Jason Epstein was always giving on behalf of Random House for authors he had corralled.

One met most of the same people—the family—at all these parties, but there was usually enough variation in the crowd to breed other invitations to other parties extending into other worlds than the literary. Thus, for example, it was at a party at the Trillings' that I was introduced to Lillian Hellman, who then invited me to a party which had an entirely different tone from that of the family gatherings I had been accustomed to. There were writers present (including Norman Mailer, with whom I had a first, and fateful for me, encounter that night), but they were writers whose books had been known to *sell,* and there were also famous theatrical personalities and many chic and beautifully begowned women who clearly could afford to pay a kind of attention to their persons that family-type women were not generally in a financial position to do. And so the circle of parties, carrying me further and further into the heart of "Manhattan," began extending outward from the family, ultimately to reach as far as the White House, and even, as these things came to be measured in the Johnson sixties, beyond.

Parties were sometimes fun and sometimes not, but fun was beside the point: for me they always served as a barometer of the progress of my career. There were other landmarks besides my first party at Lillian Hellman's. There was my first weekend at Philip Rahv's house in the country, drinking and arguing about radicalism late into the night; there was my first invitation (at last!) to Hannah Arendt's annual New Year's Eve party, where the German-speaking contingent, arriving promptly at 9:30, would congregate in one room with the marzipan and the liqueurs, and the family, filing in toward midnight, would segregate itself in another with the bourbon and the Scotch; there was my first small dinner party at Mary McCarthy's meticulously furnished apartment in the East Nineties; there was my first elegantly peopled cocktail party at Sylvia Marlowe's; there was my first black-tie affair in New York, at Louis Kronenberger's, where legendary figures from the twenties like E. E. Cummings appeared; there was my first summons to the Park Avenue salon of Mr. and Mrs. Kirk Askew, with its dazzling collection of celebrities and titled European ladies. And for the sake of these things too, I drove myself to write.

Only for the sake of these things and fame? Did I not write because I had something to say? This question rests, I believe, on a misconception of the nature of writing—or, more precisely, the nature of writers. Joseph Wood Krutch used to make a distinction between young men who want to write and those who want to have written, and although the distinction does have a limited applicability, it disappears into untenability the moment one pushes it too far. The desire to write, if real, arises in the first place from the ability to write: a child, for example, may show himself to be unusually articulate on paper and will then be encouraged by teachers or parents to exercise this power. I choose the word "exercise" deliberately, for articulateness on paper is a gift which does not differ greatly in principle from the gift of physical coordination we call athletic skill: like a muscle, it needs to be exercised not only in order for it to develop but because it exerts a pressure of its own on the possessor to use it, to keep working it out, and to no special purpose beyond the pleasure of feeling it function as it was meant to do. And just as a healthy muscle will grow restless and finally troublesome when denied the exercise it requires, so will the ability to write clamor for activity if it is kept in idleness for too long.

The urge to write, then, is there long before anything can possibly be there to write *about*—just as, to pursue the physical analogy, the urge to use the body is there long before the rules of baseball are learned—and it will continue to be there at a later stage in the absence (really apparent absence) of anything to say (for articulate people always have *something* to say when inhibition does not get in the way).

But if wanting to write means being subject to a pressure from within to exercise a skill, wanting to have written means coveting the title of Writer: the one desire is, so to speak, "natural," and the other a product of "nurture." Krutch's distinction is applicable only to those who lack the natural pressure but experience the nurtured lust. Those who truly suffer the pressure, however, are rarely free of the lust. The pressure drives them to write, but so too does the desire to merit the romantic and culturally glamorous (high-ranking, in army terms) identity of Writer—a desire which may originate from the outside but is soon internalized and transformed into a pressure from within as insistent as the pressure for exercise.

Spurred on by these mutually reinforcing and conspiratorial pressures, the writer will look around for "material"—stories, characters, themes, ideas—on which he can exercise his gift. Being no longer a child, he cannot content himself with a mere workout; for that, he may keep a journal. Being a Writer now, he must use his gift of articulateness on paper for a purpose beyond itself, as "purpose" has been defined by the traditions of the literary form to which he has found by trial and error it lends itself most readily. (Here the physical analogy would be with an all-round athlete who finally decides to concentrate on a single game.) He must, in other words, "say something," whether through plot, imagery, or idea. Now the trick becomes to find the right material— "right" meaning the material that will trigger into action what in Platonic fashion he already knows, feels, thinks, that will help him hit upon the "key" of which I have spoken before, unlock the floodgates of his mind, and free him to make as much sense of his experience (or, as I described it earlier, to achieve as much coherence) as he has the intelligence and imagination to do.

Of course I had something to say. I had ideas about literature, about particular novelists, about American society, about the cold war, about the Jews, about the character of my own generation, and being a writer whose gift functioned best in the form of the critical essay, I looked around for books to review which would give me an opportunity to express and explore those ideas. In the service of what purpose beyond my own need to exercise this gift, my own desire to be a Writer, and my own craving for the extrinsic rewards of the writing trade? In the service, I would have said, and not been lying, of standards. For I was still Leavisian enough in my thinking to believe in the supreme importance of the critic as the guardian of standards in a culture that more and more threatened to destroy them, and in the critic's sacred responsibility to expose the fraudulent while working to make the genuine prevail in the consciousness and mind of the age.

It had, to be sure, been a very long time, roughly the death of D. H. Lawrence, since Leavis himself had found anything worth making prevail, and the criteria of judgment he had trained me to absorb were in any case so demanding that very few books, whether old or new, were capable of satisfying them even partially, let alone fully. These criteria had left me with a critical vocabulary superbly fashioned for the job of explaining why, say, Pope was a greater poet than Dryden or why *The Mill on the Floss* was a lesser novel than *Middlemarch,* but I began after a while to feel that using it on most current novels was like hauling out a piece of heavy artillery to knock off a rifleman only ten yards away. It was certainly better than the bland, perfunctory, promiscuously accepting vocabulary of most journalistic criticism in America ("a beautifully written, moving novel that reveals a side of Mr. X he has never shown us before"), and its apparent unfairness and ungenerosity could moreover be justified by the thought that it grew out of the absolutistic nature of art itself and corresponded truly to one's actual aesthetic responses. Nothing, as Trilling once remarked, creates more anxiety in one than reading a novel that *almost* succeeds: to which I would add the obvious corollary that nothing is so exhilarating as reading a novel that does succeed, even if, like that most notorious of all the relevant examples, *An American Tragedy,* it suffers from gigantic flaws.

Nevertheless, I was increasingly bothered by this problem of critical overkill and increasingly preoccupied with the need to find a language in which it would be possible to talk honestly and intelligently and demandingly about contemporary literature without at the same time condemning it all to perdition. After struggling for a few weeks with a competent and inconsequential novel by Elizabeth Spencer that the *New Yorker* had given me to review, for example, all I could think of to say about it was, "If Eudora Welty is a good writer, so is Elizabeth Spencer." This may have been mildly witty, but it was not a three-thousand-word review, and I had to beg off the assignment.

One of the things that played a part in my uneasiness over the harshness of most of my reviews was meeting many of the novelists I had either written about or (worse, from their point of view) conspicuously failed to mention anywhere. In good Leavisian fashion (and this was a family trait as well) I had never thought of criticism as properly being directed at the author. I wrote with no intention of instructing the author or showing him how to improve; if I was instructing anyone, it was the "reading public," in Leavis' terminology. Now all of a sudden I was being confronted in the flesh with people whose *feelings* I had hurt, people who had spent years struggling over books to have someone like me tell them that they had wasted their time and to imply, even, that they had committed some kind of crime against humanity. A well-known young novelist whom I had handled roughly in an aside once asked me, after a few drinks had unstiffened us both, whether I admired Edmund Wilson. Certainly, I said, he was one of my heroes. Then why, asked the novelist plaintively, didn't I try to do what he had done in his time? Wilson had acted as an advocate of the writers of his own generation, whereas I was for some reason choosing to act as an enemy of the writers of mine.

I could not get that conversation out of my head, and when Allen Ginsberg, whom I had known slightly at Columbia, and Jack Kerouac, whom I was meeting for the first time, and, to my surprise, finding attractive, hurled the same charge at me after a piece of mine damaging to Kerouac's standing as a novelist had appeared in *Partisan Review*, I was thrown into a serious funk.

What was I doing anyway, and for the sake of what was I doing it? Did I really care whether or not a bunch of idiot kids thought *On the Road* was a great novel? Did it matter if they did? Did I really believe all that Leavisian stuff about the health of the culture and the fate of civilization? Did I really want to spend my life handing out failing grades to perfectly nice people who were just knocking themselves out to make a living like everyone else?

Enter sentimentality, exit criticism: whatever usefulness I might once have had as a literary critic was bound to be impaired by such questions as these. For either a critic does care, and care passionately, when a bad book is praised and does believe enough in the importance of discrimination to put all personal considerations aside in the fixing and arguing of a judgment, or he is no critic regardless of how much "criticism" he writes. But if my new mood represented a *trahison* against criticism, in its patronizing sentimentality toward writers it also expressed a far more devastating judgment of the state of contemporary fiction than my harshest published comments had ever done. Translated into plain English, the idea that wrong critical judgments do not really matter means that the literature in question does not really matter, that it lacks the power to shape the spirit of the age, to mold and extend consciousness, to heighten a sense of reality which would otherwise be dulled, to make order where there would otherwise be disorder, to bring life to the mind and imagination where there would otherwise be illness and death. I am still inclined to think that the fiction of the 1950's in America did not in fact matter in this very large way, and because it did not, there was no role for a serious critic to play except the tiresome one of setting himself time after time against the illusion that literature was once again coming to matter as it had mattered most recently in the great creative explosion of the teens and twenties.

"I will never be an orphan on the earth so long as this man lives on it," said Gorky of Tolstoy, giving the most beautiful expression I have ever encountered to the exaltation and vicarious vindication men always seem to feel at the mere knowledge that greatness is possible in the time and place of their own inglorious passage from birth to death. The insistent craving for this knowledge, I believe, lies behind many an inflated literary (and political) reputation. It is the most important single factor in the persistent reappearance of the illusion that the serious critic has to go on puncturing in a period like the fifties when the work being done is mainly a work of consolidation.

I had no wish to play so narrow and ungrateful a role. My idea of criticism was broad and ambitious, having, as I indicated earlier, been formed in college at a time when criticism seemed the most vital of all intellectual activities, when it fed into and was fed by philosophy, theology, politics, history—everything. In becoming a critic myself, I had neglected to realize that criticism had acquired this lofty character for a decade or two through its association with a great and revolutionary movement within contemporary literature that needed support (whence came the undercurrent of polemical urgency I had found so thrilling in college), that needed interpretation (which made possible the brilliance I had so lusted to emulate), and that needed legitimation (hence the impulse toward a "revaluation," as Leavis called it, of the entire literary tradition and a relation to the literature of the past the very reverse of academic). In the absence of such a movement, as I was now beginning to learn, criticism could only shrivel into academicism or take on the kind of strident negativism that had been bothering me in my own work. Because literature was no longer at the center, neither could criticism be, and since the center was where *I* wanted to be, it was inevitable that as a critic I would gradually run out of gas and then grind as a writer to a complete and miserable halt.

Meanwhile I too had to make my living like everyone else—at least eight thousand a year to be precise—and at the moment I was making my living as a practicing critic. Irving Kristol, who thought well of my work, had just returned to New York after five years in London running *Encounter* and was now editor of *The Reporter:* a fortunate circumstance for me, since *The Reporter* paid well (ten cents a word at the time) and I was in desperate financial straits as a result of the *New Yorker*'s decision to stop giving me books to review. This decision was never announced to me in so many words, but the coldness of the voice on the other end of the line where there had been warmth for the past three years and more finally got the message through to my brain, which had naturally enough been reluctant to receive it; I gave up calling them, still hoping they might call me, but the phone never rang again.

Why the *New Yorker* "fired" me I was never able to find out; perhaps they simply felt that they had had enough of my kind of writing, perhaps they had come to think me unreliable after all the assignments I had funked, or perhaps they had smelled out the change I was undergoing and did not like the odor. But whatever the reason, it was a serious blow to my financial situation and an even more serious blow to my vanity.

It did not, however, turn out to be the blow I feared it would be to my position in the world. I had wild imaginings of people fleeing from me who sometime had me sought; I felt sure that I would be in disgrace everywhere as soon as the word got around. Actually, the word would not have got around at all if I had not chosen to spread it around myself. "I don't remember seeing anything by you in the *New Yorker* lately; how come?" someone would say to me at a party. "They fired me," I would answer cheerfully, and await a comforting expression of puzzlement and surprise. Or: "I wish you would

start writing for the *New Yorker* again; I miss your reviews." To which I would reply: "I wish I could write
for them again too, but they won't let me, they fired me."
By now I was beginning in a perverse way to enjoy the
sound of this not altogether precise word, and beginning
to notice to my great relief that more people seemed
to hold it against the *New Yorker* than against me. This
of course helped to soothe my vanity, and the fact that I
was for once on the other side of the dirty little secret
and could for a change cash in on the not inconsiderable
perquisites of failure—an entitlement to sympathy, a
sense of having been wronged, and the suspicion that it is
one's virtues which are getting one into trouble—helped
to soothe my wounded spirit. Now, I told myself with
high satisfaction, they won't be able to say that the
wheels are always greased for me. I was wrong; they
would still be able to say it. But for a little while, at least,
I experienced the peculiar pleasures of that special combination of bitterness and smugness I had so often seen
on the faces of people whom Robert Rossen's film *The
Hustler* later taught me to think of as "losers."

The largest single fee I had ever earned as a free-
lance writer was seven hundred and fifty dollars for an
article commissioned by *Esquire,* which was just then in
the process of making itself over from a girlie-cum-
fashion magazine into a cultural trend-spotter (the policy change having been determined, interestingly
enough, as much by the influence of David Riesman as

by the preemptive arrival of *Playboy* on the scene: an *Esquire* editor told me that *The Lonely Crowd* had convinced them of the existence of a new kind of mass audience in America, better educated, more interested in culture and self-improvement, and that it was to appeal to this audience that they were now seeking out writers like me). While still a member of the *Commentary* troika, I had also written an article for *Harper's,* which paid respectably if not munificently and was hospitable, but none of the other magazines to which I had contributed—*Partisan Review,* the *New Republic,* the *New Leader,* the *New York Times Book Review,* the *New Statesman,* etc. —paid enough to keep me going as a full-time free-lance writer. My best bet in fending off the dispossess notice which haunted my dreams, then, was to concentrate on *The Reporter,* reviewing regularly for them, as Kristol wanted me to, and to write an article for *Esquire* or *Harper's* whenever I could think of a viable idea. At the same time I would get an advance from a publisher and start on a book.

From the moment the work of a young writer begins to appear in magazines, everyone begins hounding him for a book. The publishers, eager to snap up all the new talent they can find, naturally keep an alert eye on the magazines—and by the mid-fifties, *Partisan Review* and *Commentary,* together with literary quarterlies like *Hudson Review* and *Kenyon Review,* had very definitely joined the larger-circulation magazines as important showcases to which the publishers came to shop. Whereas in the prewar period, writers from within the family largely depended on small firms with a taste for modernism like New Directions and Vanguard, in the postwar period many of the big firms—among them Viking, Random House, Harcourt Brace, Knopf, and Farrar Straus—gradually woke up to the fact that there was not only prestige to be gained from publishing family-type writers, but perhaps even money, and not in the very long run at that. And indeed, names like Saul Bellow, Mary McCarthy, Ralph Ellison, Bernard Malamud, James Baldwin, and Philip Roth—to mention only a few—were to appear on the best-seller lists in the postwar years. At the same time, quality paperbacks were to make possible the wide sale of books by such family-type critics and intellectuals as Lionel Trilling, David Riesman, Hannah Arendt, and Paul Goodman.

Thus, as a young contributor to *Partisan Review* and *Commentary,* I was much in demand by the publishers; and when my name also began showing up in the *New Yorker* and other places too, a pressure was set up which was very hard to resist.

But it is not only the publishers who hound a young writer for a book. "Are you working on a book?" practically everyone he meets will ask. "When are you going to write one and what will it be about?" Magazine pieces are evanescent, transient; books are solid, permanent: so the idea goes. And so it also went with me. The book everyone seemed to think I should write was a novel; books were more real than articles, and novels, being "creative," were the most real of books: so the idea went on that point. But here I emphatically parted company with it. I did not believe—and had even said so in an article which gained me much notoriety in certain circles —that fiction was the only kind of writing which deserved to be called "creative," and I did not, as I have just explained, believe that the novel was at the moment the most vital form that literature was taking in America. There were young novelists around I respected— Malamud, Bellow, Flannery O'Connor, Ellison, Donleavy, the Jones of *From Here to Eternity,* and especially Mailer—but the truth was that the American books of the postwar period which had mattered to me personally, and not to me alone either, in the large way that fiction and poetry once had mattered were not novels (and certainly not poems—not until Robert Lowell's *Life Studies* came out, anyway), but works the trade quaintly called "nonfiction," as though they had only a negative existence: *The Liberal Imagination, The Origins of Totalitarianism, Notes of a Native Son,* and a host of still uncollected pieces by various other members of the family. Whether or not such writings merited the honorific "literature"—and I thought they did—they, and even lesser than they, had made an impact upon my mind, imagination, and soul far greater than anything I had experienced from reading even the best of the younger American novelists. Theirs was the company I would have wished any book I might write to join. The center, I thought, had shifted to them.

But where exactly was that? I would not have been able to say. Vaguely it all came together in my mind as "society," in opposition to the privatized universe of most current American fiction, with its increasingly boring emphasis on love as the be-all and end-all of life, with its narcissism, its self-pitying tones, its constricted sense of human possibility, its unearned wisdoms, its trivial emotional dramas. "Society" was *out there;* it was where everything after all was really going on; it was where *history* was being made. I conceived the notion at first of writing a series of long connected essays on key American ("nonfiction") writers of each decade since the twenties which, put together, would tell nothing less than the whole story of the changing role of the American intellectual in the past forty years and his changing relation to American society. For this modest little project, I got a twenty-five-hundred-dollar advance —less, probably, than I could have wangled through bargaining, but enough to pay the rent for a few months, and more than enough to give me nervous thoughts about the fix I would be in if I proved unable to write the book and had to return the money.

As anyone with any sense would have known, the project was far too ambitious. After weeks of intensive reading (to write a Book, one must do Research), I managed to turn out a fifty-page essay on Edmund Wilson, the longest single piece I had ever written, but I never got past the first paragraph of Chapter Two. In a real panic now, I desperately drew up a new plan: I would write a book, modeled on *Axel's Castle* (by which I meant an introduction, six critical essays, and a "Whither Mankind?" type of concluding chapter) on postwar American fiction, the point being not to attack it but to show how "society"—the character of the times, and especially the influence of the cold war—had made it what it was.

My then publisher was amiably agreeable (all he wanted was a book from me, he didn't much care about what), and again I set out to do Research. I read or re-read the complete works of every novelist of any pretension to seriousness who had come along in the postwar period and everything anyone had written about them, taking, in violation of my usual practice, copious (and mostly useless) notes, as though I were a graduate student doing a doctoral dissertation who had to prove the sufficiency of his scholarly apparatus. The determinedly sympathetic spirit in which I grimly tried to approach every book did not, to put it mildly, lead to the disturbance of my earlier negativism toward contemporary American fiction, but I did find myself growing more and more enamored of the cunning escape route I thought I was hacking through my dilemma as a literary critic. By reading the novelists as victims of a historical situation in which I myself was equally caught, I could write about them *from the center,* and not as an enemy but as an understanding friend; by treating them, moreover, as victims who were both describing our common predicament and testing out various ways of coping with it, whose inadequacy then showed up in their fiction as aesthetic flaws (falsities of tone, unrealized characters, willed attitudes, unresolved conflicts, mechanical resolutions, and the like), I could also write about them without playing critically false.

There was nothing especially original, not even to me, in this approach, but it *felt* original. This time I got through Chapter One—on Mailer—and almost to the end of Chapter Two—on Bellow—before running out of gas again. The other novelists I had been intending to include simply did not lend themselves to the "central" or "social" treatment which had worked, or so I thought, very well with Mailer and Bellow; or if they did, I was unable, after several fruitless and despairing starts, to figure out how. That took care of the book, and now, long overdue as these things usually go with young writers who have made something of a splash, the period of the block set in.

Blocks are to the professional writer what jails are to the professional burglar: a "normal" occupational hazard which must be taken into consideration in the choosing of the profession and discounted, as it were, in advance. What happens to a blocked writer is this: not only is he unable to finish anything he starts, but after a while he literally forgets how to write, becoming tangled in syntax and lost in grammar, quite as though he had never mastered the elementary art of constructing a sentence. Once he is in this condition, there is nothing to do but stop, for—as with the experience of sexual impotence which a writing block so closely resembles—the more he tries, the worse it becomes. Yet having stopped, he can never know if the block has disappeared unless he tries to write again, and so he goes on trying, only to be defeated again and again and plunged deeper and deeper into what must surely be the most complete condition of self-hating despair this side of insanity.

Burglars may well be as stoical about going to jail as the movies have made them out to be, but I have known very few writers who did not respond to the onset of a block with hysteria, and to its hardening over time with suicidal fantasies of one kind or another. In the case of my own first real block (I had only suffered minor ones before), the fantasies alternated between actual suicide and dreams of an escape from the loathsome self in which I felt trapped, so radical as to amount to a suicide of the spirit.

I gave considerable thought to this problem of escape. I was being punished, I told myself, for the sin of ambitiousness. What was ambitiousness? It was a lust for the things of this world. Because of this lust, I was doomed to unhappiness in the world of jobs, unable to rest content with powerlessness and yet unable to satisfy my disgusting need for power. Apparently repenting, I had then left the life of power, thinking to enter a life which would free me of these foul hungers. But had I not, cunning sinner, carried the same hungers with me under a different name? And was not writing now taking a just revenge on me for having used it corruptly for ends beyond itself—for having turned it into the servant of my ambition for fame when by the laws of its own holy nature it had been reserved as a refuge from the lust for the things of this world, and as the one domain on earth where only selflessness could prevail?

Incapable of the purity of selflessness, I was properly being banished from this refuge like a money-changer from the Temple, and ordered back into the world where the likes of me belonged. But if I went back, I knew, I would only get caught once again in the unendurable toils of power—a slave to this self of mine that I now understood to be incorrigibly susceptible to temptation. Could I renounce it altogether? Could I perhaps change my name, disappear into a strange city and take a menial job? It would have to be a very menial job, so menial that there would be no possibility whatever of rising up and out of it. Was there such a job in all the length of this Sodom, this Gomorrah, they called America? I racked my brain, dismissing one idea after another until, delighted with my own inspired brilliance, I came up with a solution that satisfied all the necessary conditions: a floorsweeper in a clothing factory. And I was deadly serious about it, castigating myself for lacking the courage to follow it through. (I still think this idea was a better one than some of the others I have heard blocked writers shyly tell about: becoming an auto mechanic, for example, would put one right back into the spiral of ambition, except at a lower level, and would therefore be no solution at all.)

William James says that Christianity is the religion of "the sick soul": my soul was sick and therefore I thought like a Christian (even explicitly so, for another of my fantasies—checked, however, by my atavistic antipathy toward the idea of a Jew converting to Christianity—was to take a vow of silence and become a Trappist monk). The secret language of the dirty little secret of success, as I was discovering from the images in which my own fantasies of failure, renunciation, and salvation were spontaneously cast, was the language of Christianity, with the saint translated into the artist, and art translated into the self-transcendent worship of God.

About one thing, however, I was right: ambitiousness, though not of the kind I meant, *was* the cause of my block. In this I was a true scion of the family. The family has produced its share of books, but its characteristic form has been the short piece, and many of its most brilliant and learned members—people who know more and can cram more ideas into a single paragraph than will be found in many whole volumes—have been prevented from writing books by overambitiousness and by the feeling that a book is something special, belonging to a different class of phenomena from articles or lectures. I am not a Jungian, but there are times when it is difficult to resist turning to the notion of the racial unconscious for an explanation, and such a time comes upon me whenever I think about the relation certain members of the family have to the problem of writing a book. Like the Talmudic scholars who were surely numbered among their forefathers, they not only regard books as holy objects but, haunted by what was perhaps the most ferociously tyrannical tradition of scholarship the world has ever seen, they seem to believe that one must have mastered everything before one is entitled to the temerity of saying anything on paper. For their forefathers, "everything" was at least delimited to "the sea of the Talmud" which could, in fact, be mastered; for them, however, "everything" means *everything,* and so the preparation to write can never come to an end and be succeeded by the act of writing itself.

For some of these more or less permanently blocked members of the family, the issue is not scholarship but rather originality and scope: they must either be Marx and Freud or not be anything at all between the covers of a book. This is, to be sure, a form of vanity—the same vanity that keeps many would-be writers from exposing themselves on paper for fear of disturbing their oceanic fantasies of superiority by a less than perfect performance. Such people go about the world with an "an' if I would" look on their faces which is more precious to them than anything they could possibly write, and they are, of course, utterly contemptuous of the piddling efforts of others. But the vanity that came into play with me when I set out to write a book was more strictly of the "Jewish" variety. I read too much, I took too many notes, I wanted to answer too many questions, I wanted to make too many connections, and I was defeated finally by an unwillingness to settle for a relatively modest job of work. I enormously admired the matter-of-fact professionalism of Edmund Wilson, which contrasted so dramatically with the disproportionate pressure we of the family seemed to put on even the smallest piece of writing we did, as though there had never been another piece of writing before and there would never be another one again. But such professionalism, stemming as it did from the calm sense Wilson had of being a participant in an ongoing enterprise, was beyond me and beyond most of the family too. We had to create, or at least discover, the world anew whenever we put pen to paper; if we could not do this, it seemed, we could do nothing.

Unless I could be professional, I could not earn my living as a writer, and if I could not earn my living as a writer, I would have to find a job and get back into the power racket again. It was a prospect I dreaded, but what else could I do in the absence of enough courage to disappear into floorsweeperdom?

Go into business and get rich, said Jason Epstein. As a result of his losing battle at Doubleday, he had gone through a crisis of his own in relation to the world of jobs and had come up with a solution exactly the opposite of mine. Jobs, he explained to me, were a form of slavery, and the system (it was called capitalism, in case I had forgotten—which, indeed, in true 1950's spirit I had) was rigged so that the only way to beat it was to join it; if you merely worked for it, no matter how much they paid you, you would always be poor—unless, of course, you had a peasant's idea of wealth.

I certainly had a peasant's idea of wealth, but Jason Epstein even more certainly did not. He was what my mother would have called "a sport," a fantastically generous young man with a real flair for the extravagant gesture and a carelessness about money which was a dream of aristocracy in action. Leaving a cocktail party, he would invite ten people to dinner and take them to some appallingly expensive restaurant, priced far beyond the resources either of his expense account or his salary as a junior executive, and never turn a hair at the sight of a bill such as would have given me a heart attack on the spot. If he traveled, it had to be first-class; if he bought a pair of shoes, it had to be from an English bootmaker who came once a year to the Plaza to fit his customers, and then he would spend thirty dollars sending them over to London by airmail to get them resoled. It was not, as I came to realize, that he enjoyed these luxuries in themselves; he was, in fact, entirely indifferent to comfort. What he loved was doing things in style, and like a Miniver Cheevy (but not at all growing lean as he assailed the seasons) he grumbled constantly over the inferior tools America gave him to work with: the restaurants were lousy, New York was ugly, the whole country stank. But he did the best he could with the materials at hand, and he was beautiful to watch.

Epstein had taken a job with Random House on the understanding that they would allow him to set up a little publishing business of his own on the side which would do for the children of the Anchor audience what Anchor had done for their parents, and he wanted me in on it with him. We could, he said, finance the operation by selling stock, but the investors would have to agree to giving us 50 percent of the ownership of the company in return for having conceived the idea and providing the talent. Madly scribbling unintelligible figures on a sheet of paper, he proved to me that the scheme was foolproof; within five years at the most we would both be rich.

My heart, still largely unresponsive to the call of Mammon, was never in it, but seeing no alternative and much impressed by the hard-headedness of Epstein's interpretation of the realities of American society, I went along. To my surprise we did actually manage to raise a

large amount of money on the very terms he had out-
lined, and we incorporated ourselves, in a ceremony in
the plush offices of a very fancy New York law firm, as
the Looking Glass Library. Having spent my childhood
mainly reading comic books and a few collections of
fairy tales, I now had to become familiar with the vast
literature for children which has been produced since
the nineteenth century, and to that end I spent three full
days a week squeezed with a book into one of the little
chairs in the Children's Room at the main branch of the
New York Public Library, avoiding as best I could the
suspicious glances of parents and librarians alike. There
I discovered that children's books, with very few exceptions, really are for children. I also came home one day
with a very high fever which the doctor said he would
have diagnosed as roseola if not for the fact that it was a
children's disease that adults hardly ever contracted.
This adult, however, apparently had, which was the only
thing besides a fairly pleasant temporary living he was
ever to get out of the Looking Glass Library.

After about a year and the publication of our first
twenty titles, it seemed obvious that for a variety of reasons the Looking Glass Library would never become
more than a modest success, and that the route through
money was about to be sealed off to me as effectively as
the routes through power and fame had been. But before
I had a chance to take careful stock of my situation
again, the curse which had been hanging over *Commen-*

tary for the past five years exacted its most ghastly trib- ute yet in the suicide of Elliot Cohen. Within a very short time, I was to find myself back in the midst of the power racket from which I had fled, but in an entirely new and unexpected way.

9 Becoming a Boss

Advice to Young Men: The best way to get a job you really want is to believe that you really don't want it.

I was certain that I did not want to become the editor of _Commentary,_ and most of my friends were convinced that it would be a mistake for me to take the magazine over if the job were offered.

Jason Epstein, in his characteristically impatient fashion, said that _Commentary_ was finished, played out, through, and wondered how I could even consider getting involved with a boring Jewish magazine. This did not strike me as a particularly cogent argument. Though it was true that _Commentary_ was no longer the magazine it had been in its early days, I thought I knew the reasons for the change, and I suspected that the process might be reversed.

Irving Kristol said that the only hope for *Commentary* was to give up straying beyond the reservation and confine itself exclusively to Jewish subject matter, and that I would not be the right editor for such a magazine. Coming from a rabbi, this would not have surprised me, but coming from Kristol it did, and in any event I held the opposite view of what ought to be done.

Diana Trilling said I was too young to put myself into a position where I would be constantly forced into a hasty overformulation of my ideas; becoming the editor of a monthly magazine of opinion would, she predicted, ruin me as a critic. Since I already considered myself ruined as a critic, however, this argument, while impressive, did not frighten me.

William Phillips said it was naïve to think that the editor of *Commentary* was free to do as he pleased with the magazine; if I took the job, I would be beholden to the American Jewish Committee and forced to turn out the kind of magazine they wanted to have. Though Phillips was himself a great editor and one of the wisest and dearest men I had ever known, I did not in this case assume that his advice came out of a disinterested concern for my welfare. I knew that he would have liked me to join the staff of *Partisan Review*, which would have been fine if he had been able to pay me a living wage, and if not for the fact that I would have been drawn into the by now ancient power struggle between him and Rahv. As young men they had been very close, even to the extent of collaborating on several articles, but the years of struggle to keep *Partisan Review* going (it had long ago broken all little-magazine records for longevity) had taken their toll, and the two former friends now resembled an unhappily married couple staying together for the sake of the child. Their favorite "grandson" though I might have been at the time, the last thing I had any intention of doing was moving into such a situation.

But if, as I thought, I did not want the job, what I definitely and consciously did want was a final triumph over my ex-demi-boss, who had remained at *Commentary*, was once again its acting editor, and was no doubt expecting an imminent appointment as Cohen's successor. I wanted the job to be offered to me, and I wanted him to know that it had been offered after I had turned it down.

Thus it was with the keenest anticipation that I watched the mounting signs that the American Jewish Committee was seriously considering me as a candidate. In response to a casual inquiry, I indicated that I was not interested in the job. Would I, nevertheless, be willing to meet with the committee that was empowered to appoint a new editor and give them the benefit of my thinking about the magazine? I would and I did, around a lunch table at a private club, where I held forth for over an hour about the history of *Commentary*, the role it had once played in American culture, and the role it might conceivably play again.

I could sense as I talked that the three members of the committee who were present at that lunch were completely sold, but again I coolly indicated—with a shrewdness of which I would have been utterly incapable had I been consciously insincere or making an effort to be shrewd—that the job did not interest me. I would lose my stock in the Looking Glass Library if I left the company in less than three years; I was working on a book; running a magazine would leave me no time for writing. Would I, nevertheless, be willing to meet with the other members of their committee, as I had with them? My remarks had been very helpful, and they were sure that the other members of the committee would find them equally so.

Again there was a lunch at a private club; again I held forth, elaborating and embroidering on my original disquisition to the point of suggesting the direction *Commentary* should take in the future; again it was clear that the job could almost certainly be mine if I wanted it; and again I expressed my regret that it would be impossible for me to shoulder so large a burden at this stage of my life. Was there any way of persuading me to reconsider? Not really. Not really? Well, I supposed I would be strongly tempted if the right terms were offered. What were the right terms? A completely free hand, an agreement to let me make the magazine more general and less Jewish in emphasis (the reason being that there was no longer enough first-rate work of the kind appropriate to *Commentary* being done within the Jewish world to nourish the great magazine it ought to become), and (this said shyly) a large salary—perhaps even as much as twenty thousand a year? But of course I was only speculating. Of course, but would I, nevertheless, be willing to meet with the executive director of the American Jewish Committee to discuss those terms with him?

Around yet another lunch table at yet another private club, the executive director of the American Jewish Committee said that my terms were acceptable, except for the salary (the sure touch with which I had instinctively handled everything else having deserted me on the question of money, I deserved to be defeated on that). He knocked several thousand off my proposed figure, but with my peasant's idea of wealth, the salary still seemed very high to me, and I was in any case so embarrassed by the mention of money and so worried that anyone might get the idea that I *cared* about such a thing, as to be incapable of bargaining effectively for it. I said I would think it all over and let him have my decision within a week.

My ex-demi-boss never had a chance. Nor, probably, would I if I had still been working at *Commentary* when the search for a successor to Cohen began. It often happens in the world of jobs that the number-two man is promoted to the top position as a reward for long and faithful service, but almost as often someone from the outside will be moved into the vacated office at the top. Why this should be so is not entirely clear: perhaps it has something to do with the appeal of the unfamiliar, especially when the enterprise in question has run into trouble; perhaps boards of directors are as prone as other human beings to be contemptuous of the familiar, even to the extent of suspecting that there must be something wrong with anyone who has been unable to do anything better with himself than work in a subordinate position for them. Having been at *Commentary* and left, I was in the doubly advantageous position of knowing a great deal about the magazine and yet being the proverbial outsider who could come in and "shake things up," as the saying goes. Having also proved—at any rate apparently—that I could make it somewhere else, I was bound to be taken as a man who was capable of making it there.

My ex-demi-boss had nothing going for him to compete with all this; indeed, the only thanks he could expect to get (besides a generous severance arrangement) for having served faithfully and long and under difficult conditions was to be blamed for the decline of the magazine. The same fate would probably have befallen him in any company under similar or analogous circumstances.

I had other things going for me too. If I had exposed an eagerness for the job—which I undoubtedly would have been unable to prevent myself from doing if I had known how much I wanted it—I might still have been offered it, but not on my own terms; and once on the job I would have been in a weaker position in my relations with the American Jewish Committee than I was subsequently able to command. The fact that I acted as though I were genuinely reluctant to take the magazine on, however, not only made me seem a more desirable catch but gave me much more bargaining power when terms came to be discussed than I would otherwise have possessed.

Finally my youth—I was not yet thirty years old—was an asset at a time when corporations all over the country were making presidents out of men in their thirties and when the electorate was preparing to make a President of the United States out of a man in his early forties. This reflected an important change in American attitudes, for not since the centuries before the Romantics discovered (some say invented) the unique values of childhood had the idea of youth been held in such disrepute or the qualities of youthfulness in such low esteem as in the decade following the Second World War. Until the Beats came along in 1957, the most prominent dissenter from this spirit was, of course, J. D. Salinger, and the young quite properly rewarded him for being their only champion by buying about a billion copies of his books. But except in the lonely universe of Salinger, "maturity" and "responsibility"—the "tragic sense of life," as it was self-flatteringly known in literary circles —were, as befitted a period of conservatism, all the rage in America. If one made a study of the imagery of American writing between 1946 and 1956 on subjects as diverse as psychoanalysis, theology, politics, and literature, one would find, I believe, that the idea of youth came to be universally associated, and on all levels of intellectual sophistication, with the idea of neurosis (even in Salinger's mind), and the idea of maturity with mental and spiritual health (except in Salinger's world, where the alternatives were either to be a doomed neurotic child all one's life or a corrupt and unfeeling adult).

Since the causes of this fascinating development were closely tied up with the cold war, it is not to be wondered at that a change should have begun setting in with the less bellicose international atmosphere that Stalin's death and its immediate aftermath temporarily brought along with it. But whatever the cause, the spiritual aspect of the ethos of "maturity" and "responsibility" was already being turned inside out by the Beats and the so-called "sick" comedians and "black humorists" whose irreverence toward American adulthood and all its works began attracting attention to them in the late fifties, just as its quietistic political assumptions were to be violently shaken up by the emergence into visibility of the civil-rights and peace movements as the Eisenhower years drew to a merciful close. "Never trust anyone over thirty," the leader of the Berkeley student demonstrations was to say in 1965, showing how far the reaction had gone in a mere ten years.

By 1959, however, the process was only just getting under way—in the minds of the leaders of the American Jewish Committee no less than everywhere else. A decade earlier, it is unlikely that they would so much as have considered putting so expensive an enterprise into the hands of anyone so young as I was when they made me the editor of *Commentary*. In the spirit of the ethos of "maturity" they would probably have thought it a reckless, imprudent, and irresponsible thing to do. But by 1959, youth was coming back into fashion and prudence and caution were accordingly going out of fashion as virtues. As the rhetoric of the Kennedy campaign, among other symptoms, was to show, "boldness" and "imaginativeness" were now coming to be numbered among the necessary ingredients of any responsible action. To appoint so young a man to head a very costly enterprise must have seemed to the American Jewish Committee a bold and imaginative step to take and therefore—such is the power of attitude changes within a culture—a responsible step as well.

As for me, I was elated by the victory I had won, and I sat around savoring it for a few days, still intending, however, to turn the job down. But the night before I was due to give the American Jewish Committee my decision, I found myself thinking what a pity it was that the opportunity to have a magazine of my own had come along at the wrong time; if only I had already written a book, it would have been great fun to see whether I really could pull *Commentary* out of the doldrums and make it great again. I began speculating in detail about the changes I would institute, the played-out features I would drop and the new ones I would create, the writers I would go after and the ones I would avoid, the questions I would air and the point of view from which I would air them, the issues I would bring to the surface and the people I would get to discuss them, the kind of manuscript editing I would do and the tone I would try to establish.

There was room for a monthly magazine such as the one I envisaged; there was so much nobody else was doing and that needed to be done. The time, if wrong for me personally, was exactly right for a new magazine. A new spirit was brewing in the atmosphere; I could feel it at work in myself, and I was sure that it must be at work in others too, still inchoate but upsetting settled ideas and feelings and stirring new ones into life. An editor who shared as I did in this spirit and who could imagine what the full range of its implications might turn out to be would have the power to shape and develop and direct it into a sustained and organized impulse to take a fresh look at all the weary ideas and attitudes whose constant reiteration in the *Commentary* of the recent past (and practically everywhere else by now) had made it so predictable and listless a magazine. Because Elliot Cohen had had something new to say, like it or not, *Commentary* had been charged with vitality for the first ten years, which according to Edmund Wilson was the natural life span of a genuine editorial impulse; all *Commentary* had done since Cohen's illness was to insist over and over again, and in an endless variety of ways, on points which had already been made, which had already sunk in, which had no further juice in them. The moment had clearly come to say something new, and the possibility for saying it through a monthly magazine was almost certainly there. What a pity I would lose the chance to be the one to exploit it.

But why should I lose the chance? For the sake of what greater good? I was making no progress with my book, and it would probably be best for me to put it aside anyway; as for my stock in the Looking Glass Library, it had cost me nothing to acquire and would cost me nothing to give up. Once again I went over the reasons for my decision to turn down the job, simultaneously recalling to mind everything my friends had said in support of that decision; and as I did so, the conviction that we were all stark, staring, raving mad began to grow in me, exploding finally into one of those furious revelations which seem to illuminate the whole universe in a single great clue.

Why had I been treating myself, and being treated by everyone around me, as though I were a sickly, delicate child who would contract a mortal illness if he so much as exposed himself to the air? Why was it that the first answer to every invitation the world ever sent me had to be No? Why was No a more virtuous word than Yes? Why was "impossible" a wiser judgment than "possible"? Why was it better to hold back than to let go? Why was prudence more advisable than venturesomeness? What were we all afraid of? What terrible dangers were we protecting ourselves against? Were magazines thrown up for grabs every day of the week that so extraordinary an opportunity should be tossed away with such smug complacency?

I was only thirty years old. Suppose it were to prove a mistake for me to take *Commentary* on—so disastrous a mistake that a year or two or even five of my life would be eaten up and wasted by it. I would still be only thirty-five at the end of the process. Was the imminence of my death so certain that I could not *afford* to waste five years? And who said they would be wasted anyway? What made everyone so sure in advance of an untried experience that he knew exactly what it would yield? It was the fifties that had been telling me to turn *Commentary* down, in the language the dirty little secret had assumed during that period: the tired middle-aged language of skepticism, pessimism, and resignation. By three o'clock in the morning—the hour Scott Fitzgerald said it always was in the deep, dark night of the soul—I had decided to say No to the dying fifties and Yes to the coming sixties, to whose more adventurous and youthful spirit my first act of dedication would be accepting the editorship of *Commentary*, and my second, the effort to transform *Commentary* into its evangelical voice. It had been a very narrow escape indeed.

The "new *Commentary*," as it was soon being called, began making an impact much earlier than I had expected. Circulation did not greatly concern me, assuming as I then did that an intellectual magazine which was further limited in its appeal by being explicitly Jewish in character could never corral more than twenty-five or thirty thousand readers (we had just under twenty thousand when I took over). What did concern me was to get the family reading it and writing for it again, most of them having fallen or been driven away during the years of trouble, and to get the magazine talked about once again in as many circles as possible. To these ends, I adopted a strategy that would, I hoped, make it instantly clear that *Commentary* was to all intents and purposes a brand-new magazine. Working some eighteen hours a day for seven days a week, and with only Sherry Abel, who had reluctantly accepted a promotion to managing editor, to help me at first (the old regime having, of course, left as a result of my appointment), I redesigned the cover and the format (badly, but at least it was different), threw out the whole backlog of manuscripts my ex-demi-boss had been planning to publish, abolished most of the old departments which had been a regular fixture for nearly fifteen years, and started putting an issue together that would both dramatically and subtly suggest the line of march the new *Commentary* meant to take.

The practical elements of the strategy were mostly given by my diagnosis of where the magazine had gone wrong. I knew, for example, that the necessity to publish a certain number of articles of Jewish interest in each issue had led to the adoption of a double standard of judgment; I resolved, therefore, that I would be as exacting about Jewish material as about any other kind of article, and if this meant, as I had warned the American Jewish Committee it inevitably would, putting out an issue from time to time with a minimum of such material, so it would have to be. Similarly with fiction: I would only print a story if I had one I considered good and would simply forget about the rule that there had to be a story in each issue. Poetry I decided (like Rabbi Plato before me, said Sherry) to stop publishing altogether, in order to evade the impossibly difficult problem of finding poems that were good in themselves and yet substantively relevant to the general preoccupations of the magazine: a problem that a literary magazine did not have, but that a magazine of opinion inescapably had to face. Finally, I determined to take *Commentary* out of the hands of the largely academic types on whom it had come to rely so heavily and to bring it back into the family, because I believed that there was more lively intelligence and more intellectual seriousness to be found within the family, and among its relatives in Europe, than among any other group in America.

These were all practical workaday policies, but I had an ideological strategy too, which was to turn *Commentary*, as I myself had been turning, in the same leftward direction that I was confident the best energies of the sixties were also preparing to move. For *Commentary* itself, this turn would not have to be executed from the Right, but rather from the position that was known at the time as "hard anti-Communism," a position virtually every member of the family held in the early fifties (though it came to embarrass some of them later so greatly that in the familiar pendulum pattern of such ideological politics as has room to exist in pragmatic America, they went all the way over to the side of those for whom the word "Communism" refers exclusively to a delusion in the mind of the State Department).

There were, of course, various kinds of hard anti-Communists: there were the old democratic socialists in the trade-union movement whose anti-Communism could be traced back to the Menshevik-Bolshevik struggle in the Russian Revolution itself and had been reaffirmed in bitter fights for union control in the thirties; there were the ex-Communists who had been persuaded of the "absolute evil" of Communism during their association with the party and whose current political views varied from the extreme right-wing sentiments of a Whittaker Chambers to the strongly liberal ones of a

Theodore Draper; there were the Trotskyites and ex-Trotskyites whose anti-Stalinism was an essential element of their intellectual and emotional heritage and who were socialist in their domestic political thinking; and there were, of course, right-wingers like McCarthy and Nixon who saw Communism as a threat to the American way of life, or were demagogically using the issue to promote their own careers and (a lovely bonus) to discredit the Democratic party.

In the early fifties, the two main intellectual organs of the hard anti-Communism which had its roots on the Left rather than the Right were *Commentary* and the *New Leader; Partisan Review* was in the same camp, but more uneasily so. Hard anti-Communism of this variety rested on two major assumptions: (1) the Soviet Union was a totalitarian state of the same unqualifiedly evil character as Nazi Germany, and as such could not be expected to change except for the worse (this idea was given its most powerful theoretical support by Hannah Arendt in *The Origins of Totalitarianism,* which conceived of totalitarianism as an "ideal" metaphysical category rather than as a system of political arrangements responsive to changing historical conditions); (2) the Soviet Union was incorrigibly committed to the cause of world revolution, to be furthered by military means when necessary, and when possible by a strategy of internal subversion directed from Moscow; only American power stood in the way of this fanatical ambition to destroy freedom all over the world, and only American awareness of the nature of the threat could generate policies that would thwart it.

Until the rise of McCarthy, family solidarity on this position was more or less complete, as could be seen from the fact that practically all of them joined the American Committee for Cultural Freedom, which was founded in 1949 for no other purpose than to rally the intellectuals behind the hard anti-Communist line, and which succeeded in enlisting such kissing-cousin liberals from Harvard as David Riesman and Arthur Schlesinger, Jr., into its ranks. But the family, like the Committee itself, split violently in 1952, one faction (the "anti-anti-Communists") contending that fighting McCarthy was a more urgent priority than fighting Communism, and the other (the "hard anti-Communists") asserting the opposite. There was also a minority position, espoused most prominently by Diana Trilling, which held that the two dangers to freedom were of equal importance.*

This split gave rise to one of those hideous polariza-

---

* While the American Committee for Cultural Freedom was affiliated for a time with the Congress for Cultural Freedom, it did not, so far as I have been able to discover, receive any financial support from the CIA, possibly because CIA funds in this area were reserved exclusively for overseas operations. In any case, the complexities of the matter were such that the American Committee, which was *not* being backed by the CIA, broke with the Congress, which *was* receiving CIA money, over a statement by Bertrand Russell, who was president of the Congress in the mid-fifties. The faction then in control of the American Committee considered Russell's statement and the policies of the Congress in general to be excessively "soft on Communism."

tions to which the American intellectual world seems periodically to be doomed. Each faction suspected the other of being "soft" on McCarthy or "soft" on Communism, as the case might be; each engaged in secret name-calling and gleefully unearthed the most sordid motives to explain the other's views. Once again friendships were made and broken on the basis of political views alone, and self-righteousness reigned supreme, as it always does, on both sides of the sectarian fence.

Why I, who had been too young to participate in the ideological battles of the thirties, should have got caught up so passionately in this hangover from those battles, I do not really know. But get caught up I did—on the side of the hard anti-Communists, who not only seemed to me to have the better arguments but who also seemed more thrillingly brilliant and moral. The charge that they were soft on McCarthyism struck me as ridiculous and, in fact, for most of them it was (let it also be said for the record that some of the most penetrating analyses of McCarthy and his methods to have been written at the time appeared in *Commentary*). On the other hand, there can be little question that the hard anti-Communists were more concerned with fighting what they took to be misconceptions of the nature of Soviet Communism than with fighting the persecution to which so many people were being subjected in the early fifties; and it shames me to say that I shared fully in their brutal insensitivity on this issue.

Thus Irving Kristol denied in 1952 that civil liberties were in jeopardy, or indeed that anyone's civil liberties had yet been infringed by congressional investigation, and I cheered; so too when Sidney Hook defended the constitutionality of the Smith Act and the right of universities to fire Communist teachers; and so too when other writers in *Commentary* saw little to be alarmed about in the practice of blacklisting, which had become so widespread in the entertainment industry. Meanwhile dangerous characters like Dashiell Hammett were going to jail and enemies of freedom like Lillian Hellman were unable to get any work.

If any single event was responsible for my own break with hard anti-Communism, it was Khrushchev's de-Stalinization speech. The famous passage in which Khrushchev explained how Stalin had got the old Bolsheviks to confess at the Moscow Trials to crimes they had not committed—"beat, beat, beat"—destroyed in one blow of its own all the subtly elaborate Koestlerian and Orwellian theories about the dehumanizing effects of Communist ideology (Koestler refused my invitation to him to write an article for *Commentary* on how he himself thought the speech had affected his picture of things in *Darkness at Noon*), while at the same time refuting the "metaphysical" theory of Communist totalitarianism according to which the system could only change in the direction of a more perfect realization of the totalitarian aim of total control. It seemed obvious to me that the hard anti-Communists would have to admit that they had been wrong on this latter point at least—that they had overgeneralized on the basis of the limited historical evidence provided by Stalinism.

But I still had much to learn about the intellectual rigidity to which the human mind is prone in politics. No sooner was the ink dry on the issue of the New York *Times* that carried the smuggled-out version of Khrushchev's speech than Bertram D. Wolfe, a hard anti-Communist of the ex-Communist variety and the author of one of the very best books ever written about the Russian Revolution, *Three Who Made a Revolution,* sent an article into *Commentary* pooh-poohing the speech's significance, calling it an obvious tactical retreat out of the Leninist manual, and denying that it portended any essential change either in the Soviet domestic situation or in the Communist commitment to the goal of world revolution.

This article, which The Boss published with great enthusiasm, took my breath away: how could Wolfe possibly be so *sure* so quickly unless he had closed his mind to any evidence which might interfere with his comfortable theories? Nor, as I subsequently discovered, was Wolfe alone among the "experts"—or Kremlinologists, as they used to be called—in being certain of the unimportance of the most important event to have taken place in the Communist world for decades. They had, Philip Rahv told me, an investment in their theories, and

I was foolish to think they wouldn't try to protect such valuable stocks and bonds.

Among the other consequences of my break with hard anti-Communism was a growing disturbance over the explicit ban—which Cohen had promulgated and to which The Boss was completely loyal—on "anti-anti-Communist" writers. All articles were carefully inspected for traces of softness on Communism: a crime of the mind and character which might even give itself away in a single word, or in some remark having no apparent connection with politics at all. I was also increasingly bothered by the disposition inherent in the hard anti-Communist position—though by no means logically necessary to it, as *Dissent* was somewhat ponderously demonstrating, and as Phillips and Rahv were making me see in private conversation—to place everything American in a favorable light. *Commentary,* to be sure, never went quite so far as *Time* in this direction, but it often went further than I could comfortably accompany it (as with Daniel Boorstin's neo-Burkean interpretations of American history), and it could always be trusted to tell its readers what was right with American society more frequently than what was wrong.

From *Commentary*—in this it was a true spokesman for the spirit of the fifties—one got the impression that the United States of America, for all its imperfections (the persistence of discrimination against Jews and Negroes being the main one), was the best society a human nature beset and limited by its own built-in imperfections (Original Sin, in other words—though a Jewish magazine could hardly permit itself to say so) was likely to be able to build. American society was, therefore, Reality (or, as William Styron was to put it in his fifties novel of the sixties, *Set This House on Fire,* "being"), and any large dissatisfaction with it was to be attributed to the Human Condition itself, against which it was of course "childish" or "foolish" or "infantile leftist" or pathological to struggle. "Two cheers for democracy," E. M. Forster had said; "Two cheers for Reality," came back the echo from the Malibar Caves of the American 1950's—and from the loft on West Thirty-third Street in which *Commentary* was then housed.

My ideological strategy for the "new *Commentary*," now mercifully housed in the American Jewish Committee's new air-conditioned building on East Fifty-sixth Street, was to say goodbye to all that: to hard anti-Communism and to celebrations, however quiet, of American virtue. Since the international situation was reasonably calm at the moment and since the discrediting and death of McCarthy had pushed the whole question of domestic security into the background, the latter half of the strategy, involving in its positive aspect an attempted transformation of *Commentary* into a center for the revival of the long-dormant tradition of American social criticism, would have to get tested out first.

The subject I had fixed on for the opening salvo was

one in which, as a parent and a resident of the Upper West Side of Manhattan, I had an intense personal interest, and which moreover was journalistically hot just then: the spread of juvenile delinquency, especially among middle-class kids who lacked the excuse of intolerable social conditions for their "deviant" behavior. In the spirit of the fifties, everyone seemed to be taking this phenomenon as a collection of unrelated incidents of individual pathology—as indeed I myself had come close to doing in my article on the Beats in 1957—to be dealt with either sternly by the cops or benevolently by the psychiatrists. Could it perhaps be interpreted in another way—as a symptom of certain radical failings in American life which could only be dealt with *politically?*

Norman Mailer took roughly this view of it, but I wanted a less apocalyptic writer who could support it in a more scholarly style than Mailer would do, and I began reading up on the professional literature in the hope of finding one. Just when I was on the point of giving up, someone told me that Paul Goodman—that prodigal genius of a first-generation son—had written a book on the subject, of which a small piece had already been published in *Dissent.* Though I had always admired Goodman's work, even succeeding in sneaking a few things by him past The Boss in the old days and later helping to get his novel *The Empire City* published, and though I had been much taken with the colloquial directness and fluency of a few of the reviews he had recently done for

Dissent, this particular piece had not struck me as especially interesting. But I contacted Goodman anyway and got a copy of the entire manuscript of his book to read. It was called *Growing Up Absurd* and had been rejected, he told me with no apparent bitterness, by nineteen different publishers.

I could hardly believe my eyes when I started reading the book. It was everything I wanted for the new *Commentary,* and more: it was the very incarnation of the new spirit I had been hoping would be at work in the world, as it had been at work in me. Enormously excited, I telephoned Jason Epstein and told him about it. Goodman? he said skeptically, that has-been? But I insisted that he read the book immediately—which he did, that very night in my apartment. Being an anarchist at heart, he was even more excited than I had been by the book, and Goodman had a contract the next day from Random House, one of the publishers which had rejected *Growing Up Absurd* before.

Goodman and I, working feverishly, carved out three long articles, representing more than half of the entire manuscript, for the first three issues of the "new *Commentary,*" and Epstein got ready to publish it in book form as soon as the serialization had run its course. The articles were so great a sensation that they put the "new *Commentary*" on the map from the very first minute, and the book of course went on to become one of the campus bibles of the sixties and to sell over a hundred thousand copies—incidentally giving Epstein and me a reputation as partners in the making of literary careers which I dearly wish were justified in other cases besides the one of Goodman, in which it indubitably was, and the earlier one of Norman O. Brown, in which in a different way it had also more or less been.

The Goodman pieces, so fresh in outlook and so surprising to come upon in *Commentary*, were probably the single most important factor in the rapidity with which the "new *Commentary*," to the delight of some and the dismay of others (including Stanley Edgar Hyman, who said that he had preferred me in my earlier role as the youngest of the old to my present one as the oldest of the young), was able to define itself. But there were other factors as well. Family names like Trilling, Kazin, Macdonald, Arendt, Rosenberg, Bazelon, Barrett, Fiedler, and Howe began appearing with much greater regularity on the cover than they had done in the past few years, and other names which had come to symbolize dullness or mediocrity or predictability in the minds of many stopped appearing altogether. The proportion of general articles in each issue grew much higher than it had ever been, while material of special Jewish concern not only played a less prominent role but tended to be less parochial in appeal. This, along with several articles I published that various interest groups found offensive, made a lot of trouble for me from the start. But it turned out to be fortunate that trouble arose so early in the game, for it plunged me immediately into the main problem I would have as a boss: how to make the power which had formally been conferred upon me into an effective reality.

The editorial independence which the American Jewish Committee had always granted to *Commentary* consisted simply in this: no person except the editor or anyone he might voluntarily wish to consult could read articles in advance of publication or could dictate what should or should not appear in the magazine. If I had never worked at *Commentary* before, I would probably have still been innocent enough to think that once the AJC had agreed to giving me a completely free hand, that would be that; but I had learned from my observation of The Boss in action that there were subtleties to the relationship between *Commentary* and the AJC which could not be comprehended within the simple phrase "editorial independence." The editor of *Commentary*, like any chief executive of any operation owned by others, only had as much freedom—which is to say power—as he was willing to risk exercising. If he did something he thought right and of which the AJC then disapproved, it was not enough merely to defend himself and hold firmly to his ground; he also had to make certain that he would not be deterred *in the future* by the fear of similar trouble from taking an action which he believed to be in the best interests of the magazine.

There was only one way I or anyone else could be

faithful to this principle: I had to be ready at any moment to lose my job. The AJC could fire me at its pleasure; that was its protection against me. My protection against it was my willingness to get fired; the minute I lost that willingness, I would lose my freedom and consequently my power to do the best editorial job I was capable of doing. Nor could such a willingness be successfully faked. In the world of power—serious power—the animal instincts get activated, so that nothing is easier to see through than bravado, and nothing is so quickly smelled out as the weakness which stems from fear. Even though I was a man much given to anxiety and disadvantaged in the world of power by a childish desire for everyone to love me and a terror of making enemies, I was able to command more than enough strength to compensate for these weaknesses simply by virtue of my genuine indifference to the prospect of getting fired.

This indifference stemmed partly from the strain which the exercise of that other kind of power, the hierarchical kind, was daily putting me under—a strain so great that it did more to exhaust me than all the actual work of getting out the magazine put together. I loved my power over the magazine itself—the power that had freed me from being subject to the power of others and that was making it marvelously possible for me to hold a job and still be a servant of "culture"—and it was wonderful having a big office and a secretary all to myself, and being deferred to. But I could not bear having to decide how much money other people should earn, or having to be concerned with the punctuality and performance of anyone but myself, or having to shoulder the full responsibility for saying no to writers (something a subordinate on a magazine always can and even should, for the sake of future relations, blame on the boss). I hated having to check over manuscripts edited by assistants and associates and having to worry about their vanity as well as the author's. Most of all, I suffered the most gruesome agonies whenever I had to fire anyone (though of course they were as nothing compared with the agonies I was inflicting). Having tried on several occasions to fire an employee "cleanly," I can understand why a leading business school should have thought it a good idea to offer a course for executives on techniques of firing which are sadistically designed to force the victim into resigning: business schools are on the side of management and they would naturally wish to spare bosses the unavoidable ugliness of the firing scene—of being forced to watch while grown men cry or to listen while they take whatever revenge they can in abuse.

Using The Boss of old as an obverse model, I had promised myself that I would run *Commentary* as a society of colleagues and peers, and I tried doing just that. The result—though it took me years to realize this—was that I turned the operation into one of those "progressive" families in which the father, instead of representing authority, becomes another one of the children himself, vying for their favor and consent. By denying the sheer fact of my hierarchical power—by refusing simply to assert my will without going into orgies of explanation —I put myself into a position of having to prove to my subordinates (a word I would never have allowed to enter my thoughts, let alone pass my lips) that I *deserved* to be the boss. I worked ten times harder than anyone who worked for me (I would have said "with me"), and at tasks I should not even have been involved in; I wasted an enormous amount of time in conferences whose real purpose was not to arrive at a decision but to make my "colleagues" see and applaud the rightness of any course I proposed to take; I was incapable of administering a deserved rebuke, and only could bring myself to fire anyone when, in consideration of the welfare of the magazine, there was absolutely no escaping the necessity; and in general, I acted and felt as though it were I who was on trial before my subordinates rather than the other way around.

I was, in short, a perfect picture of what hierarchical power looks like when "exercised" under the aegis of the dirty little secret. A perfect picture of what such power looks like when *not* exercised under the aegis of the dirty little secret can be had from an anecdote, possibly apocryphal, about Henry Luce, who, hearing that there was rebelliousness in the ranks at *Time* over the magazine's decision to back Eisenhower instead of Stevenson in 1952, called the staff together and announced as he rose to address them: "In case some of you don't know me, let me introduce myself. I am your boss. I can hire and I can fire. Any questions?"

There was a third kind of power the editorship of *Commentary* automatically brought with it: a new position in the world, and to this kind I responded with mixed feelings. *Commentary* was an institution, and as its head I was now entitled to certain of the perquisites of rank. Invitations: to banquets, to parties, to join the boards of directors of committees, to appear on television, to lecture, to consult. *Time* magazine, until it decided that I was moving dangerously far to the Left, regularly asked for my opinion on a variety of subjects and printed my picture as one of a group of "distinguished intellectuals"; reporters often interviewed me and quoted my statements in the press; and people in general treated me with a degree of deference greater than anything I had experienced before.

I piously hoped that I was worthy of all this, but I knew that my own worthiness or lack of it had nothing to do with the case. For I was beginning to understand what position meant in America and how it worked—how truly it resembled an officer's uniform and how faithfully the whole society followed the principle of saluting the uniform and not the man. As the editor of *Commentary,* I was no longer simply a person with a particular set of qualities, and on my own in the world; I was now a personage, with an identity extrinsic to myself to which people responded more immediately and even more fully, whether with like or dislike, than they did to *me*.

To be sure, some responded in this way because they identified me as the person—not the personage—who was responsible for a magazine they admired or hated; others did it because they wanted something of me that was now in my power as a personage to give. But many just did it because that was how they related to the world: they wanted to meet or associate with the editor of *Commentary,* whoever the present incumbent of that office might be, because it was an office that carried its own esteem in their eyes.

Experiencing such treatment, I also began to see that much the same principle regulated the distribution of honors and deference in many other areas, including several in which the only "offices" were intangible. The possession of wealth was such an "office," for example, for if the rich were often pursued because money might be got out of them, they were at least as frequently cultivated for no other reason than that they were rich. A more subtle application of the principle was professional reputation: there always had to be a "leading" this and a "leading" that in every field and in every generation, and if the leader happened not to be very good at his trade, he would still reap the benefits of the "office" he was filling by virtue of his position in the relative scale of things, and so much the worse for the field. Even in the field of ideas themselves, an article or a speech was considered newsworthy not according to how interesting or original it might be, but according to the size of the constituency assumed to be behind it.

But the very broadest of all the applications of the principle was the informal system of pluralism by which American society was ruled—far more despotically than it ever admitted to itself. However much liberal theory might go on insisting through the editorial columns of the New York *Times* that an individual must be judged on his own merits alone, and no matter how loyally the courts might adhere to that noble ideal, there was no such creature in American life and culture as this abstract individual. In the eyes of society, if not of judges, each person was a composite of extrinsic identities—regional, religious, ethnic, occupational—every one of which played a determining role in his fate greater than "his own merits alone" could possibly play, unless those merits happened to be very great indeed.

The American "individual" lived in a particular locale, worshiped, or came from a family that had worshiped, in a particular church, derived from a particular ethnic or racial group, and held a particular job: by these things was he known. Within those various communities, the amount of money, power, and repute he could acquire was indeed determined by "his own merits alone" but—again excepting those of extraordinary talent—in the society as a whole his progress was limited by the status of the particularistic communities from which he came in relation to all other particularistic communities. For each of these communities was itself an "office" of greater or lesser power, higher or lower rank in the national life. The "black power" movement of the mid-sixties was to be based on a perception of this reality, just as in another field the labor movement of the thirties had been, and in yet another the effort of the Jewish organizations to have Judaism officially recognized as one of the three major American faiths.

A long way back in this book, I compared the pluralistic social contract which was implicitly negotiated between the white Anglo-Saxon Protestants and the various immigrant groups in the post-Civil War period with the written Constitution which had come out of an analogous negotiation between the less populous and more populous regions of the country. But the bargain the immigrants got was not so favorable as the one the small states had been able to strike in their time, for whereas the latter had at least been accepted as equals in the Senate, the former were not accepted as equals at all. Instead, by the terms of the brutal bargain given to them, they were promised only freedom from gross discrimination, and only to the extent that they succeeded in turning themselves into facsimile WASPs. I also said, however, that the immigrant groups, having at first submitted to this "colonial" cultural arrangement, later fought back and got qualifying clauses—or amendments, as we may call them—written into the contract.

Thus there came a time when political tickets had to be "balanced" in ethnic terms, making it possible and even necessary for politicians to exploit their ethnicity as a resource instead of repudiating it as a stigma, and when appointments to a wide variety of actual offices, from cabinet posts to university presidencies, could only be had by a member of one of the more recently arrived ethnic groups, just as other executive appointments, both public and private, were reserved exclusively for members of the oldest of the ethnic groups, the WASPs. In similar fashion, some of the occupational groupings which had suffered from low status were in time able to negotiate qualifying clauses into the contract that governed their relations with the business community—most notably the academic profession.

All this brought the pluralistic ideal closer to reality in America, but it did not yet mean that the personal qualities deriving from ethnic and occupational particularisms all enjoyed equal status, or that an individual no longer needed to turn himself into a reasonable facsimile of an East Coast patrician WASP (or, if he was an academic making his way in government, a "hard-headed" —i.e., businesslike—"realist") to get ahead outside the confines of the local community. For outside each community stands the "neutral" territory, beautifully symbolized by the legal status of Washington, D. C. as an abstraction not even belonging to the Union, on which their leading representatives all meet—the national government in political life, the mass media in culture—and the language and manners of that neutral territory can be described as at the minimum having been purged of all the different particularisms except those of WASP-dom (and except, significantly, in comedy). Ralph Bunche would not have become Ralph Bunche if he had looked and spoken and dressed like a lower-class Harlem Negro; Arthur Goldberg would not have become a Supreme Court Justice or a UN ambassador if he had still had the manners of a second-generation Jewish boy from the streets of Chicago; and even John F. Kennedy would probably not have been elected President of the United States if he had been an Irish Catholic like Al Smith instead of a fantasy of patrician elegance.

Elliot Cohen's *Commentary* instinctively, or perhaps with some measure of calculation, followed through on the principles regulating this pluralistic system. By making itself into the leading Jewish magazine in America, it had also been able to win a place as a recognized institution of the national culture, for the particularistic ethnic community out of which *Commentary* came had by the postwar period acquired enough status or rank to command the general attention. If *Commentary* had not been a Jewish magazine, it is doubtful that it could have established itself at all, but if the tone of its Jewishness had not at the same time been largely an acculturated one—a product of the brutal bargain—or if its style had smelled too strongly of immigrant origins or been less facsimile-WASP than it actually succeeded in becoming, it would certainly never have gained the widespread acceptance it gradually did as a magazine of general interest. My own policies as editor of *Commentary* simply pushed the logic of Cohen's strategy further than he himself had done: the "new *Commentary*" bespoke, and reflected, a more advanced stage of acculturation than the old, and was accordingly more general than Jewish in emphasis, but it remained explicitly Jewish in part of its contents and identifiably Jewish in the intellectual style (that of the family) with which it treated even subjects of a wholly general nature.

I had at first thought that both these kinds of Jewishness would severely limit the growth of *Commentary*'s reputation and influence, because no more than anyone else had I anticipated how chic the idea of Jewishness was soon to become in America—especially as that idea was represented by and mediated through the family. Ten years earlier, as I have already indicated, Jewishness had still been associated in many quarters, and not only Gentile ones, with vulgarity and lack of cultivation, but the 1960's witnessed a startling transformation of attitude on this point as on so many others. American Jews had in past decades played a minor role on the literary scene (though a major one in the entertainment world), but now suddenly they were replacing the Southern writers as the leading school of novelists and so dominating the field of serious fiction that a patrician WASP like Gore Vidal could complain whimsically of discrimination: there was room, he said, on the lists of the important American writers of his generation for only a single "O.K. *Goy.*"

The spreading vogue of the New York Jewish intellectual (the family) reflected the same change. Almost all the members of the family, including some of the most difficult or allusive writers among them, like Hannah Arendt and Harold Rosenberg, were now beginning to appear in places other than *Partisan Review* or *Commentary* or *Dissent* or *Encounter.* Their pieces could be found in such unexpected magazines as *Vogue, Life, Playboy,* and the *Saturday Evening Post,* not to mention a more and more hospitable *New Yorker* and a similarly receptive *Esquire.* Articles in such magazines as the *Hudson Review* were already beginning to make dark backlash references to the existence of a "Jewish Establishment" which (of course) was in a conspiracy to take over and (this only intimated) corrupt American culture. Such references, appearing at first in muted or euphemistic guise ("New York" was the main code word employed in the New York *Times Book Review* by J. Donald Adams in accusing Lionel Trilling of the outrage of having tried to appropriate even Robert Frost, *his* poet, by misrepresenting Frost's work as belonging to the modernist tradition), eventually became altogether explicit, and in a few cases moved dangerously close to involving the same accusations against the Jewish influence in culture as those made by the Germans in the 1920's and after. (One piece I myself have particular reason to remember, it having been an attack on me personally, managed the *tour de force* of echoing every single one of Richard Wagner's charges in that *locus classicus* of cultural anti-Semitism, *The Jews in Music*.)

Backlash or no backlash, however, for the moment Jews were culturally all the rage in America, no doubt in part because ethnicity was beginning to take the place of region as the main source of color and individuality in an age when the progressive eradication of regional differences was threatening to leave the country with an otherwise blandly homogenized culture. Among the other consequences of this change in the relative position of the Jews was the growth of *Commentary* into an "office" of more than marginal significance. Year by year the circulation mounted, from about twenty thousand at the start of 1960 to an undreamed-of sixty thousand at the end of 1966; and it promised to reach a hundred thousand before the decade was over. Compared to the mass magazines, of course, this was still a ridiculously small figure, but for a magazine of its type *Commentary* seemed to be making it on a scale previously unimaginable.

But the newly chic status of Jewishness was not the only factor at work in this development. *Commentary* was thought of not simply as a leading representative of a particularistic ethnic community which, under a

qualifying clause written into the implicit American social contract, now had the right to command the general attention; the magazine was also seen as emanating
from an occupational community, "the intellectuals,"
whose once lowly standing had been similarly improved
by yet another amendment to the secondary American
Constitution which was finally ratified when John F.
Kennedy became President. Under this amendment the
intellectuals were recognized as an occupational group-
ing that mattered in American life: from having carried
a faint aura of disreputability, the title "intellectual" all
at once became an honorific, and much began to be made
in Washington as elsewhere of leading representatives of
this particularistic class.

The family did not regard certain of these "leading" representatives who were being honored with invitations to the White House and appointments to government task forces as intellectuals at all—they were, the
family said, academics or high-level technicians—and
within the Kennedy administration itself, only Schlesinger, Galbraith, Goodwin, and Moynihan really were
acknowledged as intellectuals in family eyes. Nevertheless, the family shared in the benefits of the new amendment: they may not have regarded others as deserving
of the title "intellectual," but no one doubted *their* in-
alienable right to it. For the first time in their lives, they
were in a relation to political power that could not be
characterized as hostility reciprocated by indifference.

All of us in the family knew and were even friendly with members of the White House staff; they read our magazines and the pieces and books we ourselves wrote, and they cared—it was even said the President himself cared—about what we thought. Would Roosevelt have cared? Would Truman? Would Eisenhower? Sometimes we were consulted directly—and made extremely uneasy by the kind of thing we discovered was expected of us. Once, for example, I myself was summoned to Washington by a *very* high member of the Kennedy administration who wanted to hear my "ideas" (that was the word he used) about the situation in Harlem. I had, as it happened, a great many of what I would have called "ideas"—and interesting ones as I thought—on this subject, but I noticed while expounding them over a very good lunch that the great man was growing restless and bored. This puzzled me, for I had thought I was speaking well. Faltering a bit in response to his impatience, I asked him whether he disagreed with what I was saying. "No, no," he answered, "what you're saying is all very well, but what should we *do* about it?"

Do? I was not accustomed to thinking in such terms; I was accustomed to making critical analyses whose point was to understand a problem as fully as possible, not to affect or manipulate it. Marx once said that the effort of philosophy until he came along had been to understand the world, whereas he was using philosophy as an instrument for changing the world. In this

conversation in Washington, I was the philosopher and
the official on the other side of the table the Marxist—
but a Marxist operating within very stringent limitations indeed. For if I had said to him when he asked me
what to do: "Why, get ten billion dollars, tear down
Harlem, and build it up again as a decent place to live
in," he would have dismissed me without further ado as
a fool and a visionary. He wanted politically viable pro-
posals for programs which could be drafted into bills
and had a chance of getting through Congress; what he
meant by "ideas" (and being an "intellectual," I was
supposed to have them) was something to be dropped
into the company suggestion box.

I had a similar experience when, upon Johnson's
accession to the Presidency, I was asked, as one of six
"intellectuals," to write a letter outlining the things I
would like to see him do. I have never had so much trouble writing anything, and in the course of working on the
letter I came to realize that the trouble stemmed from
feelings of alienation from the country of my birth so
deep that I could not even overcome them when they
were decreed away for me personally by the President of
the United States himself. By "alienation" in this context I meant simply the feeling that this was not *my*
country; I was not really a part of it; I was a citizen,
and a highly interested one, of a small community in
New York which lived by its own laws and had as little
commerce as it could manage with a hostile surrounding

environment. As an intellectual I was as ghettoized as my ancestors in Eastern Europe had been as Jews. It was not I (nor they) who had built the ghetto, but it would take more than a mere tearing down of the walls to get me out of it. I could not tell the President of the United States what to do except in the vaguest rhetorical terms—the prose of my letter kept threatening to sound like the Preamble to the Constitution or a refined Fourth of July speech—because I had never given enough serious thought to the possibility that the country could be shaped in accordance with my "ideas." I had never, in other words, felt anything but completely powerless in relation to what might or might not go on "out there."

To be endowed suddenly with *this* kind of power was the most unsettling experience of all. In time I came to feel that the way for me to exercise what little of it I seemed to possess was to go on doing the "philosophical" job I had been trying to do all along, and not—as several second-generation members of the family, most notably Daniel Bell and Irving Kristol, proposed—to shape my thinking or the direction of *Commentary* in accordance with what Bell called "the ladder of practicality." Bell and Kristol were to found a new magazine of their own, *The Public Interest,* in line with this principle. Thanks to Kristol's great editorial talents and Bell's insatiable curiosity, it was to be much better than a company suggestion box, but it would still operate, like the art of politics itself, strictly within the limits of the immediately possible and the terms of the given situation. Quite apart from my theoretical objection to their notion that "ideology" was dead and that all problems were therefore now technical (a notion resting ultimately on the fifties belief that the system under which we were living in America was the best a fallible human nature was likely to be able to build), I did not believe that intellectual discourse, even within the realm of politics, need limit itself so masochistically in order to be "relevant" or influential, even in the short run.

Indeed, the thinking behind *The Public Interest*— to pursue the analogy between European Jews and American intellectuals—seemed to me to resemble the idea of the radical assimilationists who thought the "Jewish problem" could be solved by the disappearance of the Jews into the surrounding environment. The proposed Bell-Kristol solution to the problem of the intellectuals was assimilation into the surrounding environment of "hard-headedness" and "practicality"—to doff the intellectual's equivalent of the gaberdine (shall we say the sports jackets and dark wool shirts affected by those members of the first generation who still lived in Greenwich Village?) and to don a well-cut business suit.

On the other side, however, I found myself less and less able to go along with the completely apocalyptic sixties notion that American society was hopelessly, incorrigibly corrupt. The "new *Commentary*" was perhaps the first magazine of any size to pay serious and sympathetic attention to the various phenomena which came to be known collectively as the New Left—radical political activism on the campuses, the emergence of the militant wing of the civil-rights movement, and the consolidation of the movement to "end the cold war"—and in the first two or three years of my editorship many articles, either directly or indirectly related to these phenomena, were published. But as time went on, I began to be disturbed by a certain tone or emphasis in these more and more coalescent movements which seemed to me to be turning them away from the necessary impulse to reexamine the clichés of the fifties and toward a disastrous surrender to the equally vicious clichés of the thirties.

It was one thing, for example, to insist in revisionist fashion that the United States had not been entirely innocent of blame for the start of the cold war and that American foreign policy had not in the postwar period been the model of benevolence and good intentions which our propaganda (and hard anti-Communism) made it out to be; but it was another thing to argue that Stalin had been entirely innocent of blame and that it was the United States which carried full responsibility for the cold war. It was one thing to urge that the United States do everything it could to work for treaties of multilateral nuclear disarmament, and another to advise it to adopt a policy of unilateral disarmament. It was one thing to say that the programs of the old-line civil-rights organizations had not been adequately responsive to the needs of the Negro masses, and another to accuse them of being in secret coalition with the racists to keep the Negroes down. It was one thing to say that the American educational system was failing in its responsibilities to the poor, and another to sentimentalize dropping out of school as an act of social protest. It was one thing to be critical of American society, institutions, and foreign policy, and another to be nihilistically dismissive of the democratic system as a total fake.

When I thought of these ideas and attitudes as the return of the repressed clichés of the thirties, I meant that they seemed to have no purpose beyond proving how rotten America was. When in the pre-Popular Front days the Stalinists adopted the same tactic (in the Scottsboro Case, to cite only one instance, they ran into conflict with the NAACP because the latter's objective was to save the railroaded young Negroes in the case from the electric chair, whereas the objective of the Communists, while apparently the same, was to create martyrs and to demonstrate that bourgeois justice was incapable of working), it had at least been in the belief that this tactic would help to bring the revolution a little closer. But in the sixties, when it was triumphantly demonstrated that a particular act of legislation did not go far enough or that American policy in a given area of the world was based on stupid or venal assumptions, no revolutionary strategy was involved; the only purpose frequently being served was to pile up evidence of the fraudulence of American democratic processes and pretensions: to prove that America was racist or imperialistic or counterrevolutionary. (William Phillips once told the New Left-minded English critic Kenneth Tynan that he could not argue with him about politics, because Tynan's arguments were so old that he, Phillips, could no longer remember the answers.)

As *Commentary* had been the main center, along with *Dissent,* for the family-style airing of the spirit of the early sixties, *The New York Review of Books* became the main center for a sophisticated articulation of the spirit of the mid-sixties. Jason Epstein had had the idea for a paper like *The New York Review* for a long time, but it had originally been a fifties idea in the sense that its aims were defined in relation to the belief that aesthetic taste and critical standards were issues of overriding significance as well as of primary journalistic interest. There was no effective guardian of taste and standards in America, and *The New York Review*—beginning publication on a regular basis in 1963—meant to fill that gap. At first it did indeed devote itself primarily to that task, relying so heavily on members of the family that for a while it was jokingly characterized by some as *Partisan Review* on newsprint.

As to *Partisan Review* itself, it was plagued by continuing financial troubles and internal dissension, and it had begun to be damaged by some of the very factors which had worked to the benefit of *Commentary*. In its essence, it had always been a "ghetto" magazine, and although it would continue to print good articles and stories and poems, its energies were bound to be slowed by the "acculturation" of so many of its children and the triumph of so many of its ideas, attitudes, and tastes. It had been the greatest magazine of its kind in the history of America, and for a longer period than is usually given to magazines to be great, but it was weakened by the scattering of the family in the third generation and by the concomitant development of a "post-middlebrow" culture. The quintessential highbrow magazine could scarcely be expected to flourish in such a culture; and it did not, its founding editors having to suffer the bitter pain of watching others gorge themselves on the fruits of what they had planted and nourished, while they continued to live on meager rations indeed.

The New York Review was edited by a veteran of that most post-middlebrow of all literary magazines, *The Paris Review,* Robert Silvers, and by Barbara Epstein, the wife of the Columbus of the post-middlebrow reading public, and it was financed by a group of wealthy patrician WASPs whose willingness to back such a venture in itself constituted a measure of the extent to which the influence of the family had spread and the degree to which the traditions of its intellectual style had become chic. Only in the third generation could backing of this nature have been found, and only in the third generation could a periodical of this character have achieved so rapid a success. Silvers was an intimate friend and had been a close professional associate of the editor of *The Paris Review,* George Plimpton, whose return to New York in the waning hours of the fifties deserves a place in the social annals of the American literary intellectual as proportionately important in its own context as de Gaulle's return to France in another. For Plimpton, besides being a writer and an editor and an overwhelmingly charming man, was also the scion of a distinguished family and a full-fledged member of the world which later came to be known as "the beautiful people"—and it was he, more than anyone else (except perhaps Richard Goodwin after Kennedy's election), who acted as the matchmaker in the forging of a genuine, if highly unstable, British-type Establishment in America. He brought writers and intellectuals into contact with the rich, the powerful, and the fashionable for the first time in any of their lives, and thereby did much to increase the standing and power of the former, if not the comfort and happiness of the latter.

The cultural tone of *The New York Review* reflected all this, though it took a political position so far to the Left of anything that could legitimately be called "Establishment" that Irving Howe could say of some of the people associated with it that they were "guerrillas with tenure." Yet even this did not disqualify the paper from being thought of as establishmentarian in the new sense, any more than the similar mixture of radical politics and Bloomsbury aesthetics in the *New Statesman* ever led anyone to dispute its place in the British Establishment. In any event, *The New York Review* outflanked *Commentary* on the Left in the mid-sixties with its (in my view) uncritical celebrations of such things as the Berkeley student demonstrations and a stance of opposition to the Vietnam war which (again in my view) was mainly serving the objective of proving how dreadful the United States was. *Commentary* had been publishing articles severely critical of American policy in Vietnam since 1961 (most of them going unread by many of the people who later vied with one another for the honor of being the most outraged by the war), and although the magazine was so far from the old hard anti-Communist position as to incur the suspicion in certain quarters of having gone soft on Communism, it was still anti-Communist enough to be out of phase with a climate of opinion which, as Norman Thomas put it, loved the Vietcong more than it loved peace. *The New York Review* was not pro-Vietcong but it was more closely in tune with this ethos (a much more powerful one within the culture, and especially among the intelligent young, than the newspapers or the public-opinion polls ever could see) than *Commentary*.

Except in a small way, however, this did not hurt *Commentary*'s standing in the world, or the reputation it too was acquiring as an organ of the new Establishment. Since the arrival of a new and brilliant business manager named Martin Edelston, moreover, the deficit had been going down at a rapid rate, and there was a good chance that we would—fantastic prospect—actually be making a profit within a few years. All this had been achieved, to the best of my knowledge, without any concessions to popularity; indeed, if anything, *Commentary* was a more difficult magazine to read than it had been when its circulation was ten thousand and it was losing a hundred and fifty thousand dollars annually. What then was I to make of the idea that the ambition for success was a corrupting force in American culture?

10 That Last Infirmity

Like retired athletes who cannot bear to be away from the field and will settle for coaching jobs rather than hang up their uniforms altogether, blocked writers often think of editing as a way out of the painful fix of needing to write and being unable to do so. During a period of blockage in the early fifties, for example, Mary McCarthy got Dwight Macdonald and Richard Rovere to collaborate with her in working up a prospectus for a new magazine (it was to be called *The Critic* and would be "anti-anti-Communist" in spirit) and even succeeded in raising most of the necessary funds. But no sooner had her block disappeared than she lost interest, and *The Critic* never got off the ground. Some years later, similarly, when Macdonald was having his troubles with writing and I was having mine with The Boss, he and I went into a temporary and abortive editorial partnership, getting as far as the prospectus for a new magazine of our own before he started writing again and decided to skip the whole thing.

Editing, however, is no escape for the blocked writer, unless, like Elliot Cohen, he is permanently blocked and uses his magazine as a means of coercing others, in effect, to do his writing for him. I was sufficiently aware of this temptation—and aware that yielding to it rendered an editor capable of refusing to publish good pieces for no better reason than that he disagreed with them on a point or two—to take preventive measures against it when, during my own period of blockage, I became the editor of *Commentary*. I made up my mind to circumvent both the temptation and the block by doing a short monthly column in which I would comment on the major articles in each issue, expressing whatever disagreements I might have with them or elaborating on points the author had chosen not to discuss. This was not "real" writing, I thought, so the block would not get in the way; at the same time I could use the column to help define the new character of the magazine more clearly.

"The Issue" lasted for eight months. When I was asked why I had given it up, I would say that it had taken too much out of me or some such thing, but the ironic truth was that I had stopped doing it because the trick I had been playing on myself had failed to come off. I had cunningly managed to get around my block by persuading it that in writing "The Issue" I was not really writing at all, but when I discovered that many of my friends took exactly this view of the matter ("Why don't you write for *Commentary* yourself?" they would ask, just when I was sweating out a column), I was unable to go on with it. For about two years thereafter I wrote not a single word, throwing myself with even greater fury into the work of the magazine, and making sure to drink enough at the end of the long day to keep me from giving in to any inclination that might arise in the unguarded night to brave the mockeries of my own literary impotence.

The characteristic form of hypocrisy in the pre-Freudian age, when principles and duty reigned supreme, was high-mindedness—the ascription of purer motives to oneself than one was actually acting upon; in the Freudian age, when everyone thinks he knows how sordid we all are inside, hypocrisy more often takes the form of ascribing baser motives to oneself than one is in fact being driven by. In my relation to writing, I was a perfect specimen of the low-minded hypocrite. Feeling proud of my courageous honesty (low-minded hypocrisy always prides itself on its honesty, as the high-minded variety does on its nobility), I would tell myself that I had only become a writer in the first place to attract attention and to acquire status; writing had done its job, it had carried me to a position where I could get along very nicely without it—a position in which I could satisfy my craving for attention and status more efficiently, more reliably, less neurotically. Why then should I go on torturing myself? What did I need writing for anyway?

As it frequently is on low-minded hypocrites, however, the joke was on me in this case. It was certainly true that I had always written to attract attention and acquire status—to become, in a word, famous—but it was equally true that my need to write had an independent existence of its own and would, like any other natural hunger, go on demanding to be fed, whether rewards extrinsic to the sheer relief and pleasure of being fed came along with the meat or not. Nor, by the time I was in my thirties, was there any longer a possibility that I could, without doing serious damage to the health of my soul, escape the demands of that "nurtured" lust to be a Writer which had lived inside me ever since I could remember. It was simply too late for me to get away with constructing a new identity for myself—the identity of Editor—to take the place of the identity of Writer. I was stuck with being a Writer, and the only question was whether I would be a Writer who wrote or a Writer who sickened for lack of writing. For two years, then, I sickened, even to the extent of despising such fame as my work at *Commentary* was bringing me, because it was the fame of the personage I had become and not the fame of the person—the Writer—I was.

I have already described how in the worst days of my block, when *Commentary* had not yet been there to distract me from it, I had convinced myself that I was being punished for having turned writing into the instrument of my craving for fame. I had yearned in those days to be able to adopt an attitude of matter-of-fact professionalism in my writing, to be modest in my aims, to think of myself as a journalist instead of a writer. I blamed all the trouble on the religiosity in which the nineteenth century had soaked the idea of writing: if only I—we—could get back to the eighteenth-century view of writing as a craft no different in kind from carpentry, there would be an end of insane ambitiousness, and there would be no more blocks (did a carpenter ever fail to fill an order for a cabinet because he had forgotten how to handle his tools?). I was a craftsmanlike editor; I had a job to do and I did it, sometimes in an inspired way, sometimes not, but there was never any question that the job would get done, and if this month's issue was not so good as I would have wanted it to be, I would have another chance with the next. Why was it impossible for me to feel the same way about writing?

As fate in the form of Huntington Hartford's notorious millions would have it, I was soon to be given an opportunity to experiment with precisely that possibility. Hartford had started a glossy new magazine called

Show, which was supposed to be devoted to the performing arts, and was now (1962) being run by Frank Gibney, whom I had once met when he was occupying
another of the innumerable editorial posts he had held
in his vigorous time, and a young refugee from the staff
of *Look* named Robert Wool. Gibney and Wool had decided to expand the concept of "performing arts" to include literature; they wanted a monthly column on
books and they asked me if I would be willing to take it
on. No, I said, I couldn't and I especially couldn't review current fiction every month. Not even for seven
hundred and fifty dollars per piece, and not even if they
allowed me to write about any kind of book I wanted,
including political ones? The price was staggering, like
everything about *Show* having to do with money (it reportedly lost six million dollars before folding after four
years of publication). How could I turn down such an
offer? I now had a fourth child (John having broken the
string of girls in our family in 1961), I was living in a
bigger and more expensive apartment, and though I was
making twice as much money as I had been earning a
few years earlier, I seemed to have less rather than more
to spend, and I was always broke.

My friend John Thompson, who had at different
periods of his life been very poor, very rich, and a middling wage slave, had an explanation for this puzzling
state of affairs. All of us, he said, were broke because we
had an insufficient appreciation of how rich the rich

were. We thought we could afford to eat in their restaurants, to buy our clothes in their stores, to drink the brands of liquor they drank, to send our children to their schools, to take vacations in their watering places, to entertain our friends in the special mode they had created. In fact, however, only the rich could afford these things, and on less than sixty thousand a year, *after* taxes, even they had a hard time managing the style of life our undisciplined taste for the best—in the world, where it cost a fortune, as in the arts, where it was at least free—had got us all caught up in.

The answer, Thompson said—the loophole in this fine-print clause of the brutal bargain—was to "think poor." It was true that the rich had a wonderful style of life, and that there was no tradition of decent poverty in New York as there was, say, in Paris, where "cheap" did not necessarily mean bad or ugly or tasteless, but aping the rich was just another way of enslaving yourself to them. They had it rigged so that you would never be able to make enough by working for them to pay for a style of life modeled on theirs; if you did not have what David Bazelon called "a shrewd birth certificate," your alternatives were to go into business and get rich yourself, work like a dog for the few crumbs of style they would throw you in exchange for making them even richer, or take it a little easier and settle for three-dollar shirts and the cream-cheese sandwiches at Chock Full o' Nuts.

Thompson had a point, I knew, but in view of the fact that he often preached this sermon in the Palm Restaurant (where he and I and Jason Epstein, calling ourselves the Newport Reading Club, would meet once a week to whine and giggle at one another about just such problems as these over many martinis, applejacks, and the best and most expensive steak which can be had in New York or anywhere else in the world), it made little impression on me. In any case, to think poor would have been to put myself back in Brooklyn, and I was now too much at home in Manhattan, too much in possession of it—and the more, not the less, in love with it for being in possession—to retrace, even in a single aspect of my soul, the steps of that long journey I had undertaken in blindness more than half my life ago. Manhattan was a costly place to live, in more ways than one, but to me it was worth every penny.

Worth it or not, however, I had to be able to afford it, and so for the first time in my literary career I set out to write not for fame but for money—and made the wonderful discovery that money could not only buy steak at the Palm but could break through a block as well. I wrote about twenty long reviews for *Show* in almost as many months, pushing myself time after time through difficulties which would have defeated me before with the thought of that seven-hundred-and-fifty-dollar check I would never receive if I failed to finish the piece. So enamored was I of this new mode of operation, this new professionalism that had taken writing out of the realm of "psychology" and deposited it so beautifully into the world of real work (the kind one did for the sake of the pay), of meeting obligations to others (they were depending on me to get my pieces done on time), and of supporting a family (the money was of course being spent, Manhattan-fashion, faster than it was being earned and was now mysteriously indispensable, even though we had been getting along without it only a few months earlier)—so enamored was I of all this that I took a positive pleasure in the fact that hardly anyone I knew read *Show* and that its audience, for all I could tell, was taking no notice whatever of my reviews.

There was an added benefit in this situation for me: no one was looking over my shoulder as I wrote, making faces, telling me that it was no good. I might tell myself that it was no good, but that was different from shuddering at the thought of what Philip Rahv might say. Exhausting though the pace was of turning out *Commentary* while writing a three-thousand-word piece every month, I went on with it, and little by little my confidence as a writer started to come back. After about a year with *Show*, I was beginning to feel ready to emerge from the relative anonymity of its pages and to appear in "public" again.

This readiness, of course, signified a return of the lust for literary fame that had got me into trouble before, and that I had resolved to squelch in the future. But thanks once again to Huntington Hartford's millions, fame was soon to join money (and, with conditions, power) in being granted my own personal parole from the prisons of the dirty little secret in which success and its constituent elements have for so long been kept. In the fall of 1962, *Show* convened a conference with the aim of bringing North American artists and intellectuals into closer contact with their Latin American counterparts, and Hartford not only agreed to pay the considerable travel expenses involved but also offered to house the participants for the length of the conference on an island he owned off the coast of Nassau. This property, formerly known as Hog Island, he had begun to develop at an unthinkable investment into what was envisaged as becoming the most luxurious and beautiful resort in the entire Caribbean area; all the plans had not yet been executed, but Paradise Island, as Hartford had rechristened it, already deserved its name by the time the *Show* symposiasts, of whom I was one, arrived there.

The five days I spent on Paradise Island had an effect on me so far out of proportion to anything describable that occurred there that the experience might be said to have lacked an objective correlative. Yet something snapped in me the minute I set foot on the island, and for the next five days I felt as man is supposed to have felt before being expelled from the original Paradise called Eden. Like a healthy four-year-old child who still inhabits that state—the memory of which, according to Freud, is the source of the legend of Eden—I was in total command of all my energies at every moment, uninhibited in the use of them, unwearying in their exercise. I could drink all night without getting drunk and still wake up after only two or three hours of sleep without being in the least bit tired. My senses had never been so alert, my brain never so alive, my spirits never so high. I loved everyone, and everyone loved me. I did not blame them; I even loved myself.

What did it? I think it was that Paradise Island represented a realization of the fantasy I had always carried about in my soul but had never been daring enough to picture in vividly concrete detail: *this* was what Success looked like, all its various components brought together in one dazzling display, and the look of it made me drunker than all the gallons of rum I consumed that week. This was what it meant to be rich: to sleep in a huge bright room with a terrace overlooking an incredibly translucent green sea, to stretch one's arms out idly by the side of a swimming pool and have two white-coated servants vie for the privilege of depositing a Bloody Mary into one's hand, to sign checks (which we had to do, though of course we would never have to pay them) without giving money a second thought. All around me, too, was the evidence of what it meant to be famous (for the North American delegation was mostly composed of people whose fame far outweighed my own meager measure of it): it meant that a serene self-assurance had been injected into the spirit to combat the uncertainties and anxieties which, to be sure, remained, but no longer had the field to themselves.

Norman Mailer once remarked that the most subtle sociologists in America are the promoters who allot ringside seats to a heavyweight championship fight: as between, say, Frank Sinatra, Truman Capote, Johnny Unitas, and Robert Kennedy (my examples, not Mailer's), they know who outranks whom. But if only the fight promoters are capable of mastering the higher calculus of fame in America, we are all amazingly skillful at its arithmetic. Anyone who is reasonably literate can walk into a room full of well-known people from different fields and know which are the generals, which the majors, and which the lieutenants; and the people themselves can usually make even more precise measurements than that. They instinctively stay away from those of lesser rank, for fear of being aggressed against, and, unless they themselves are either aggressive or very foolish, from those of higher rank, for fear of being patronized or made to feel uncomfortably humble. They will tend instead to congregate with their peers, and they know exactly who those are. "Butt out, buster, I'm talking to one of my peers now," the first movie star I ever met said to me at a party when I tried to join in a conversation she was having with another movie star who had interrupted the highly unsatisfactory one I had been having with her for the past ten minutes. This was, of course, a monstrous thing to say, but the monstrousness was in the saying, not in the feeling, which is very common among the famous.

There are many individual exceptions to this rule, Mailer himself being a prominent one, and yet I have only been at two gatherings where it did not generally apply. One was a state dinner at the White House—the only large party I have ever attended that included not a single person who was not visibly and absolutely beside himself with delight to be there (not even members of the cabinet who might have been expected to be blasé). The result was that everyone took everyone else's presence as a mark of peerage in that neutral territory on which all of us, coming from "different walks of life," were meeting: we were all generals that evening simply by virtue of having been invited, and no uneasiness as to rank arose.

The other such gathering was the conference on Paradise Island, and it gave me a taste I would never forget of what it was like to be a general among generals. Not everyone in the group may have been what Mailer calls major league so far as intrinsic achievement was concerned, but major league most of them certainly were in terms of the kind of fame that in America was directly convertible into wealth. I looked upon those who possessed such fame, and I liked what I saw; I measured myself against them, and I did not fall short.

"From now on," says a character in the movie by Clifford Odets and Ernest Lehman, *The Sweet Smell of Success*, "the best of everything is good enough for me." I left Paradise Island with those words ringing in my head. Think poor? I had been thinking poor, I could now see, all my life. Even when I thought I had stopped doing so— when, for example, I had triumphantly silenced the voice of depression-Brooklyn (which, like Goneril and Regan with Lear's knights, tells one that nothing is necessary to have) by entitling myself for being a good boy to such wonders as a three-dollar extension cord on the telephone or even an eighty-dollar suede jacket—I had still been taking it for granted that the best of everything was not for the likes of me, that thinking rich and even thinking famous were dangerous habits of mind, and sinful ones as well.

King Lear's "O reason not the need" speech became my favorite passage in the whole of English literature for a time, but of course in this new mood, I was again responding, as so frequently I had done since moving into the Manhattan condition of life, to an actual possibility in the world to which my instincts and emotions —shaped in a period when no such possibility had been imagined—had not been trained. And as my instincts and emotions had been educated in childhood to stifle hungers which it was assumed in the 1930s could never be satisfied, so my ideas and attitudes had later been shaped in college in accordance with the same principle. I was taught—not quite in so many words, but very

337

nearly—that the serious life of the mind I wanted to lead was, in America, inevitably a life of relative deprivation. It carried its own rewards, but except in very rare cases, the rewards were not of this world. One must not expect money, and one must not expect fame and power outside the tiny circle of the similarly inclined: expectation was the first step to a betrayal of integrity. Like the excellent student I was, I got the point of the lesson, and with a veritable vengeance I learned not to expect: only to begin discovering that in an affluent society and a post-middlebrow culture, not to expect was a way of not demanding *what was now there to be had,* and that not demanding was the surest way of not getting. I left Paradise Island resolving to demand.

Resolutions of this type, to be sure, do not get made in a day—or even five days in Paradise—and I suffered many relapses. Moreoever, there was no obvious action for me to take in obedience to the resolution: how, precisely, was I now supposed to express my demands on the world? Should I go around, like Henderson the Rain King, announcing, "I want! I want! I want!" to everyone I met? Should I hire a press agent? The high of Paradise Island was followed by a cyclically foredoomed low, including the first serious illness I had experienced since childhood and the first really vivid intimations I had ever glimpsed of my own mortality. If Hazlitt was right when he said that no young man believes he is going to die, I stopped being a young man at the age of thirty-three: and about time, I thought, too. If I was sick of anything, I was sick of living in a perpetual state of Becoming: it was time, as Saul Bellow said, to stop Becoming and to start Being. Being oneself, of course.

It was not long before an occasion arose which provided me with an opportunity to perform a concrete action in the service not only of demand but of Being as well—though I did not at the time recognize the occasion as such, preoccupied as I was with the troublesome details of it rather than with what it might signify for me. A year or so before my trip to Paradise Island, I had asked James Baldwin, many of whose early articles and stories had been published in the "old *Commentary*," to write a piece for me on the Black Muslim movement, then beginning to attract notice because of its anti-white separatist ideology, its spreading influence within the Negro ghettos, and the apparently successful techniques it had developed for turning criminals, drug addicts, and prostitutes into models of middle-class morality. Baldwin liked the idea and, to my great editorial delight, said he would do it. We met for drinks several times to discuss the approach it might be best for him to take and some of the points he ought to try covering. Because Baldwin was a man whom it had always been, and would always be, difficult to reach on the telephone, I wrote him several letters during the next few months inquiring about the progress of the piece and reiterating my belief in the crucial and growing importance of the subject.

Shortly after returning to the office from Paradise Island, I telephoned him on the off chance that he might be in; to my surprise, he answered the phone. How was the article coming along? As a matter of fact, it was finished, but it was very long, too long for *Commentary*. Nonsense, length was no problem at all; I was dying to read it, and I would send a messenger for it immediately. No, there was no use doing that, he had given his copy to his agent. Fine, I would send a messenger to his agent. Well, he didn't think his agent had the manuscript either. Who had it then? He wasn't sure, but he thought his agent had submitted it to William Shawn at the *New Yorker*—not that they would want it, of course, and as soon as they returned it, he would send it right to me.

I was thunderstruck. No greater violation of the ethics of the trade could be imagined than Baldwin had committed in taking an article he had been invited to write by the editor of one magazine and giving it to the editor of another. I considered taking legal action but dropped the idea as unseemly; I considered protesting to the *New Yorker,* but gave up in despair when I learned that they had in fact already accepted and scheduled the piece by the time of my conversation with Baldwin and were paying him about twelve thousand dollars for it—more than twenty times as much as I would have been able to do. The price tag on family writing had risen steeply in a mere ten years, no doubt about that.

Like the Ancient Mariner himself, only even more demented, I stopped one of three all over town, ranting and raving against the unspeakable thing Baldwin had done, until the fantastic realization began dawning on me that a good many people in the publishing world who would have been outraged if any other writer had acted in similar fashion were ready to forgive or "understand" Baldwin because he was a Negro. This made me, if possible, even angrier, and when the piece came out a few weeks later—it was, of course, *The Fire Next Time*—and I saw what a precious item had been stolen from me, my fury knew no bounds. As if my cup of gall needed an additional poisonous ingredient, Hannah Arendt—feeling understandably benign toward the *New Yorker* for having just agreed to send her to Jerusalem to cover the Eichmann trial—told me solemnly over lunch before I had had a chance to recount my tale of woe that the *New Yorker* was the *only* magazine in America which would have had the courage to publish so inflammatory an article as Baldwin's; I, "of course," could never have risked printing it in *Commentary*.

Baldwin and I had known and liked each other, in a slightly suspicious sort of way, for a long time, so that when he called me and proposed that we have a drink to "talk this thing over," I agreed, happy to get a chance to tell him exactly what I thought of him. Not even the contrition he showed, nor his minimally honorable refusal to justify what he had done, could stop me. I said that he had dared to commit such a dastardly act because he was a Negro, and had been counting on the white-liberal guilt that he knew so much about, that he was such a great connoisseur of, to enable him to get away with it. And he had gotten away with it—he who went around preaching the virtues of "paying one's dues." Even I had let him get away with it by my failure to sue, but I was at least not going to be blackmailed in my feelings. If he thought I felt guilty toward him or any other Negro, he was very much mistaken. Neither I nor my ancestors had ever wronged the Negroes; on the contrary, I had grown up in an "integrated" slum neighborhood where it was the Negroes who persecuted the whites and not the other way round. I told him several stories about my childhood relations with Negroes and about the resentment and hatred with which my experience had left me, and as I talked, Baldwin's eyes blazed even more fiercely than usual. "You ought," he whispered when I had finished, "to write all that down."

I had been thinking of it, I said; in fact I had even made a few unsuccessful passes at it out of my irritation with all the sentimental nonsense that was being talked about integration by whites who knew nothing about Negroes, and by Negroes who thought that all their problems could be solved by living next-door to whites.

The problem went deeper than the integrationists seemed to understand; there was something almost psychotic in the relation of whites to Negroes in America, resembling in its resistance to rational analysis the feeling of Christian Europe about the Jews. Integration was not the answer, not only because the liberals were deceiving themselves in believing that white America would agree to it, but because it could only work if the Negroes themselves gave up the secret dream of escaping the condition of blackness. Some day, perhaps, the Negroes would disappear through wholesale miscegenation into the white population; it would be the best conclusion to the whole sorry story, if only it ever could happen. Baldwin, becoming more and more excited in that earnest way of his, urged me again to tell it on paper as I had been telling it that evening to him. It was important, more important than I knew, for such things to be said; and they had to be said in public.

"My Negro Problem—and Ours," as I called the essay in which I tried to tell it on paper as I had told it to Baldwin, turned out to be a major event in my literary career. After several years of being unable to get it started, I wrote it finally—or rather it wrote itself—over a long weekend at home, in three hot, blissful sessions at the typewriter. It would, I knew, offend many people, and would cause me much trouble if published in *Commentary*, but I was prouder of it than anything I had ever done as a writer, and as an editor I was too keenly aware of the value of a sensation to give it to any other magazine. Its appearance in *Commentary* in February of 1963 created an even greater sensation than I had anticipated, however: we got over three hundred letters (as compared with the ten or twenty a controversial article would normally provoke), calling me everything from a racist to a moral hero. Dozens of articles and editorials commenting on the piece were printed in other magazines and in the newspapers, and for nearly a year I was unable to walk into a room without being assaulted by some intense young woman demanding to know why I was against the Negroes. Almost daily I would receive requests from television producers asking me to join various civil-rights leaders on discussion programs, but I stopped accepting such invitations as soon as I realized that I was being cast, for lack of anyone better suited to the part in New York, in the role of the bigot on the panel.

After a while, I wearied of explaining to people that the article had been intended as a critique of the unrealistic assumptions behind the integrationist strategy for solving the problems of the Negroes (on this point most of what I said was borne out by the events of the next few years), that I had not been *proposing* miscegenation as a solution but rather expressing my belief that it would be the most desirable outcome (here I was probably wrong, though not, I think, morally), and that my main purpose had been to cut through the hypocrisy with which the whole issue of civil rights had come to be surrounded (in that I succeeded with some, and made things worse with others).

The words most frequently used in praise of "My Negro Problem," when it was praised, were "courageous" and "honest." Indeed the piece was both, but not at all in the sense its admirers meant. It required no great courage on my part to voice unpleasant truths; nor, given the milieu in which I had grown up, was it difficult for me to acknowledge that my feelings toward Negroes were less than perfectly benign and were sharply in conflict with my moral and political convictions. What did require courage was the decision I made to appear in "public" again after concealing myself so timidly in *Show;* to act again on the lust for fame I had been trying so hard to suppress; to interject myself (or "put in my two cents," as they used to say in Brooklyn) into a major contemporary issue without hiding diffidently behind a book; and most of all, to assert without apology that *my* experience, however unrepresentative or peripheral or exotic it might seem, was a valid sample of life in America which could be used to illuminate even the most centrally significant of American problems. The honesty of the essay, similarly, consisted in the fact that it was the first piece I had ever written in a voice that belonged entirely to me, and that it was an act I was performing in the service of the demand for that broader and wider attention to which I had decided at Paradise

Island I was now entitled and for which I had determined to make a bid.

I was, then, risking something important in writing "My Negro Problem," but it was neither my job as editor of *Commentary* nor my reputation as a good liberal. In announcing as I in effect did in that piece, "This is who I am, this is the best I can do, not as a precocious and promising young person, but as a grown man writing as truly and bravely and skillfully as it will ever be given to him to write," I was taking the risk of being told that I simply was not good enough to merit the kind of fame I was after and that the best of everything was much too good for me. The results, of course, were inconclusive, but they were far more cheering than not. "My Negro Problem" was certainly the best piece of writing I had ever done, and had also attracted more attention—some of it, to be sure, not entirely flattering —than anything else of mine: a further proof out of my own experience that success could be had without tinkering with the holy inner light. Was it perhaps even possible that success had become a roughly accurate measure of intrinsic quality in the post-middlebrow world of American culture?

For this temporary flirtation with the nihilism of the extrinsic, I was soon to be duly punished. By the end of 1963, I had been writing professionally for over twelve years and had published almost a hundred pieces, but I had yet to publish a book. It was clear that the one

I had started on postwar American fiction would never get done, and my then publisher suggested that I fulfill my contract with him by putting together a collection of my essays instead. My first answer to any proposition had always been No, but this time the No was especially vehement. The idea that my maiden voyage into the world of books would be astride a collection violated my sense of literary propriety, and moreover I dreaded the prospect of having to read through all my past work with a cold editorial eye: who knew what I might find there? My publisher, however, insisted, and since the only alternatives to a refusal were the equally impossible ones of writing another book or returning the advance he had paid me, I gave in.

Putting the collection together was, as I had anticipated, an unpleasant experience, the only redeeming feature being that my *Show* pieces seemed better to me than I had supposed when writing them. For the rest I alternated between feeling miserable at the scanty progress I thought I had made as a writer in all those years, and embarrassed at the callowness and gaucherie of some of my most fondly remembered past performances. Gritting my teeth, I made a selection, organized it as best I could into something more unified than a random collection, and wrote an introduction calculated to arouse the anger of certain types in the literary world, which it succeeded beyond all expectation in doing. (*Advice to Young Critics:* In reviewing a collection of essays, *never* take what the author says about himself in the introduction at face value; if you do, you will write a boring and unintelligent review. You will show yourself off to much better advantage, and probably be much closer to the truth, if you devote your review to demonstrating how radically—whether for good or for ill—the essays themselves contradict the statement of principles in the introduction.)

By any normal standards, the book, *Doings and Undoings: The Fifties and After in American Writing,* fared very well. It was widely and for the most part favorably reviewed, and it even enjoyed a good sale for a collection of critical essays, going into a third hardcover edition within a year. But I was not operating by normal standards. I responded even to the most enthusiastic reviews as though they were attacks (in this acting exactly like many other writers I had always despised for their childish behavior in the face of criticism) and to the attacks as though they had been written with murder in the heart (which, in truth, a couple of them had).

I had never been much given to paranoia, but all my potentialities for it were now activated. A well-known English critic who was teaching that year in an American university and whom I had met only once and very briefly wrote me a note about the book which was full of the most extravagant praise; when he reviewed it a few weeks later in much more moderate terms, I flew into a rage and spent the better part of a week making up scenarios to account for the discrepancy. (English critic to American colleague: *"Doings and Undoings* is the best critical collection to have come out in America in years." American colleague: "You really think so? How extraordinary. I would say that it's a middling specimen of New York journalism." English critic: "Hmm. Would that be the general opinion in this country?" American colleague: "Certainly." English critic: "Excuse me, I've got to get back to my office to revise a review I've just written.")

The depth and bitterness of my disappointment with the reception of *Doings and Undoings* was, of course, a measure of how large my demands on the world had grown. Only a few years earlier, on the principle of "It doesn't matter what they say about you as long as they spell your name right" (no easy condition in my case), I had been delighted to see my name mentioned in print, even if the reference was unflattering. Now, unless a reviewer went into raptures over me, I thought him my enemy. I had been dreaming that the appearance of the book would become the occasion for a general proclamation of my appointment to the office of "leading young critic in America"; instead it became the occasion for several people to present me with the first installments of the bill for all those glorious years when everyone had been on my side.

I should have anticipated that this would happen, for I had seen it happen often enough to others before me, but I was too hungry by now to have perspective. Later, all passion spent, I understood that I had been around too long, and that the "early eminence" of which one reviewer spoke had aroused too much resentment for the book to be treated in the way I had hoped it would—and in the way it probably would have been treated a few years earlier. By 1964, however, the time had come for a second look at my reputation; and by the laws of the literary world, a second look always means revision: the devaluation of a reputation now discovered to have been inflated in the past, or the establishment of a reputation now seen to have been understated, as the case may be. All writers who make a splash go through these ups and downs, which have much less relation to the true worth of their work than to such factors as changing fashions in taste, shifting climates of opinion, and the highly complicated politics of literary envy and literary adulation.

Every morning a stock-market report on reputations comes out in New York. It is invisible, but those who have eyes to see can read it. Did so-and-so have dinner at Jacqueline Kennedy's apartment last night? Up five points. Was so-and-so *not* invited by the Lowells to meet the latest visiting Russian poet? Down one-eighth. Did so-and-so's book get nominated for the National Book Award? Up two and five-eighths. Did *Partisan Review* neglect to ask so-and-so to participate in a symposium? Down two. Because of the dirty little secret, many of the most avid readers of this daily report would indignantly deny having a subscription to it, and would act if caught poring over it rather as a vicar in Victorian England might have acted if caught drooling over a volume of de Sade. In the months following the publication of *Doings and Undoings,* I hardly dared look at the listings for fear of finding myself wiped out, but when I finally worked up the courage to take a sidelong glance at them one morning, I discovered to my surprise that after much active trading my stock had registered an impressive gain. It had started moving hesitantly with a page-four review (and picture) in the Sunday *Times;* rose again slightly with a picture and a flattering piece in *Newsweek;* fell off somewhat after a vicious assault on me in *The New York Review of Books* (unaccompanied by a Levine caricature, which cost me another point); but then rose sharply when the unusual honor of being attacked at great length in the *New Yorker* was paid me in spite of their long-standing rule against reviewing books containing material, as *Doings and Undoings* did, which had originally appeared in their pages; went up still further when *Partisan Review* featured their piece about me on the cover; and eventually leveled off at a new high as the publication date of the book receded into the past.

The whole business of reputation, of fame, of success was coming to fascinate me in a new way. Everyone seemed to be caught up in it, and yet no one told the truth about it. People capable of the most brutal honesty in other areas would at the mention of the word success suddenly lift their eyes up to the heavens and begin chanting the most horrendous pieties imaginable. Some of them were obviously protecting themselves from the anxiety that thoughts of worldly success and failure in relation to their own work would inevitably arouse. But others reminded me of Communists who had long since given up believing that their faith corresponded to anything real in the world but were desperately afraid to let go of it lest they lose their intellectual and emotional bearings entirely.

The major dissenter from this spirit—the only man in America, I sometimes thought, who was capable of perfect honesty on the subject of success—was Norman Mailer. Long before meeting him in 1958, I had admired Mailer's work enormously, and had always been puzzled by the low esteem in which he was generally held by the family. But Mailer was a best-selling novelist and therefore not to be taken seriously. By 1958, he had redeemed himself somewhat by writing *Barbary Shore,* an obscure allegorical novel which sold badly, and then *The Deer Park,* a novel about Hollywood which had been rejected by several publishers on the ground that it was too obscene; and he had also helped his reputation as a serious writer along by joining the family to the extent of associating himself with *Dissent.* Nevertheless, more than one of my friends thought I was crazy when I made what was perhaps the first large-scale critical effort to argue for his importance (an effort, incidentally, I was already engaged in by the time I met Mailer), and it was only with great reluctance that *Partisan Review* agreed to publish the essay.

The better I got to know Mailer personally—and we became very close friends—the more extraordinary I found him. He was, as the saying goes, a walking bag of contradictions: pugnacious in temperament and yet of a surpassing sweetness of character; foolish beyond belief about people, and yet unbelievably quick to understand the point of what anyone was up to; obsessed with fame, power, and rank, and yet the freest of any man I had ever encountered of snobbishness in any of its forms. Like most famous writers, he was surrounded by courtiers and sycophants, but with this difference: he allowed them into his life not to flatter him but to give his radically egalitarian imagination a constant workout. He had the true novelist's curiosity about people unlike himself—you could see him getting hooked ten times a night by strangers at a party—and his respect for modes of life other than his own was so great that it often led him into romanticizing people and things that might legitimately have been dismissed as uninteresting or mediocre. He would look into the empty eyes of some vapid upper-class girl and announce to her that she could be the madam of a Mexican whorehouse; or he would decide that some broken-down Negro junkie he had met in a Village dive was a battalion-commander at heart. Mailer assumed in the most straightforward way that everyone was out for all the power he could get at every minute of the day, and that from the most casual confrontation between two people, one emerged with a victory and the other with a defeat; he even had a hypochondriacal theory involving the birth and death of cells to cover for the assumption. He himself wanted everything: he would "settle for nothing less" than making a revolution in the consciousness of his time, *and* earning millions of dollars, *and* achieving the very heights of American celebrityhood. He respected the position of celebrityhood precisely as he respected people, sometimes romanticizing a particular "office," but never making the more common and worse mistake of underestimating how much it took to get anywhere big in America or pooh-poohing the qualities of mind and character required for staying on top.

Mailer, I thought, was performing an experiment on himself in public: he was trying to prove that the best way for an American to deal with the ambition for worldly success—an ambition the American male can as easily escape as he can get away with not going to school —was to throw himself unashamedly into it in the hope of coming up again on the other side. "Make me chaste, O Lord, but not yet," prayed Saint Augustine, and he was a more effective saint for having been vouchsafed the granting of his request. Mailer, it seemed to me, might some day transcend the problem, and even if he never did, he was still following a nobler and more honorable course than the prigs of the *New Republic* school of criticism who were forever clucking their tongues over his refusal to bow down before the icons of selfless purity to which they so stridently protested their own righteous devotion, often in the form of fearless exposés of the venalities of Hollywood and the Broadway theater which would, of course, but for their ever vigilant eyes, have gone altogether unnoticed.

Mailer was supposed to be an artist, they said, but he was a bad little artist because a good little artist would sit at home working at his art instead of hanging around the poolroom every night with bums who played hookey from school. If he were a good little artist, they said, he would be thinking all the time about his art instead of thinking about his career; he would embrace the profound realization, to which they in their own selfless wisdom had come, that only by despising success could he ever hope to achieve the greatness he was ambitious for.

It did not occur to these lovers of literature while preaching such sermons that the bad little artist had just refuted every single assumption on the basis of which they were scolding him by producing, in *Advertisements for Myself,* one of the great works of confessional autobiography in American literature; nor could these irrepressible praters about aesthetic values recover long enough from the shock of hearing an artist admit how much sales and reviews mattered to him to notice how beautiful a blend of irony, rhetorical richness, and intellectual resonance had gone into the act of admission. But of course *Advertisements for Myself,* not being a novel, was not art; in fact, it counted so little even for writing that in the very act of reviewing it, they wondered when Mailer would stop running for President or for Mayor of New York and "get down to writing again."

For several years I toyed with the idea of doing a book about Mailer that would focus on the problem of success, but in the end I decided that if I ever did work up the nerve to write about this problem, I would have to do it without hiding behind him or anyone else. Such a book, I thought, ought properly to be written in the first person, and it ought in itself to constitute a frank, Mailer-like bid for literary distinction, fame, and money all in one package: otherwise it would be unable to extricate itself from the toils of the dirty little secret. Writing a book like that would be a very dangerous thing to do, but some day, I told myself, I would like to try doing it.

I just have.

INDEX

Abel, Lionel, 112
Abel, Sherry, 154, 198–99, 205, 206, 286, 287
Adams, J. Donald, 118, 310
Agee, James, 110
Algren, Nelson, 239
Anderson, Sherwood, 112
Arendt, Hannah, 89, 99, 111, 179, 233, 247, 260, 289, 298, 310, 341
Aristotle, 104
Arnold, Matthew, 81
Askew, Mr. and Mrs. Kirk, 248
Auden, W. H., 173
Augustine, Saint, 104, 140, 143, 354

Babbitt, Irving, 118
Baker, Dorothy, 148
Baldwin, James, 86, 110, 120, 260, 339–43
Barrett, William, 110, 120, 298
Bazelon, David, 111, 120, 298, 330
Beauvoir, Simone de, 238
Beerbohm, Max, 169
Bell, Daniel, 42, 89, 111, 120, 246, 315–16
Bellow, Saul, 99, 110, 120, 122, 123, 155–56, 159–65, 260, 261, 264, 339
Bereday, George Z. F., 23n
Berryman, John, 110
Blackmur, R. P., 40, 73
Boorstin, Daniel, 294
Brogan, D. W., 89
Brooke, Rupert, 77
Brooks, Cleanth, 40
Brooks, Van Wyck, 112, 117, 131
Brown, Norman O., 298
Bunche, Ralph, 308
Burke, Kenneth, 114, 73, 91, 294

Cagney, James, 85
Camus, Albert, 238
Capote, Truman, 335
Cawelti, John G., xiiin
Cézanne, Paul, 27
Chambers, Whittaker, 288
Chase, Richard, 41, 110, 120
Chaucer, Geoffrey, 73
Chiappe, Andrew, 41, 78
Cohen, Elliot, 99, 100, 101, 103, 111, 127, 128, 129, 130, 132, 133, 134, 135, 152, 161, 175, 197–98,

Cohen, Elliot (*continued*)
200–201, 207–8, 210, 211, 212, 229–30, 232–33, 273, 276, 278, 283–84, 294, 308, 325
Coleridge, Samuel Taylor, 144
Conroy, Jack, 113
Cowley, Malcolm, 114
Cozzens, James Gould, 241
Crabbe, George, 92
Cromwell, Oliver, 159
Cummings, E. E., 248

Davis, Robert Gorham, 110
Dell, Floyd, 112
Dewey, Thomas E., 133
Disraeli, Benjamin, 104, 105
Donleavy, J. P., 261
Dos Passos, John, 112
Draper, Theodore, 289
Dreiser, Theodore, 114
Dryden, John, 251
Dupee, F. W., 41, 42, 78, 110, 111, 112, 113

Eastman, Max, 112, 114
Edelston, Martin, 323
Edman, Irwin, 34
Eisenhower, Dwight D., 281, 313
Eliot, T. S., 41, 72, 75, 76, 77, 78, 79, 112, 113, 114, 157
Ellison, Ralph, 110, 260, 261
Epstein, Barbara, 320
Epstein, Jason, 173, 197, 217–19, 233–34, 246, 270–72, 274, 297–98, 319, 331

Fadiman, Clifton, 128, 173
Faulkner, William, 191, 238
Fiedler, Leslie, 89, 99, 120, 122, 123, 298
Fitzgerald, F. Scott, 285
Forster, E. M., 295
Fraiberg, Selma, 183
Freud, Sigmund, 57, 121, 122, 125, 268
Frost, Robert, 310

Galbraith, John Kenneth, 312
Gibney, Frank, 329
Ginsberg, Allen, 39, 215, 253
Ginsberg, H. L., 45
Glazer, Nathan, 101, 111, 120, 197
Goldberg, Arthur, 308
Goodman, Paul, 111, 112, 113, 119, 122, 260, 296–98
Goodwin, Richard, 312, 321
Graves, Robert, 233
Greenberg, Clement, 99, 101, 111, 112, 113, 119, 129, 147, 152

Hadas, Moses, 34, 44, 148–49
Hammett, Dashiell, 292
Hardwick, Elizabeth, 110, 120, 167
Harrington, Michael, 6, 110
Hartford, Huntington, 333
Hazlitt, William, 338
Heilbroner, Robert L., 5–6
Hellman, Lillian, 247, 292
Hemingway, Ernest, 112
Herrick, Robert, 92
Hiss, Alger, 87
Hobbes, Thomas, 89
Hollander, John, 39
Hook, Sidney, 89, 99, 111, 112, 292
Howe, Irving, 88, 120, 122, 136, 152, 298, 321
Hurwitz, Henry, 129
Hyman, Stanley Edgar, 298

Jacobson, Dan, 144
James, Harry, 85
James, Henry, 100, 123, 150
James, William, xiii, 267
Jarrell, Randall, 40
Johnson, Lyndon B., 59, 314
Johnson, Samuel, 145
Jones, James, 261
Jonson, Ben, 142
Joyce, James, 78, 114

Kaufman, George S., 118
Kazin, Alfred, 99, 120, 122, 123, 167, 170, 298

Keats, John, 26, 27, 39, 92
Kempton, Murray, 109
Kennan, George, 89
Kennedy, Jacqueline, 350
Kennedy, John F., 38–39, 282, 308, 312–13, 321
Kennedy, Robert F., 38–39, 335
Keppel, Frederick P., 46–48
Kerouac, Jack, 215, 253
Khrushchev, Nikita, 125, 293
Koestler, Arthur, 89, 116, 292
Kristol, Irving, 101–2, 111, 120, 136, 152, 175, 256, 259, 275, 292, 315–16
Kronenberger, Louis, 248
Krutch, Joseph Wood, 248, 249

Lawrence, D. H., xvi, 141
Lawrence, T. E., 143
Leavis, F. R., 76–81, 91, 95, 105, 158, 251, 253, 254, 256
Leavis, Q. D., 76
Lowell, Robert, 110, 167, 261, 350
Luce, Henry, 302–3
Lynn, Kenneth S., xiii*n*

Macdonald, Dwight, 89, 110, 111, 112, 113, 119, 157, 167, 168, 170–71, 241, 298, 324–25
MacLeish, Archibald, 118
Mailer, Norman, 247, 261, 264, 296, 335–36, 352–56
Malamud, Bernard, 101, 105, 152, 260, 261
Marcus, Steven, 153, 172
Marlowe, Sylvia, 248
Marston, John, 104
Marx, Groucho, 152
Marx, Karl (Marxism), 113, 115, 118, 121, 125, 126, 268, 313
Mayer, Louis B., 118
McCarthy, Joseph R., 87, 125, 289, 290, 291, 295
McCarthy, Mary, 99, 110, 120, 124, 125, 127, 154–55, 167, 246, 248, 260, 324

Melbourne, Lord William Lamb, 67
Mencken, H. L., 112
Meredith, George, 104
Merleau-Ponty, Maurice, 116
Miller, Glenn, 85
Milton, John, 104, 243, 244
Morgenthau, Hans, J., 89
Moynihan, Daniel Patrick, 312
Mozart, Wolfgang Amadeus, 27

Newman, Joseph Cardinal, 19
Niebuhr, Reinhold, 89

Oakeshott, Michael, 89
O'Brien, Pat, 85
O'Connor, Flannery, 261
Oppenheimer, J. Robert, 125
Orwell, George, 89, 116

Paul, Saint, 26
Phillips, William, 113, 119, 120, 151, 239, 246, 275, 294, 319
Plato, 104
Plimpton, George, 321
Pollock, Jackson, 130
Pope, Alexander, 251
Popper, Karl, 89
Pound, Ezra, 112
Proust, Marcel, 78

Rahv, Philip, 111, 113, 119, 121, 123, 125, 152, 165, 167, 173, 176, 239, 247, 276, 293–94, 332
Ransom, John Crowe, 114
Reed, John, 112
Reich, Wilhelm, 162
Riesman, David, 75, 101, 258–59, 260, 290
Rischin, Moses, xiii*n*
Roosevelt, Franklin D., 118, 313
Rosenberg, Harold, 99, 110, 111, 119, 122, 298, 310
Rosenfeld, Isaac, 99, 110, 120, 122
Ross, Harold, 168, 169
Rossen, Robert, 258
Roth, Philip, 172, 260

Rovere, Richard H., 324

Salinger, J. D., 169, 280–81
Samuel, Maurice, 48
Sartre, Jean-Paul, 88
Schapiro, Meyer, 110, 111, 112
Schlesinger, Arthur, Jr., 290, 312
Schwartz, Delmore, 110, 120, 122, 125, 160
Shakespeare, William, 37, 78, 89, 142, 181
Shaw, George Bernard, 143
Shawn, William, 168, 340
Silone, Ignazio, 116
Silvers, Robert, 320–21
Sinatra, Frank, 335
Smith, Al, 308
Solow, Herbert, 128
Sontag, Susan, 154–55
Spencer, Elizabeth, 252
Spender, Stephen, 116, 136
Stalin, Joseph (Stalinism), 88, 113, 114, 115, 118, 120, 124, 129, 131, 135, 289, 292, 317
Steinbeck, John, 118
Stengel, Casey, 100
Styron, William, 295

Tate, Allen, 40, 114
Thomas, Norman, 322
Thompson, John, 110, 329–31
Tocqueville, Alexis de, 59, 126, 232
Trilling. Diana, 94–97, 100, 275, 290

Trilling, Lionel, 41, 42, 48n, 78–81, 89, 94–96, 99, 100, 111, 112, 125, 126, 127, 128, 134, 157, 160, 173–74, 201, 214, 247, 260, 298, 310
Troy, William, 110
Truman, Harry S, 125, 313
Tynan, Kenneth, 319

Unitas, Johnny, 335

Van Doren, Mark, 34, 39
Vidal, Gore, 310

Wagner, Richard, 311
Wallace, Henry, 89
Warren, Robert Penn, 114
Warshow, Robert, 89, 99, 101–2, 104, 111, 120, 123, 135, 147, 148, 149–50, 153, 155–59, 166, 173–75, 191, 197, 200, 210, 239
Welty, Eudora, 252
West, Nathanael, 238
Whyte, William H., 37
Wilde, Oscar, 240
Wilson, Edmund, 112, 114, 116, 117, 147, 170, 205, 253, 263, 269, 284
Wolfe, Bertram, 293
Wool, Robert, 329
Wordsworth, William, 81, 103

Yates, Richard, 213
Yeats, William Butler, 38, 78, 114